The EMPRINT Method

A Guide to Reproducing Competence

Leslie Cameron-Bandler
David Gordon
Michael Lebeau

FuturePace, Inc. • San Rafael, California

Ignorance is the night of the mind,
Without moon or stars.

Confucius

When you wish upon a star,
It makes no difference who you are. . . .

Jimminy Cricket

To Mark and Alex and Kyra

Published by FuturePace, Inc., P.O. Box 1173, San Rafael, California 94915

ISBN 0-932573-02-9

Library of Congress Catalog Number 85-80457

Cover design by Bill Fulton.

Contents

Preface

This book is intended to change your mind about what is possible for you to achieve. By the time you finish reading the first chapter, you will be aware of the possibility of acquiring a wide range of new skills, talents, and aptitudes. By the time you finish the final chapter, you will have the tools you need to master an accelerated skill acquisition process—the EMPRINT™ method—that you can use to turn those possibilities into accomplishments.

The purpose of this book, then, is to provide you with tools that will enable you to identify and acquire (or transfer to others) desirable human aptitudes. The purpose of this preface is to introduce you to the approach we used to create the EMPRINT method, as well as to create other methods and self-improvement formats that are described in other books by the authors. We call our approach Mental Aptitude Patterning™·SM. While it is not necessary to have an understanding of Mental Aptitude Patterning to learn the EMPRINT method, knowing at least a little about Mental Aptitude Patterning will enable you to better appreciate both how we created the EMPRINT method, and how the method can be used to enhance the skills of individuals, as well as of large groups of people. Our overall approach is not discussed in the presentation of the EMPRINT method, so if you would like to proceed immediately to the introduction of the method, skip to Chapter 1. If you would like a brief introduction to Mental Aptitude Patterning, read on.

Using Mental Aptitude Patterning, we code the patterns that underlie a particular human aptitude, which we then transform into a sequence of instructional experiences that, when followed, result in the installation of that particular aptitude in anyone.

Let us break that mouthful down into a couple of smaller bites.

We code the patterns that underlie human aptitudes.

An "aptitude" is any excellent ability that an individual manifests, including the ability to stick to a diet, learn calculus, play music, organize presentations, motivate oneself to action, recognize and understand patterns, and so on. In short, anything that people naturally do well is an aptitude.

Aptitudes are composed of *constellations* of specific perceptions and internal representations (ways of thinking). It is the kind of perceptions and representations, and how they interact with one another, that combine to manifest a particular aptitude. When we speak of "the patterns that underlie human aptitudes," we are referring to these constellations.

In essence, we have created a new language for describing aptitudes. We take the patterns that underlie aptitudes and code them into this language. The vocabulary of our language consists of the set of distinctions that represent those elements that combine to form the basis for any aptitude or talent. The ways in which those distinctions interact with each other and the world comprise the syntax of our language. With this language we are able to "write sentences" that usefully describe (in terms of understanding and replication) the specific constellation of perceptions and representations underlying a particular aptitude. In other words, we generate an internal processing-based description of how a person is adept at problem solving, or planning wisely for the future, or managing people well, or caring for personal health, or maintaining fulfilling relationships, or doing algebraic proofs.

In a way this process is like cooking a meal. Each aptitude "dish" is the result of specific perceptual and representational "ingredients" being combined in a certain way (in a particular sequence, under certain conditions of heat or cold, for specified lengths of time, and so on). By specifying the ingredients and cooking methods we come up with the recipe for a particular dish. This recipe allows us not only to know how the dish was made, but also to reproduce it ourselves. The goal of Mental Aptitude Patterning is to discover recipes for the various human aptitudes that are worth making available to others.

This process may also be compared to writing a musical score. The notes are akin to the perceptions and representations that make up human experiences. Like perceptions and representations, these notes can be combined in thirds, fifths, and ninths, as chords and arpeggios, in various tempos and keys, to create unique musical experiences. The resulting score provides not only a way of analyzing the structure of a particular composition, it also provides a means of transferring the ability to reproduce the music itself to anyone capable of reading the score.

We transform the coded information into a sequence of instructional experiences that, when followed, result in the installation of a particular aptitude in anyone.

The "instructional experiences" we are talking about are akin to the sequences of learning experiences that are often used to help a person become skillful in a sport. For instance, in skiing, tennis, swimming, and golf, the movements at which one must become skillful have been modeled and then specified as sequences of small, incremental pieces of behavior, each of which is relatively easy to grasp. Mastery of these incremental pieces leads eventually to the skillful manifestation of whole behaviors fundamental to each of these sports.

In sports, the incremental external behaviors that make up skills are readily accessible by watching (either in person or on film or tape) a person who exemplifies the skills to be learned. Thus the relationship between foot placement, bend of the knee, position of the thumb and elbow, and so on can be modeled, observed, copied, and taught. Not long ago sports skills were acquired through practice and osmosis by those who had "talent." Now these skills are available to almost anyone who is willing to take lessons and practice. What Mental Aptitude Patterning does is to move *inside,* to the arena of the mind, doing for previously unacquirable aptitudes what has become standard practice for acquiring athletic skills.

As an approach, Mental Aptitude Patterning (and the methods and formats it has generated) seems to us to be a great improvement over the way that most abilities are passed on to others, which is generally through a mentoring process. That is, when a person wants to become adept at something (whether it be algebra, tennis, or being motivated), he or she usually seeks an apprenticeship with a mentor, someone who already demonstrates an aptitude for the ability the person wants. This apprenticeship may be either explicit or implicit, and may be carried on through personal contact, media, books, seminars, or classes. Regardless of how it is done, however, the process of learning to think as the mentor thinks is almost always the result of a long period of intimate exposure to the mentor's model of the world. Even then, the mentor's aptitudes are rarely passed on, and the apprentice must be satisfied with copying the mentor's behaviors and techniques.

Our approach is an improvement over mentoring in that it provides any interested person with access to compilations of the thinking patterns that make up the aptitudes of talented people. This is more efficient in terms of time, effort, and results, and provides tremendous independence as well.

What does all this mean? The aptitudes that an individual naturally manifests can be coded and formatted so that they can be deliberately and efficiently acquired by others. The implication is that an individual can do well at anything he or she chooses (anything, that is, that has been coded and for which a sequence of instructional experiences has been generated). For us, however, this is more than an implication—it is an assertion, and it is a goal.

We believe that realizing that goal will provide a means of advancing personal, cultural, and societal evolution by making the pool of human talents available *to any one person.* This seems to us to be the most viable way of making it possible for the human mind and experience to keep pace with the winged sandals of technological development.

And, perhaps most important, Mental Aptitude Patterning has the potential of creating for every individual possibilities that would not otherwise exist. Every individual longs for certain skills, traits, abilities, and attributes for which he or she seems to lack the aptitude. That longing too often goes unfulfilled, unnecessarily. The pool of human experience available to be tapped is broader and deeper than we can presently imagine. Whether that pool is tapped depends first upon our recognition that it exists, and then upon our development of a process capable of describing and transferring those experiences to others. This book is intended both to convince you that this pool does indeed exist, and to present the EMPRINT method—an accelerated skill acquisition process that will enable you to tap into that incredibly rich reservoir of human talent.

San Rafael, California
July 7, 1985

Like the creative composer, some people are more gifted at living than others. They do have an effect on those around them, but the process stops there because there is no way of describing in technical terms just what it is they do, most of which is out of awareness. Some time in the future, a long, long time from now when culture is more completely explored, there will be the equivalent of musical scores that can be learned, each for a different type of man or woman in different types of jobs and relationships, for time, space, work, and play. We see people who are successful and happy today, who have jobs which are rewarding and productive. What are the sets, isolates, and patterns that differentiate their lives from those of the less fortunate? We need to have a means for making life a little less haphazard and more enjoyable.

Edward T. Hall
The Silent Language

PART I

Introduction

1 Taking Camera in Hand

In the early 1400s the Chinese emperor Yung Lo launched the most immense armada ever seen on our planet to that time. Yung Lo's historic seafaring expedition employed a crew of thirty-seven thousand, sailing in a flotilla of over three hundred ships. The largest vessel, the Treasure Ship, was 444 feet long with a beam of 180 feet and carried nine masts. With its several stories and high overhanging stern galley, it was much larger than any ship ever before seen in the West. Europeans who encountered it were astonished at the armada's overall size, and simply flabbergasted at the enormity of the Treasure Ship. No western construction methods or theories could account for the seemingly impossible reality that confronted them.

Equally remarkable to western observers was the ingenious construction that prevented water in one part of the hull from flooding the whole ship. Although bulkheads were novel in Europe as a way to prevent the spread of water or fire, they were an old trick of the trade in China. The Chinese had been constructing their ships with bulkheadlike transverse members for centuries. The material that had suggested the concept to them was a familiar part of their life, one which they used in countless cultural, religious, household, and decorative applications. That material was bamboo. The design inspired by bamboo gave the strength and resilience that made possible the towering ships that dazzled the foreigners.

It didn't take long for the Europeans to adapt this design to their own ship construction. Soon they were sailing their own colossal ships to new and old destinations in greatly enhanced safety, style, comfort, and economy. Today we still build ships—as well as skis, aircraft, spaceships, and hundreds of other modern products—that incorporate the elegant design suggested to the ancient Chinese by bamboo.

In the early 1980s another unique expedition was launched. Compared to Yung Lo's armada it was tiny. It consisted of only three people: the authors of this book. The vehicles we used to reach our destination were mundane: automobiles and telephones. But then the people we set out to encounter were often as close as the house next door. They were present at our lectures and workshops, at the businesswomen's Tuesday lunch at the Holiday Inn, and at our friend's weekly backyard barbecue. As co-members of the same national and local culture they were similar to us; but because the cargo we brought to them was so unfamiliar they could only perceive it at first as something foreign.

Our cargo consisted of a *concept* and a *tool*. The concept was that the pool of human talents is a reservoir of resources that can be tapped by anyone; we need no longer be limited by the abilities that were bestowed upon us by heredity and childhood environment. These talents are the incredible range of aptitudes, knacks, propensities, and seemingly natural abilities that exist within human beings. We further suggested that there exists the equivalent of a *language of the brain* that can be learned and then used to code one person's competence or brilliance in such a way as to make it available to any other person.

The tool was a method we used to demonstrate that our concept is sound. We applied our method to a man in his mid-thirties whose life had no purpose or direction. He changed from being financially dependent on others to being independent, able to set worthwhile goals, and innovative in generating lucrative professional opportunites. A painfully shy forty-year-old woman was so worried about the opinions of others that she was almost incapable of speaking or acting.

Using our method, she quickly reoriented her thinking so that her self-esteem hinged on her own thoughtful opinion, enabling her to express her best personal qualities with confidence, even in situations that previously had been stressful. Another woman was convinced she was destined to be destitute in her old age, even though she was still young and competent. She had always spent money as quickly as she earned it, and now she imagined herself ending up penniless and unable to care for herself. With the help of our tool, she took control of her future by seeking out and adopting the talent for fiscal responsibility, long-term financial planning, and investing. A middle-aged man, frustrated and discouraged at repeatedly falling into the same traps, finally learned how to avoid repeating his mistakes—by learning how others are able to recognize, evaluate, and learn from them.

Over time, the people we encountered became familiar with our message and our method. They observed their friends and colleagues demonstrating new competencies, and they also experienced their own new abilities to succeed in previously frustrating areas of their lives. It didn't take long for many of them to adopt our new concept and tool, and soon they were using their continual harvest of new resources to build brighter and more fulfilling futures.

The purpose of this book is to acquaint *you* with that method of recognizing and using for yourself this great untapped resource: the skills, talents, and attributes of others. Our tool, the EMPRINT method, is based on a set of distinctions that shed the light of understanding on the perceptions and thought processes underlying experience and behavior. The organization of this set of distinctions within the EMPRINT method provides *the basis for the transferring of competence and excellence* from one person to another.

Edward T. Hall eloquently set us our task twenty-six years ago when he prophesied "the equivalent of musical scores that can be learned, each for a different type of man or woman in different types of jobs and relationships, for time, space, work, and play." The EMPRINT method is a tool for creating the equivalent of those musical scores. It is method for creating clear and concise maps of success and fulfillment, and it opens the door to a land of *choice* that awaits those who

3

undertake to follow those particular maps to the destinations they project.

Before discussing how to use the EMPRINT method, we will introduce the distinctions and organizing principles upon which it is based. Perhaps the easiest way to understand these distinctions and organizing principles is to regard them as comprising a *model* for understanding human thinking and behavior. What exactly is a model? A model is a description of something that strictly corresponds to the structure of the thing being described. This description may be physical, as in the case of a miniature city used by city planners, the colored wooden balls strung together to show the configuration of DNA, or computer circuits demonstrating aspects of neural functioning. The description may also be conceptual, as in the case of the mathematics that describe black holes, the patterns of social interactions by which an anthropologist characterizes a particular culture, or the psychological theory a therapist uses in assessing the development of a client's personality. Whether physical or conceptual, what makes such descriptions models is that they functionally and structurally correspond to the system that they represent.

The set of distinctions—or model—each of us uses acts as a filter and organizer of experience. In terms of perception, for instance, Eskimos make dozens of distinctions about snow. Because of the crucial role that snow plays in every aspect of their lives—from walking to hunting to building shelters—they have learned to make distinctions that other cultures have not. A westerner and an Eskimo looking at a field of snow would differ not only in *what* they notice, but also in its meaning. This difference in perceptual distinctions is reflected in the fact that Eskimo language has nearly a dozen simple words for our "snow," indicating that it is falling snow, snow on the ground, drift snow, soft, loose, hard-packed, frozen, crusted, melting, etc. Eskimos also differ from members of our culture in that they do not eat bread. To the Eskimo, bread is not one of the distinctions—not one of the parts of the Eskimo model—for food. Thus Catholic Eskimos have an interesting variation on the Lord's Prayer which runs "Give us this day our daily fish." (Pei, 1965, p. 222)

Another example of how the models we use act as filters and organizers of experience was furnished by an acquaintance whose grandmother was transported as a young woman from the candle-lit Russian *shtetl* of her childhood to the electrically lit city of New York. For years she knew nothing about the mystery of electricity and was content with the fact that if she "made the switch," the light went on. One day her young nephew decided to explain the mystery of electricity to her, using a hydraulic model. ("The wire is like a hose with water running through it....") She followed the explanation very closely, and for the rest of her life she made sure to keep bulbs in unused light sockets and tape across unused electrical outlets, "so I shouldn't let the electricity run out on the floor." This example should not be dismissed as the naivete of a simple immigrant. The situation is no different among educated and knowledgeable individuals who, though the content may be beyond the garden-hose model of electricity, are still subject to the pervasive influence of models.

An investigator who hoped to learn something about what scientists took the atomic theory to be asked a distinguished physicist and an eminent chemist whether a single atom of helium was or was not a molecule. Both answered without hesitation, but their answers were not the same. For the chemist the atom of helium was a molecule because it behaved like one with respect to the kinetic theory of gases. For the physicist, on the other hand, the helium atom was not a molecule because it displayed no molecular spectrum. Presumably both men were talking of the same particle, but they were viewing it through their own research training and practice. (Kuhn, 1970, p. 50)

It is not the case that one of the two scientists in Kuhn's example is wrong about the nature of helium atoms. The chemist and the physicist operate out of different models of the world—different sets of distinctions—and therefore perceive and respond differently to atoms of helium. Neither of their models is a representation of the truth about helium atoms; rather, each is a representation that is in accord with, and useful to, the distinctive endeavors of chemistry and physics. The perceptions and behaviors that each of us uses to bring character to the chaos of the world, and our ability to control or influence those perceptions and behaviors, are a direct result of the distinctions we use.

Useful models are made up of distinctions that describe the functional or structural relationships within a particular system. Understanding the functional relationships that operate within a particular context provides you with a set of perceptual and conceptual filters that make it possible for you to make sense out of your experiences. For instance, after years of gathering and correlating information regarding weather patterns, meteorologists have constructed some very well-defined models describing those weather patterns. Knowing the model underlying the production of rain clouds saves the trouble of having to investigate anew each time a cloud appears on the horizon. Instead, the meteorologist can turn to the model for a description of the high and low pressure systems that produce those clouds.[1]

Furthermore, understanding the functional and structural relationships operating within a system may make it possible for you to reproduce the effects of that system. Edward Hall offers a fine example of using a model in just this way.

Some years ago in the town of Grand Lake, Colorado, on the snowy western slope of the Rockies, there was a tradition that everyone had to use skis to get around in the winter time. New schoolteachers transferred into the area had to learn to ski, and even the school principal and the school band were on skis. Small children learned how to ski soon after they could walk. When one watched these people move about it was as though the skis were an actual extension of the foot, a highly adapted organ for locomotion. Each person had developed his own highly individualistic style, just as everyone had his own way of walking. When skiing competitions took place some of the villagers were better than others, while many did not compete at all.

. . . At the same time, there were a few hardy souls in Denver and other nearby towns who used to take to skis for pleasure, as a part-time activity . . . . Some of them had very real talent, others weren't so skilled . . . . They were not highly conscious of how they skied, what technique they used, or how the skill could be taught. They would say, "Watch me," or "Do it like this," and that was about as far as they could go. I never will forget the time when one of my friends who had been watching this weekly trek to the mountains finally decided to come along. He was an excellent

athlete who had once been a Golden Gloves champion, so he had no lack of natural coordination and control. However, when he first put on skis the result was comic and disasterous at once. As soon as he tried to take a step, down he went. Encumbered by his skis, he could barely get up. The newcomer was beset by all sorts of problems which demanded skilled and technical analysis if they were to be solved quickly. Unfortunately the best that these Sunday skiers could manage was something like this: "You bend your knees and take off. Eventually you'll get the hang of it."

. . . At the same time . . . thousands of feet of film were being taken in the Alps of wonderfully skilled skiers rushing down slopes, turning, climbing, and coming to a stop. These films were analyzed, and the whole process was broken down into its components or isolates, as they can be called. In addition to the components, broader patterns were also analyzed. After a while it was decided that skiing was not an art which had to be restricted to the gifted. Anyone with patience and a modicum of control could be taught to ski, since the components had been so well identified that they could be talked about and described technically. Moreover, the uniformity of skill that could be achieved by these new technically trained skiers was so amazing that it made possible the later tremendous popularity of the sport. (Hall, 1959, p. 64)

As this example makes clear, one may possess a skill and yet not understand the elements underlying the manifestation of that skill. Those who had learned how to ski knew *implicitly* how to ski, but not *explicitly*. The folks with the high-speed cameras used their footage of skilled skiers to identify the patterns that those skiers shared in terms of how they used the various parts of their bodies while skiing. Taken together, the investigators' descriptions of the functional elements underlying competent skiing constituted a *model* for skiing. As Hall notes, the two great virtues of this particular model are that it contains those elements that are necessary and sufficient for competent skiing, and that those elements are described at a level of body movement that most people can readily duplicate. For instance, there is a huge difference between saying, "Turn left," and the instruction, "Keeping both knees bent, gradually press your right knee forward so that your weight shifts more to your right ski; as you shift your weight to your right ski move your right knee slightly to the left so your weight falls more on the left edge of your right ski; keep pressing forward like this until you are through your turn, then straighten your right knee until your weight is once again equally distributed on your left and right skis."

Accurate models, then, make it possible for us to understand a subject with respect to the distinctions used in that model. The distinctions that comprise the model will therefore orient your experience along certain lines (as illustrated above with Eskimo snow distinctions, the immigrant grandmother, and the scientists, with many other examples to follow). Thus we can use a sufficiently isomorphic map of Yosemite showing roads, trails, and points of interest to gain some idea of how the park is laid out. And, if we are in the park, we can use that map to navigate. A map of Yosemite that identifies no roads, trails, or landmarks, but shows only vegetation types and densities, will be much less useful than the road map for getting around the park, but will be much more useful for understanding Yosemite's ecology. The usefulness of a model, however, often extends far beyond its value in simply explaining a thing or a phenomenon.

Models As Extensions

Perhaps the only organisms that evolve as fast as insects do (as they must to keep one crawl ahead of the chemical companies) are human beings. While the rapidity of insect evolution is largely due to their rapid generational turnover, which provides frequent and massive oportunities for genetic recoding, the rapid rate of human evolution is due to our ability to make frequent changes, as a species, in our technical and conceptual worlds. Our personal evolution—our ability as individuals to understand and influence ourselves as well as to affect the world around us—grows each time we as a species expand our understanding and alter our view of the world. In this way we can change without having to resort to genetic reshuffling.

The basis for such extragenetic evolution is our propensity for extending our sensory, perceptual, cognitive, and physical abilities beyond the boundaries of our bodies. For instance, we use telescopes and microscopes to extend our eyes, and X-rays and infrared detectors to broaden our range of visual perception. Similarly, books extend our memories, computers extend our ability to manipulate information, knives extend the cutting power of our teeth, wrenches extend the gripping power of our fingers, and automobiles extend the locomotive force of our legs. In describing this process of externalization, Edward Hall used the term "extensions." Although there are other animals that use extensions, such as male bower birds that use alleyways made of sticks festooned with brightly colored berries and flowers to enhance their attractiveness to females, or chimpanzees that use sticks to dig termite snacks out of their mounds, none of them has elevated the extensional process to the artfulness—and mania—shown by human beings. The bower birds have nothing on us when we start donning our designer jeans, hats and ties, rings, earrings, bracelets, necklaces, fragrances, and makeup.

For our purposes here, the significance of extensions is that they are relatively free of genetic constraints. For the most part, your eye is as it is, and cannot be structurally or functionally changed. But once the eye is extended (in the form of a telescope, for instance), it enters the realm of technology, which *is* manipulatable. While the eye may not be alterable, a telescope can be made to gather more light, or light only of certain wavelengths, or it can be handed to others to be used, or it can be sent into space. Hold a telescope up to your eye and instantly your abilty to discern distant objects has evolved to a level that would have taken your coiling strands of DNA millions of years to duplicate, assuming it could be done at all. Our extensions make it possible for us to evolve technologically at an astounding rate.[2]

But our extensional technology is not all that evolves. Concepts and abstractions can also become extensions, and are therefore subject to such external evolution. For instance, the concepts of right and wrong have taken on the extensional form of the legal code. Once thus extended as a set of codes, the laws that are accepted by large numbers of people as part of the real world can be changed to suit legislative or popular needs. In this way it is possible to quickly alter the legal worlds of the people who are under its sway.

Like telescopes, calculators, books, and laws, models are also examples of extensions. Telescopes are not eyes and calculators are not brains, but both of these extensions perform some of the same functions as do the eye and brain. Similarly, psychological, behavioristic, cybernetic, and holographic models of human psychology are not the brain and behaviors they portray, but they do share to varying degrees some of the same functional and structural relationships as can be found in our brains and behaviors. And, like telescopes and laws, once removed from the boundaries of the body such models become tools that can be used to influence the world and oneself, that can be changed, that can be evolved, and that can also stimulate evolution in the person using them. Darwin's description of evolution through natural selection, Freud's theory of an unconscious mind, and Einstein's notion of space-time relativity are benchmark examples of models that have profoundly affected not only scientific and philosphical thought, but now permeate and are largely taken for granted in nearly everyone's thinking.

As an extension, then, a model—and therefore the set of distinctions that comprise the model—also becomes available to others and therefore becomes part of their personal evolution. It is rarely the case, however, that the skills that we want to emulate or empathize with in another person have been modeled (by anyone, including by the exemplar). We usually must rely on some kind of apprenticeship in order to learn to operate in the world as does the exemplar. The exemplar may become our mentor impersonally (as when we read books by and about this person and try to readjust our world to match the one revealed in those writings), or the relationship may be personal (as when we interact with and ask questions of the mentor in an effort to discover how to repattern our own models to match the mentor's). In either case, learning the mentor's model of the world is slow and uncertain because it is being transferred *implicitly*. That is, by operating in the same contexts that the mentor operates in, reading and saying the same things the mentor reads and says, and attending to and trying to understand the mentor's point of view, eventually you *might* have those experiences that are critical to perceiving the world in a way that is similar to your mentor's perceptions.

A method that allowed you to create an *explicit* model of sufficient fidelity, on the other hand, would allow you to quickly acquire those perspectives that underlie your exemplar's model of the world, and so permit you to evolve as an individual far more efficiently and effectively than you could through implicit learning during an extended association. If you have a means of effectively discerning and reproducing the behavioral and experiential models of others, then *anyone can be your mentor*. This is the goal of the EMPRINT method.[3]

Like the camera-equipped investigators of Hall's skiing example, we have studied a great deal of human footage and from it we have extracted some patterns that seem to consistently underlie behavior. And like those modelers of skiing excellence, we can describe to you the resulting distinctions in terms that you can use to understand your own behavior and the behavior of others.

Unlike the skiing modelers, however, we are also giving you the camera. That is, we will place in your hands a method—the EMPRINT method—that you can use to model your own behaviors and those of others in a way that makes those behaviors transferable. Camera in hand, toward what shall we point it first? What shall we model?

Skills

The most startling revelation we see as the first light passes through the lens of our modeling camera is that our greatest resource constantly eludes us, often vanishing even before we are able to recognize it. And even when we are presented with an example of such luminous quality that we do recognize it, we have no way of preserving or propagating it, and must be satisfied with the warmth and light it brings us before it disappears. The resource we are talking about is you, your friends, your neighbors, associates, poets, entrepreneurs, teachers, mystics, engineers, dancers, card sharks—each and every human being.

Examples of luminous human beings come easily to mind. Einstein, Shakespeare, Barishnikov, Galileo, Newton, Mozart, Hawking, Faulkner, Streep, Curie, King, and Erickson are easy to recognize as individuals excelling in their particular endeavors. We are grateful for the ways in which their efforts have contributed to the quality of our lives. We admire them, and often we try to emulate them as well. These people are like very tall peaks—intimidating, but worth the climb. Unfortunately, the trail always seems to disappear halfway to the summit, leaving the climber to roam about the granite faces and talus slopes, seeking a way to continue to the top.

As dramatic and daring as assaults on the heights of human accomplishment are, most of us face the daily challenge of scaling mountains that, though mere foothills by comparison, are no less significant and can be as baffling and difficult as the highest peaks. Rather than following and attempting to overtake Einstein, many of us would simply like to feel comfortable with basic mathematics. Some of us would like to be efficient in our work, understanding with our children, able to play an instrument or paint a pleasing picture, appropriately plan a day, a vacation, or a career, eat properly, exercise regularly, negotiate a raise, enjoy making love, fulfill commitments, forget about commitments when on vacation, save money, invest money wisely, give a speech, and so on. The vast majority of the thousands of outcomes that people desire do not belong to the range of Einsteinian Matterhorns, but to the more immediate foothills of daily experience. Search through your own shortcomings and yearnings, and you will quickly discover that there are many outcomes that you wish and even strive for that are (or have been) of great personal significance, but that nevertheless seem elusive or even unattainable.

No matter how personally unattainable an outcome may seem, though, the fact remains that some people have attained it. How do we account for that fact? The most abused explanation is that "He is that kind of person and I am not." We may ask that person for advice, and emulate him as much as we can; but this course is often unsuccessful, and culminates in resignation to being "not that kind of person." We are like aspiring furniture makers who, despite having the same tools as the Master Furniture Maker, nevertheless seem incapable of making a chair that we can safely sit on.

And yet we cannot deny that there are those who enjoy the very kinds of situations and experiences that we have wished for ourselves. That our neighbors have the ability to exercise or eat properly, write well, comprehend mathematics or the mechanical problems of a car, consider obstacles as welcome challenges, treat their spouses with kindness, and so on, is not *initially* believed by most of us to be due to their genetic endowments. After years of wanting such experiences for ourselves and being continually frustrated in attaining them, however, we do often take refuge behind the curtain of genetics, attributing the successes and qualities of others to some innate "gift." You might think, "That's just the way they are, and I'm not like that." You may even feel that you were not there when the Folks Upstairs handed out those particular attributes.

Once the genetic curtain is drawn shut, however, it does more than help cut out the glare of striving and personal responsibility—it cuts off the warmth of hope as well. The shadow that thus falls is one that we, in our work, have discovered again and again to be unnecessary, and one that we continually try to dispel. It is true that there are marked differences among us as to our abilities, behaviors, and responses to life's situations. As we will demonstrate, however, it is *not* true that these differences are necessarily innate. Most of them are the manifestation of certain ways of thinking and perceiving on the part of the individual, and were *learned*—though not necessarily intentionally.

Ignoring genetic factors for a moment, let's look at an example. Say that your neighbor is able to negotiate well, while you consistently get taken to the proverbial cleaners. This fact can only be attributed to differences in your personal histories and in what each of you has learned over the course of your lives. In other words, if you had had some of the same significant formative experiences as your neighbor, you would have learned similar lessons about negotiation situations and would now be more skilled in that context. But you do not have your neighbor's personal history and can never have it. Now suppose that you need to learn about negotiating. Just what is it that he has learned that is worth *your* learning?

What your neighbor has learned as a result of his experiences is a way of perceiving and thinking—that is, a set of internal processes—within the context of negotiations. For instance, it not only occurs to him to create bargaining leverage (an outcome any budding negotiator knows to strive for), but he is also consistently able to figure out *how* to create that leverage. How can you go about learning what you need to learn about negotiating (and so change in the ways you need to change)?

It is commonly understood that a "skill" is something that one has acquired, either intentionally or unintentionally, and therefore is also available to others who are willing to spend the time and energy necessary to acquire that skill. Readily recognized as skills are the ability to ski, read, drive a car, cook, and so on. It seems obvious to most of us that becoming competent at such skills is a matter of learning what to attend to and what to do when, and then practicing until the required behaviors become automatic. Our collective experience and belief is that just about anyone can become competent at these skills if they have the necessary information and they work at it. This point was exemplified in Hall's skiing example.

Such endeavors as spelling, math, making a marriage work, and raising children exist in a shadowy realm somewhere between skill and endowment. Initially they are treated as skills, and so spelling and math drills are pressed upon children, and self-help books, magazine articles, and psychotherapies are pressed upon adults, with the intention of teaching the skills of spelling, mathematics, relating, and parenting. Failure to acquire such skills often leads quickly to the dismissive and dismal explanation that one is just not "a good speller," or "marriage material," and so on. Nevertheless, the fact is that books, classes, and therapists do exist that are able to teach the necessary discriminations and behaviors, and to motivate their use for a sufficient period of time. They can be very successful in assisting one to become a good speller, a math whiz, a loving mate, and so on. In other words, once made functionally explicit, these endeavors become *learnable skills*.[4]

Going further out on the limb of what is learnable, the aspects of human beings that apparently have the least to do with skill are those qualities generally called "personality characteristics." People just *are* optimistic, generous, tidy, affectionate, frugal, patient, trustworthy, etc.; or else they are not. You may be dissatisfied with being pessimistic and want to be optimistic, but the means to that sunny end rarely go beyond the strong-arm tactic of merely *trying* to be optimistic. Unlike skills, personality characteristics are assumed to be *endowments* rather than *attainments,* so no effort is made to discover the necessary distinctions and behaviors that make possible the ongoing experience of optimism.

Even so, all of us know people who have changed some aspect of their personalities. You can probably find an example of a change in your own personality if you search through your personal history. So at least some aspects of personality have not been mandated at the fall of the genetic gavel.

All of your character traits are the codification of *behaviors* that you have, the manifestation of which corresponds to your (or society's) notions of what behavior is indicative of that trait. For instance, if you consistently show up late for engagements, fail to return borrowed books, and promise to do things for others but fail to follow through, you might come to think of yourself as an "inconsiderate" person. Had you instead followed through on your various commitments to others you might have concluded that you are a "considerate" person. In either case you are assigning to yourself a character attribute which, as an attribute, is usually assumed to be inherent in your "self" and must therefore simply be "put up with."[5]

In resorting to the shorthand of characterizing ourselves and one another according to traits, we must remember that we are characterizing *behaviors*. As we use the term throughout this book, "behavior" includes what people do on both the outside (externally) and on the inside (internally). External behaviors are those that can be observed by others, such as smiling, practicing a tennis stroke, putting a desk in order, arguing, and so on. Internal behaviors include emotions and thought processes. To feel panicky when handed an exam is an internal behavioral response. Similarly, responding with curiosity to a novel situation, or with confidence when faced with an interview, are internal behaviors (internal behaviors that probably are manifested externally as well). Cognitive processes such as computing the product of two fractions also constitute behavior. Deciding what to do tomorrow, making a judgment about a friend's treatment of you, and considering the significance of life are all cognitive (internal) behaviors.[6] Thus everything that we *do* as human beings is a behavior.

It is not possible to know that a person possesses a particular trait unless that person exhibits behavior that is considered a manifestion of that trait. Traits, then, are names for *patterns* of behaviors, like skating and spelling, and as such can be considered learnable skills, provided that we have a sufficiently exhaustive method for specifying the processes underlying their manifestation.

All skills, including character traits, are made up of patterns of internal and external behaviors. In order to make any skill a *learnable* skill, then, we need to point our modeling camera at behaviors in a way that will capture and bring into focus the specific internal processes that interact to result in those behaviors. If we can recognize and understand the set of components (or, as we call them, "internal processes") that are the building blocks of behavior, we can organize them into a model and use them to create the kinds of behaviors—and therefore the kinds of skills and traits—we desire. What we want to discover and model is the set of internal processes that underlie any behavior.

Experience, Structure, and Transferability

While researching the internal processes of individuals in a wide variety of contexts we discovered that:

■ Between individuals who manifest the same behaviors within a particular context, there is remarkable similarity of internal processing patterns; and

■ *Usefully* describing those internal processes consistently involves a certain set of variables.

The discovery that different people who manifest the same behavior evidence similar underlying internal processes is significant for two reasons. First, certain patterns of internal processing are largely *responsible* for the manifestation of certain behaviors. And second, behaviors therefore can be learned by appropriately changing one's internal processes— that is, by matching that constellation of internal processes underlying a particular behavior.

The other discovery—that a consistent set of internal processing variables underlies all of our behavioral responses— means that it is possible to generate a useful method of skill acquisition. The "usefulness" we are referring to here is the ability of our method both to shed light on the origins of an individual's behavior, and to provide the information necessary to *transfer* that behavior to someone else.

It is our experience that almost any behavior can be transferred from a person who already manifests it to a person who does not but would like to—*provided* that the internal processes underlying that behavior are made explicit and put in a form that can be matched by the "learner." Before going further, we want to give you a personal experience of what we are talking about. The following exercise will be most potent if you actually do each step *as it is described*.

1 Search through your experiences and find some occurrence or feeling that you never want to experience again. For instance, you might want to never again be rejected, or to be taken advantage of, or to be without money; or you might want to never again feel angry, or hurt, or incompetent.

2 Spend a few moments *hoping* that "it" will never happen again.

3 Now take a deep breath and spend a few moments *anticipating* that "it" will never happen again. If your reason rejects this as a possibility, simply pretend for a moment that it is possible to anticipate such a future.

What was the difference for you between *hoping* and *anticipating* that *it* would never happen again? Comparing the two, you will probably notice that anticipating made you feel *certain* of being free of future occurrences of that unpleasant experience, while hoping made it seem *uncertain* that you could avoid the unpleasantness. Thus the subjective experience of hoping to never again be rejected is an unsettling mixture of wanting acceptance and recognizing the possiblity of being rejected anyway, while anticipating not being rejected is the pleasant state of *knowing* that you will never be rejected. The internal process underlying the subjective differences between hoping and anticipating is that when we hope, we *simultaneously* maintain internal images of both getting what we want *and* not getting what we want. (You can verify this by calling up some of your own hopes and noticing just what you are imaging as you hope.) When we anticipate, however, we maintain an internal image of only *one* possibility. (If other possibilities are imagined, they are not imagined simultaneously with the one that is anticipated. Again, we encourage you to explore this by noticing the content of your imaginings as you consider some of the experiences, events, and activities you are anticipating.) Now let's take our experiment one step further.

1 Select a *hope* that you currently have. (For instance, that you will remain close to a friend, that you will make a lot of money, that you will travel, that you will master a sport or musical instrument, etc.)

2 Now erase all but one of the possiblities about which you had hope, making a picture of only that one remaining possibility, and notice how your subjective experience changes. (For example, imagine *only* that you will make a lot of money, or *only* that you will not make a lot of money.)

You probably noticed that, when you left yourself with but one imagined possibility, your experience immediately shifted toward anticipation of that future. (Whether your anticipation is fearful or pleasant depends upon whether you are imagining only the unwanted possibility or only the wanted possibility.) This pattern cuts both ways.

1 Select some decidedly unpleasant occurrence that you are currently *anticipating* (making a fool of yourself while on a date, the arrival of a big tax bill, being a procrastinator the rest of your life, etc.), and anticipate it happening.

2   Now make a picture of things not turning out the way you are anticipating (being charming on a date, the arrival of a small tax bill, getting your work done early the rest of your life, etc.), and hold both pictures before you simultaneously. Notice how your subjective experience changes.

In this case you probably noticed that suddenly you were hoping. While previously you were anticipating, say, making a fool of yourself on a date, now (holding beside it the imagined possibility of being charming) you *hope* that you will not make a fool of yourself (or hope that you will be charming). A substantial difference in subjective experience takes place with this change from anticipation to hope, as you can verify for yourself by experimenting with the pattern. *This difference will be manifested in behavior.* The person who anticipates being a fool on a date will respond very differently to the possibility of going out than will the person who *hopes* not to be a fool (or to be charming).[7]

The distinction between hope and anticipation with which you have just been experimenting is one of dozens that we have discovered by modeling the internal processes of many individuals who were either hoping for or anticipating something. Once we understood the underlying pattern, we were able to purposefully (and often profoundly) affect our own experiences and the experiences of others by using this pattern. That is, we have represented the internal processes underlying "hoping" and "anticipating" in a way that can be *transferred* as an ability to anyone who needs or wants such an ability. Thus a middle-aged acquaintance of ours who lived an unhappy life of almost monastic seclusion became more gregarious when we had him add the picture of a happy marriage to his long-standing anticipation of dying a bachelor. As soon as he added that picture he felt more hopeful of finding a love—a change in perspective that manifested itself as increasingly gregarious behavior. Similarly, a woman who hoped for many things but, fearful of the unwanted half of the hope, rarely did anything to help those hopes be realized. She learned to erase her internal images of those fearful possibilities. Left only with the desired outcome before her, her experience turned to one of anticipation. For her, this was behaviorally manifested as getting on with doing everything she could to help make that future a reality.

Examples like these and countless others (not only from our own work) have led to the formation of a supposition that is the foundation of all our inquiries, and that underlies the development of the EMPRINT method. In its most general form, that supposition is that *if it is possible for someone, it is possible for anyone*. More specifically, the fact that some one person (an exemplar) is able to manifest a particular behavior means that his or her internal processes are organized to make that behavior possible; therefore, if other individuals organize their internal processes in the same way as the exemplar they too will manifest that behavior. We are not saying that you can become an Einstein (you do not and can not have his personal history), but that you *can* learn to enjoy and be competent at physics.[8]

The Approach

The underlying assumption in all that we have been discussing is that one's behavior is a manifestion of one's internal processes. Joe's pessimistic responses are the natural manifestation of thinking like Joe, and Sam's optimism is the natural manifestion of thinking like Sam. How each of them thinks becomes worth discovering when Joe would like to manifest optimism (or Sam would like to manifest pessimism). In short, Sam has what Joe needs in terms of internal processes in order to be able to *naturally* respond optimistically. Of course, in an effort to be like Sam, Joe could simply ape Sam's optimistic words and responses, but if those words are not congruent with Joe's *experience*, they will never come naturally and, more important, Joe will still not have what he really wants, which is to *be* optimistic. Of course, it's possible to go through the motions of a desired behavior, trying to transform oneself by groping for what to do and the force of will to do it; or, when that approach becomes too disappointing, to "realize" that one is simply "not that kind of person." But our position is that it's better to discover the particular internal processes that naturally lead to the manifestation of the desired behavior in those who already possess it.

These variables *can* be known, and the primary instrument of this knowledge is language. As Korzybski, Whorf, Sapir and others have extensively described, there is no neat way to separate a culture's language from the perceptual worlds experienced by members of that culture. Language is not an indifferent and lifeless medium for the reporting of internal experience.

We dissect nature along lines laid down by our native languages. The categories and types that we isolate from the world of phenomena we do not find there because they stare every observer in the face; on the contrary, the world is presented in a kaleidoscopic flux of impressions which has to be organized by our minds—and this means largely by the linguistic systems in our minds. We cut nature up, organize it into concepts, and ascribe significances as we do, largely because we are parties to an agreement to organize it in this way—an agreement that holds throughout our speech community and is codified in the patterns of our language. (Whorf, 1956, p. 213)

All languages have a structure of some kind, and every language reflects in its own structure that of the world as assumed by those who evolved the language. Reciprocally, we read mostly unconsciously into the world the structure of the language we use. Because we take the structure of our own habitual language so much for granted, particularly if we were born into it, it is sometimes difficult to realize how differently people with other language structures view the world. (Korzybski, 1951, p. 22)

Thus the words that a person uses are representations of his or her internal experience and are comprehensible by those individuals who organize their thinking according to the same linguistic patterns. (In general, these individuals will be from the same culture—an outsider does not necessarily need to think in another language in order to speak and decipher that language. See Whorf, 1956, pp. 134-159, 207-219.) The variables used in the EMPRINT method are distinctions characteristic of the internal processes of everyone raised in this culture. Furthermore, all of the internal processing variables are implicitly or explicitly represented in the grammar, syntax, and lexicon shared by those of us raised in this culture.

For example, in our culture we perceive a world that is organized in a particular way with respect to the past, present, and future. To those of us who have spent our lives organizing our perceptions and understandings with respect to those divisions of the time line, they seem self-evident and no more in need of justification or proof than does the observation that there are rocks in the world. However, although *we* may take for granted the distinctions past, present, and future, our *language* does not, never failing as we speak or think to assign verb tenses to the various experiences we are expressing ("I *ran*," "I *run*," "I *will run*"). By way of contrast, Whorf cites the example of the Hopi, who do not perceive their world in terms of the past, present, and future (and so have no such tense distinctions in their language), but instead organize according to *duration*. To a Hopi, two different men may age at two very different rates—one as "corn," the other as "lightning." In fact, to a Hopi it would not really be "rate," but more like *intensity*.[9] (See Whorf, 1956.)

The words and syntax each of us uses to describe our experiences are neither random nor arbitrary. They are, instead, verbal analogues of our ongoing experiences and as such they reveal the nature of that experience to the extent that we are able to accurately decipher what is being said and to empathize with the perceptions that are decoded. (By "empathize" we mean the ability to comprehend the perceptions of someone else in the same way that that person comprehends them. Again, knowing the lexicon of another language is not the same thing as being able to empathize with the experiences of someone who has grown up in that linguistic culture.) The method described here specifies those variables that our work has shown are significant in the manifestation of behavior and that are therefore worth deciphering. The deciphering itself is for the most part made possible by the patterns in our language through which we express our experiences. As we will see in the chapters to come, by consciously using our cultural decoder rings (an endowment from the breakfast cereal box of childhood) we can begin to unlock some of the functional secrets of our internal processes— processes that we normally and naturally take for granted.

Reeling in the various lines we have cast, then, our catch consists of the following suppositions and observations upon which the EMPRINT method is based:

■ Many of the abilities and qualities that are commonly believed to be innate characteristics are in fact simply a function of behavior and therefore should be learnable skills.

■ An individual's behavior is a manifestion of internal processes.

■ Internal processes can be expressed as a set of functional variables that are shared by all of us who grew up in this culture.

■ How each of us fulfills those variables can be known by the linguistic distinctions we use in describing our experiences.

■ Since the variables are the same for all of us, and the differences between us lie in the distinctions we make within each of those variables, it is possible for one person to change his internal processes to substantially match those of another person/exemplar within a particular context and thereby greatly increase his ability to manifest the same behavioral skills as those manifested by the exemplar.

This approach and the method that has grown out of it provide a means of at least beginning to fulfill Hall's prophecy that "Some time in the future, a long, long time from now when culture is more completely explored, there will be the equivalent of musical scores that can be learned, each for a different type of man or woman in different types of jobs and relationships, for time, space, work and play."

2 The Organizing Principle

Your ability to control or influence your personal experience (and, as some believe, the world itself) is the direct result of both the distinctions that you make and the model you use to organize those distinctions. A "distinction" is any perceptual or conceptual discrimination—any recognition of differences. Anything that you attend to in your internal and external environments can qualify as a distinction. In terms of perception, for instance, modern western languages make literally hundreds of color distinctions, whereas the American Indian language of Maidu makes only three such distinctions— *lak*–red; *tit*–green/blue; *tulak*–yellow/orange/brown. Native speakers of Maidu and of English will differ in what they notice when seeing, for example, the leaves of a sycamore tree and a clear mid-day sky. For the English speaker the leaves and the sky are two different colors (green and blue), while the Maidu Speaker will notice that they are varying shades of the same color (*tit*). The differences lie in how the two cultures draw the lines that distinguish one color as being different from another.

Similarly, cultural differences exist with respect to distinctions made about "time." Western cultures distinguish between past, present, and future, and those of us weaned on western culture perceive the world as exemplifying those three time frames. In fact, it is difficult for us to imagine a world without past, present, and future distinctions. We do not consider time as something tangible, as something we have made, or as something that we can change. Time in the form of the past, present, and future just *is*, like the universe just *is*.

Had you been raised as a Hopi Indian before the turn of this century, however, you would have spoken a language with only a present tense. As we discovered in the previous chapter, time for the Hopi was not divided into discrete instants belonging to the past, present, or future, and therefore was not in motion. Instead, the Hopi made distinctions about duration, such as "lightning flash" (short duration), "the life of a stalk of corn" (longer duration), and "the life of a man" (long duration). *Distinctions are the recognition, or creation, of differences.*

Beyond the distinctions of past, present, and future lie the significance and utilization of each of those time frames. A Hopi who is taught to perceive the future as distinct from the present or past will not necessarily know how to *use* that distinction. A westerner would encourage the Hopi to speculate about the future, while an Arab would instruct the Hopi that the future is *not* to be speculated about. A Hopi who speculated about the future would be praised for his practicality by the westerner, while the Arab would suspect that same Hopi of being insane. The Arab understands that only God knows the future, and for a man to think he could predict what only God knows means that man is very disturbed. The set of tacit and explicit rules that govern how the individual is to use and make sense of those time frames constitutes a framework—or organizing principle—for those distinctions. It is the organizing principle that arranges the distinctions in such a way that they become relevant to one's behavior and experience. Taking our language as an analogy, the *vocabulary* constitutes a set of distinctions, which are organized with respect to a syntax (the organizing principle). Without the organizing principle of *syntax* to sequence and assign relational significance to the vocabulary (the distinctions), the vocabulary is merely a list of names for "things."

Perhaps you can recall a nearly universal example of what we are talking about here: the first year of high school. For most people, entering high school was like moving to a strange and bewildering country. At first, high school was an alien culture, with its novel distinctions and interactions. You had to learn to distinguish between teacher, department head, counselor, activities director, attendance secretary, vice principal, and principal. Then there was the pep rally, pep squad, cheerleader, mascot, spirit, team captains, detention, prom, homecoming, senior lawn, passes (both kinds), periods (both kinds), semesters, grind classes, cinch classes, "easy A" classes, dress code, finals, ditch day, jock straps, class annual, going steady, going all the way, car clubs, service clubs, cutting, Associated Student Body, expulsion, shop, petting, necking, swats, mags, baby moons, dingle balls, the head, headers, heads, greasers, surfers, studs, jocks, brains, and wimps.

These myriad distinctions were in the service of the social interactions that were characteristic of high school. Thus it was not enough to be able to recognize the difference between a car club and a service club. You also had to learn the behaviors, sequences of behaviors, and expectations that constituted the *interactional* syntax of those distinctions. For instance, how you act around a "head," as opposed to a "brain," as opposed to a "sosh," will depend upon what "type" they consider you to be, what type you consider yourself to be, whether you are alone with them or in a group, and so on. Which lawns, clubs, and dances you are welcome at, and when, are vital learnings. And when the girl you want to ask for a date is wearing a ring that is too big for her finger, you had better know what that means.

The distinctive thread providing the warp for all of this social weaving is that of "class." Being at a dance, playing a sport, talking to a girl, ditching a class, registering for a class, or just walking down the halls, are not the same experiences for a freshman as they are for a sophomore, or a junior, or a senior. When you are a junior, bumping into someone in the hall and knocking his books out of his hands is a minor incident if the bumpee is a freshman, but it's a good time to break out your kneepads for groveling if the bumpee is a senior. Of course, the senior bumpee might be a wimp, while you are a jock, and so you end up ignoring rather than kneeling. Even so, the fact that you are a junior and your victim is a senior is nevertheless taken into account and becomes significant in terms of your perceptions and behavior (after all, you ignored a *senior*). Almost everything that goes on socially in high school is organized with respect to "class." In the context of high school, then, "class" is an *organizing principle*.

An organizing principle is a distinction that is significant to all of the various operations of a system. In the above example, consideration of "class" figures significantly in all of the social interactions (operations) that go on in high school. Analogously, the caste system in India provides an organizing principle that significantly influences most social interactions. Another example of an organizing principle is the presumption of innocence until proven guilty in the context of our legal system, affecting the operations of apprehending suspects, obtaining evidence, prosecution, jury selection, and so on. Until relatively recently, physicists operated within a Newtonian universe that was in part based on the organizing principle that phenomena could be measured, defined, and predicted, provided that you have identified the relevant variables. With their efforts organized with respect to this classical view of matter, physicists made certain discoveries about the nature of matter and its possible manifestations and interactions. When some experimental evidence seemed irreconcilable with this view of matter as being rigid with clearly defined boundaries, many physicists regrouped around another organizing principle—the *uncertainty principle*—which asserts that it is not possible to make accurate observations of all of the variables that underlie the manifestations and interactions of matter. Organizing their investigations and understanding with respect to the uncertainty principle has led physicists to previously uncharted territories, such as the "tunneling" of black holes.

Many different organizing principles have been used in creating models and theories of human experience and behavior. Confronted with the bewildering complexities, as well as the awesome task of understanding and changing those experiences and behaviors, those intent upon creating coherent models of human psychology have searched for conceptual threads which they perceive as running through human experience. The Freudian psychoanalytic model is organized with respect to the id, ego, and superego. In gestalt psychology the organizing principle is the distinction between figure and ground. Among behavioral pyschologists the principle that organizes experience and behavior is that of stimulus-response. Transactional analysis uses as its organizing principle the distinctions of child, parent, and adult. Miller, Galanter, and Pribram (1960) built their model around the organizing principle of behavior at all its various levels being subject to a "TOTE" (Test-Operate-Test-Exit). As organizing principles, each of these threads weaves for us its own unique set of patterns in terms of human experience and behavior.

There is one thread, however, that is pervasive in its influence on us. No other aspect of our experience is more easily or more often manipulated by us; no other aspect of our experience keeps us so bent to its service. It is also, as you will soon discover, one of the easiest to identify and understand. That thread, which we have chosen as the organizing principle for the EMPRINT method, is that of the *time frames of the past, present, and future.*

Accurately or inaccurately, for better or worse, we are beings whose consciousness recognizes *time* as an experiential dimension. Once we get the bit of time between our conceptual teeth (usually when quite young) we run with it, creating the past, present, and future as we go. So compelling is the experience of these time frames that their significance quickly permeates virtually all the psychological operations that make up our ongoing experiences and that direct our behaviors.

The ways in which time frames are used play an influential and even a decisive role in creating our personal experiences and in determining our behavioral responses. This will become evident to you if you take a moment to consider some decision you have made—any decision—and notice what time frames you considered and how you used them. As an example, take a few moments right now to decide where you will eat lunch tomorrow.

On what basis do you make your decision? Is it based on what tomorrow's activities and weather are likely to be (that is, the future)? Is it based on what foods appeal to you now as you think about possible eating places (that is, the present)? Or is it based on where you are accustomed to eating (that is, the past)? Regardless of any other specifics of your considerations about where to eat lunch tomorrow, you will find that those considerations take you at various times and in various ways into the past, present, and/or future.

The significance for us of time frames was originally heuristic. In the course of applying and testing other methods for the purpose of understanding and transferring behaviors we discovered that our clients and subjects not only *always* represented their experience in relation to the past, present, or future, but that they did so in a way that was *characteristic* of each of them within a particular context. This pervasive and individually characteristic representation of time frames became a practical consideration—and the organizing principle of the EMPRINT method—as we gradually discovered that time frame representation was significant in terms of determining subjective experience, directing behavior, and being able to transfer useful behaviors from one person to another.[1]

Before launching into a description of the method itself, then, we need to present the method's organizing principle— the time frames of the past, present, and future.[2]

Time Frames

Of course no one knows for certain, but human beings probably created the concept of time as a result of acquiring the cognitive ability to consciously recognize that since TODAY has always followed YESTERDAY there will be a TOMORROW. Once we recognized the reliability of those relationships we were liberated from the confines of responding only to our current internal and external environments. The existence of a ponderable past and at times a predictable future created sequence and continuity, and those two perceptions in turn engendered *planning*. Instead of being trapped in "I'm cold; I'm hot; Something is growing there," our progenitors could have seasons and other periodic events that could be measured and anticipated. Whereas before they could only respond to the exigencies of the environment, now they also had access to the past and the future as sources of information. They could therefore set priorities for behaviors in accordance with what could be expected in the near or distant future (for example, what the weather will be tonight, or preparing for the birth of a child). People could respond to what *had been* and to what *could* or *will be*.

As pervasive and fundamental as the past, present, and future seem to be, they are, as we previously mentioned, influenced by subjective intercultural differences.[3] No one has done more than Edward T. Hall to enlighten us about those differences. Through his many books describing the experiential and behavioral contrasts between cultures, Hall has revealed the tremendous diversity and influence of differing cultural perceptions of time.

In the social world [of the United States] a girl feels insulted when she is asked for a date at the last minute by someone whom she doesn't know very well, and the person who extends an invitation to a dinner party with only three or four days' notice has to apologize. How different from the people of the [Arab] Middle East with whom it is pointless to make an appointment too far in advance, because the informal structure of their time system places everything beyond a week into a single category of "future," in which plans tend to "slip off their minds." (Hall, 1959, p. 3)

The far-sightedness of Americans is myopic, however, compared to the future as seen by some Asians, who look to futures that span *centuries*. For the Navajo the future has no reality; there is only the ever-unfolding present. An offer of some great future reward will be utterly ignored by the Navajo in favor of something that can be had immediately. The past never recedes for the Trukese in the Southwest Pacific. Upon recalling a wrong committed five, ten, twenty years before, a Truk Islander will experience and respond to that memory as though it had just happened. Hall also describes the Hopi's lack of verb tenses. For the Hopi, time is not a series of discrete instants, but a "getting later" of the same time, a time in which events are accumulating. Thus the rising of the sun is a return of yesterday in another form. The Trobriand Islander does away with sequence altogether, preferring a history that is anecdotal and heedless of chronology, in which events are shifted in time and sequence as it suits the individual.[4]

All of these are very different from the western perception of time as being sequential, unidirectional, inexorable, and spanning a distinct past, present, and future. The many different distinctions that various cultures make regarding time are neither frivolous nor arbitrary, nor are they superfluous. The distinctions that human beings make are the extensions of our perceptual and cognitive experiences of the world, and so *reflect* our individual and cultural experiences (our models of the world), as well as *guide* those experiences (as Hall illustrated above in his comparison of American and Middle Eastern appointment-making). Cultural perceptions of time also influence the values, skills, and attributes that are respected and sought after in each culture.

In the culture of American business, for example, a hot topic of conversation in board rooms, cherished by investors, and responded to on Wall Street is *this quarter's* profits. With its focus on present (or very short-term) results, it is only natural that the skills and attributes that are highly valued are those having to do with the ability to get immediate results. This is in sharp contrast to the business community in Japan, in which present or short-term profits are not given the same importance as future growth and stability. In America we have a best-selling book that suggests that the efficient manager can sufficiently instruct, criticize, or praise his or her subordinates in *one minute*. The tremendous respect and admiration currently shown for Lee Iaccoca in this country exists, to a great extent, not only because he was able to fight seemingly impossible odds to rescue the Chrysler Corporation from the jaws of bankruptcy and make it a viable company again, but that he did it *in a very short period of time*.

As compelling as cultural comparisons of the effects of time perception are, you have only to turn to your own memories and experiences for some potent examples of the subjective and behavioral impact of time. Soldiers at war and civilians under siege, for instance, are often faced with little or no possibility of a future. The result is a sudden preoccupation with satisfying present needs and wants, without concern for subsequent self or societal condemnation. Men and women who were previously law abiding, considerate of others, and respectful of behavioral norms (whether out of fear of consequences or consideration for how things should be) suddenly find themselves involved in rape, plundering, stealing, and purposeless destruction. That personal gratification often takes such violent and destructive forms during wars is largely due to the context in which it occurs, for people who are told that they have only a short time to live as the result of a terminal illness do not generally go out and rape, steal, and destroy. But those who are terminally ill do often become hedonistic in the sense of setting aside their normal routines to devote their remaining days to enjoying life, gratifying whims and desires, and so on.

You can provide your own examples of the influence of time frames. Like most people, you have hopes and plans for the future. There are things that someday you want to do, to experience, to be. Imagine what you would do with your time if you had only one month to live. What considerations suddenly become trivial, and which become important?

Now imagine that you discover that you have one hundred years left to live. How does that prospect alter your hopes and plans? Some individuals take a very broad view of their lives, a view that extends beyond death. Artists, authors, and scientists, for example, tend to view their works as extensions of themselves—extensions that will survive their creator's death. People with such a perspective are likely to continue their normal activities until they die.

An example of what happens when one has no past is furnished by the indoctrination practices of many of the religious and social cults that are burgeoning in this country. These cults undermine an initiate's beliefs regarding his or her own morals and motivations, as well as the morals and motivations of their families and the society in general, by altering the initiate's perceptions of the past. For some of these groups, this disowning of the past as a lie and an hallucination is symbolized and abetted by bestowing a new name on the initiate. The past is to a great extent necessary for maintaining one's identity. Without the past to rely on, the task of shaping the new member to conform to the goals and perceptions of the cult becomes much easier. In describing his own brush with cult indoctrination, a well-known de-programmer put it this way: "You start doubting yourself. You start to question everything you believe in. Then you find yourself saying and doing the same things they are."

Young children (to the age of two), are familiar examples of individuals who have not yet had much access to the past *or* the future. To a young child, anything that happened yesterday or even earlier in the day happened "a long time ago," if indeed thay reflect on it at all. This is not to say that young children do not have memories or stored information, only that they tend not to go into the past to consciously evaluate their present situation. Rules must be repeated for them many times before they sink in. The future is even more unknowable to them, so that having to wait for things becomes a seemingly endless torture, and the immediate gratification of wants and needs has top priority.

If you have forgotten what it was like to be two years old, perhaps you still recall your teenage years. For most of us, that hormone-ridden time between childhood and adulthood was characterized by a scoffing disinterest in the past and a disregard for the future. Perhaps the sudden changes in our bodies and in our social interactions disconnected the past from what we had become. Perhaps the feeling that we had all the time in the world ahead of us made the future irrelevant. Whatever the reason, most teenagers are steeped in the present. We wanted what we wanted *now*, we did what we did for the experience of the moment, and the entity that compelled our tastes in clothes, food, entertainment, values, and morals was our current peer group.

We have offered these examples of time frame deletion and extension as a means of illustrating that there are different ways of experiencing time, and to illustrate that otherwise culturally determined experiences of time can be contextually altered. Let us now bring these observations closer to home by considering your own temporal experiences.

Imagine that an acquaintance walks up to you and pinches your arm very hard—hard enough to cause pain. How do you respond? Instead of immediately reacting with hurt or bellig-erance to the pinch, you could access the past, quickly reviewing your history with that person, previous experiences of being pinched, and where various responses of yours have previously led. You could also imagine the future to consider various ways of responding to the pinch, how the pincher will in turn respond, what you want your relationship to be with the pincher after the current situation is resolved, and so on. You could do all those things, but *do* you? Do you examine the future, or the past, or the present, or all three? And how do you use the times frame(s) you do attend to? How would your response be different if you changed the time frames you were using to evaluate the situation? And, if you use more than one time frame, how would your response differ if you changed the order in which you refer to each time frame?

A few minutes of experimentation on your own of stepping into the various possibilities of time frame deletion and extension will provide you with personal examples of the significant impact of time frames upon your subjective experience. The fact that we take time frames for granted as we go through our daily lives does not in any way dismiss the fact that they are significant in determining our experiences and behaviors. Rightly or wrongly, we perceive time as distinctly past, present, and future, and each of those distinctions is imbued with certain experiential characteristics that we must define if we are to be able to coherently use these distinctions as an organizing principle for the EMPRINT method. We now turn to the definition of those characteristics. Along the way, we will also discuss some of the appropriate and inappropriate ways in which we use the past, present, and future.

Past

But I did not only talk of the future and the veil which was drawn over it [to my fellow prisoners in the concentration camp]. I also mentioned the past; with all its joys, and how its light shone even in the present darkness. Again I quoted a poet—to avoid sounding like a preacher myself—who had written, "Was Du erlebt, kann keine Macht der Welt Dir rauben." (What you have experienced, no power on earth can take from you.) Not only our experiences, but all we have done, whatever great thoughts we may have had, and all we have suffered, all this is not lost, though it is past; we have brought it into being. Having been is also a kind of being, and perhaps the surest kind.

> Viktor E. Frankl
> *Man's Search for Meaning*

The past is the repository of memories. Although each of us is sure that we had a past and that there is a past to have had, the fact is that other than artifacts that we can examine now, such as a photograph, a tape recording, or some initials carved in a tree, the only evidence of our pasts are our memories. The notorious unreliability of most people's memories in terms of accuracy is too well documented to need repetition here. But despite this documentation and the implications of the endless family arguments in which we have all engaged about what "really" happened, we all tend to rely on our memories as being representations of what really happened in the past.

The importance of knowing what "really happened" is that it provides the basis for *patterning*—the process of discerning dependably recurring phenomena. ("Phenomena" includes anything from what constitutes a chair, to a person's curiosity about relationships, to the behavior of neutrinos.) A child who witnesses the breaking of an egg for the first time may be amazed to see a yellow blob come out, but he will not necessarily know that he can expect to see another yellow blob plop out of the next egg he sees cracked. Instead, he stores the experience as a memory, a piece of information. After witnessing the yellow blob appear from inside the broken egg several more times, the child will have a set of memories that are all the same in terms of what's inside an egg. This provides the child with the basis for generating the expectation that all eggs contain yellow blobs. In other words, the child has discerned a pattern.

If it seems incredible to you that the child might fail to immediately realize that the next egg he saw broken would also spill out a yellow blob, that is only because you have forgotten that at some point in your own early development you distilled a higher order pattern which states that "Objects that are apparently the same are likely to exhibit the same properties." Lacking this generalization, which makes it possible for us adults to make so much of our lives predictable, toddlers are able to be endlessly thrilled by a game of peek-a-boo. Your ability to pattern on the basis of past experience makes it possible for you to put your feet on the floor without worrying whether or not the floor will support you, to drive your car, to know when it's a good time to talk to your lover, and so on. In fact, the greatest use of the past is as a pool of information that can be tapped and arranged into patterns.

Although everyone can and does pattern, individuals vary in the extent to which the past is used for pattern information. You know that the chair you are sitting in will support you—it always *has*. You know that the books on your shelves do not move of their own accord—they never *have*. But imagine for a moment that you could not depend upon the past for patterns. Now what would your world be like? How secure can you feel, sitting in that chair? How sure can you be that your books will stay put on the shelf? We had a client, Tom, who lived in just such a world. As we sat talking with Tom about what he wanted, which was to be in control of his life, he periodically became nervous and started scanning the floor of the office. When we asked him what he was looking for, Tom informed us that he was checking to see whether or not the nap in the carpet had changed during the time he had not been looking at it. Undoubtedly a Cambodian farmer who has fled his mountain home and made his way to the United States is in a similar position for at least a while as he discovers that very little in his past is relevant to dealing with the wall outlets, traffic jams, and social conventions that we understand (have patterned) so well.

Unlike Tom, who had an undependable past, another client had the experience that there was no past, there was only the present—a perception that withstood every test we could devise. At one point we opened the door and asked him to see what was in the next room. We then closed the door and asked him what would be there when we opened it again. He reported that he had no idea what he would see. As far as he was concerned it could be anything. Perhaps there would be no room at all. How should he know what was on the other side of the door? For us, there was a way in which his ongoing experience was delightful and even enviable, for when he stood up and the floor *did* support his weight he was pleasantly surprised. He was the epitome of the happily awestruck child—perhaps a perfect state when walking in the woods, but obviously not an appropriate state for the mundane tasks of daily living and relating with others, which are based on the recognition and observance of patterns.

Like so many things, the past can be used both as plowshare and as sword. The past becomes a sword when it is used to justify or vindicate, rather than to inform. The most common example of a misuse of the past occurs when an individual explicitly or implicitly says, "I can't do this because I've never done it before." This person is precluding the possibility of attempting something for the first time *because* he or she has no history of having done it. Frieda is such a person. If you ask her to bake a cake, change a tire, help with an algebra problem, or make herself feel happy, her response is always the same: She searches through her personal history for information that can be used to determine whether or not the task being asked of her is one that she has tackled before. That is appropriate. Such determinations are precisely what the past is for. Frieda gets into trouble (in the sense of unnecessarily limiting herself) when her search reveals that she lacks in her personal history an example of having done the task before, and she then uses that vacancy as a justification for not trying it now (which, if she did try it, would of course *provide* her with that piece of personal history). Frieda operates and constrains herself in exactly the same way as that bane of job seekers everywhere, the employer who says that you must already have experience to be hired. Well, how are you supposed to get the experience if they won't let you do the job to get it? Frieda fails to recognize that she can now do countless things despite the fact that (if she goes back far enough in her personal history) there was a time when she had *no* previous experience with anything.

A second, more insidious misuse of the past can be stated as, "I can't do that because I have failed at it before." This misuse is more insidious in that it is a reasonable and seemingly appropriate use of personal history patterns. This misuse of the past was characteristic of a client of ours named

John. John had been through a divorce, so he was sure that he was not cut out for married life. He had been fired from a sales job, so he was no good at selling. He had tried landscape painting once, earned the scorn of his teacher, and therefore realized that he was not artistic. When he was a kid he could not hit a basketball hoop with a truck, let alone a basketball so, of course, he was no good at basketball. In each instance, John had experiences in his personal history that, when examined for patterns, seemed to demonstrate that he could not do "it," whatever "it" might be.

This apparently appropriate use of the past becomes a trap when you use it under the assumption that the present or future task being considered *is* or *will be* the same as those you have attempted in the past. For instance, John is in love and would like to ask his lady to marry him, but as he considers the possibility of marriage he recalls only examples of his incompetence as a husband. He could give up his dream of marrying his lady on the pattern-based justification that he is not good at sustaining a marriage.

It seems to us, however, that the generalization to be drawn from his personal history is not that he is poor at being a husband, but that *he HAS BEEN poor at being a husband given the contexts in which it HAS occurred* (the particular woman who was his wife, their particular living situation, age, sophistication, etc.) *and the way in which he approached being a husband* (that is, his behaviors and his understanding of their significance and impact on himself, on women, and on relationships). The difference is that in the first example John uses the past as a reason for not acting, while in the second suggested example he would be using the past as *information* regarding possible factors that made those previous experiences unsatisfactory. Using the past as the determiner of what is possible can lead to inaction and feelings of inadequacy and incompetence. Using the past as a source of information, however, is more likely to lead to a productive evaluation concerning what things need to be changed—and *how* they need to be changed—in order to fulfill your hopes and needs.

In general, people repeat what has worked well for them in the past. If, when practicing your tennis serve, you happen to toss the ball slightly forward of where you normally place it, and this toss is followed by a particularly accurate shot, you will probably try placing the ball slightly forward again. If bending your knees and arching your back produces even a few additional successful serves, you will probably install that maneuver as part of your regular serving form. Similarly, a young man whose sorrowful behavior is rewarded by eventually attracting a girlfriend, will very likely continue to use pining misery to attract women when he once again finds himself alone—not because being sorrowful is enjoyable, or the best of attractants, but because it has worked before.

One way in which the past is treated as the present is revealed in how we often respond to others as though they are the same as they were last month or last year or even ten years ago. Those of us who have greeted husbands, sons, sisters, brothers, and friends returning home from a war have had to recognize, respect, and respond to the ways in which those men and women have changed. You don't need a war to change people, though. Any profound experience—college, living independently, first love, a new job—exerts its influence on us, changing us in ways that may not be appreciated by those close to us. This is especially marked in the response of many parents to their grown children. A mother who fusses about the diet of her six-foot, thirty-six year old son is probably responding to him as though he were still who he was thirty years ago.

Most psychotherapies have been built in response to the very pattern we have been discussing. Psychoanalysis, transactional analysis, gestalt therapy, primal therapy, and rebirthing, as well as the "pop" psychotherapies such as est, Lifespring, and Scientology, are all designed to deal with the past as the source of problems. According to their tenets, you are the product of your past. We agree with this to a certain extent. What we don't agree with is the assumption that you are trapped by that past, an assumption that is held explicitly or implicitly by all of the approaches listed above. Every one of these therapies has as its primary technology/intervention some form of personal history alteration. All of them take the client back through traumatic or unsatisfactory events in an effort to alter that personal history in some way. As an example, take a moment to experience the following exercise.

1 Identify some incident in your personal history that you believe has a continuing and undesirable influence on your experience and behavior. Perhaps there was a moment of derision or failure on a playing field or in a math class that, to this day, keeps you wary of sports or math-related tasks. Or perhaps a close relative left unexpectedly, leaving you with an enduring mistrust of the permanence of relationships, or the need for continuing reassurance of your lover's affection. The incident should be one that, if it had not happened, you would be in some way different today.

2 Once you have identified that incident, consider what resource you have now that, if you had had it then, would have made a world of difference in your experience at the time. A resource can be a piece of knowledge, an understanding about the world, a belief, a behavior, a skill, or the like.

3 With that resource in mind (and well in hand), go back to that earlier incident and relive it *with the exception that* you now have at your disposal the resource from your future. Notice in what ways your experience changes when you do this. Using the resource, run through the experience a few more times, expanding with each run-through your representation of what is happening. Then "grow up" with that new memory—that is, bring yourself up through your personal history with that changed, remembered experience intact.

4 Now think of some related future situation in which you are likely to find yourself. Imagine being in that situation and notice in what ways your responses are different from those you would normally have.

A change may be effected by changing your personal history (as was done in the exercise you just tried, and as is done in gestalt therapy and rebirthing), or by catharsis (as in psychoanalysis and primal therapy), or by creating dissociation (as in transactional analysis and most of the pop therapies). The point is that all of these therapies exist as a response to the phenomenon of individuals using their past experiences as reasons or justifications for their limitations, rather than as information.

Remember that the past we are describing is the past as it is conceived in American culture. Part of our cultural understanding of time is the presupposition that what is past is over and done with. This presupposition transforms our ongoing experiences into events, which can end, as contrasted with processes, ways, or practices, which are continuous, ongoing experiences. The fact that our society operates within a syntax that specifies a discontinuity between the past, present, and future is reflected in our perception and handling of growth and maturation as divided into discrete stages, in our insistence on definite endings in our movies and television shows, and so on. (Soap operas and serials take advantage of this need of ours by leaving us with situations that are *not* resolved.)[5] Hall reminds us, however, that our perspective on the continuity of time frames is not inherent to time, but is a cultural filter.

There are also times when a given culture develops rhythms that go beyond a single generation, so that no one living person hears the whole symphony. This is true of the Maori of New Zealand, according to a friend, Karaa Pukatapu—a Maori who, when this was written, was Under Secretary for Ethnic Affairs in New Zealand. He described at some length how the cultivation of human talents was a process that required anywhere from generations to centuries to be completed. He commented: "What we know takes centuries, you try to do overnight!" The consequences of trying to compress long rhythms into short time periods result in [American-European] peoples feeling that they have failed, as they do when their children don't turn out just the way they wanted. The Maori realize that it can take generations to produce a really balanced personality. (Hall, 1983, p. 173)

By turning our experiences into events that end and then recede into the past we create the possibility of evaluating those events as either successes or failures. Left as ongoing experiences, there simply would be no occasion to say, "O.K., now *that* was a failure (success)!"

In pointing out these differences we are not implying that our culture's discontinuous view of the past and present is less valuable or valid than a view that perceives the transitions between past, present, and future as unbroken and continuous. For instance, the perception of the past and present as distinct realms is, in fact, important in generating the internal states of "disappointment" and "frustration." We respond with disappointment when we believe that it is no longer possible to attain what we wanted (that is, the opportunity has *passed*). We respond with frustration when we are not getting what we want, but nevertheless believe that it continues to be possible to attain (that is, the pursuit is still occurring in the *present*).[6] On the other hand, if something is really in the past, then it is not part of the present. This makes it easier for us in our culture to put behind us such things as tragedies, failures, mistakes, hard times, and so on.

Present

"Here," whispered Leo Auffmann, "the front window. Quiet, and you'll see it."

... And there, in small warm pools of lamplight, you could see what Leo Auffmann wanted you to see. There sat Saul and Marshall, playing chess at the coffee table. In the dining room Rebecca was laying out the silver. Naomi was cutting paper-doll dresses. Ruth was painting water colors. Joseph was running his electric train. Through the kitchen door, Lena Auffmann was sliding a pot roast from the steaming oven. Every hand, every head, every mouth made a big or little motion. You could hear their faraway voices under glass. You could hear someone singing in a high sweet voice. You could smell bread baking, too, and you knew it was real bread that would soon be covered with real butter. Everything was there and it was working.

Grandfather, Douglas, and Tom turned to look at Leo Auffmann, who gazed serenely through the window, the pink light on his cheeks.

"Sure," he murmured. "There it is." And he watched with now-gentle sorrow and now-quick delight, and at last quiet acceptance as all the bits and pieces of this house mixed, stirred, settled, poised, and ran steadily again. "The Happiness Machine," he said. "The Happiness Machine."

Ray Bradbury
Dandelion Wine

The present is the source of *direct sensory experience* and the time frame of action. You are certainly having experiences when delving into the past or imagining the future, but the sensory impressions you receive when doing so are secondary, the result of *representations* of experience, rather than direct, primary experience. Recalling your most vivid and affecting memories or fantasies, you may be hearing, seeing, smelling, and feeling just what you did (or would have) in that incident. Still, those experiences are a function of internally generated representations, rather than coming from sensory impressions of your present environment. Direct sensory experience occurs only in the present. (This is not to say that such memories and fantasies are not compelling. By *compelling* we mean subjectively real enough to elicit responses. As we will describe in Chapter 7, for some of us those memories or fantasies can be every bit as compelling—in terms of subjective responses and the behaviors they precipitate—as the present environment.)

Being in the present is good for having direct experience of your environment. Such contexts as love-making, eating a fine meal, smelling a flower, playing tennis, and listening to music are examples of times when it is appropriate to be in the present (that is, sensorially aware). This does not mean that you should not go to the past or future during any of these activities. While tasting a particular dish, for instance, you might note a flavor and then search through your memories in order to identify it. However, if, while you are tasting that dish, you are lost in some memory or fantasy, you are probably not being aware (note present tense) of the taste of the food. There is nothing remarkable about this experience. We have all had it—common examples are eating something without being aware that we are doing so, or driving by our destination while "lost in thought."

There are obvious implications to not being in the present in those contexts that are inherently "now" experiences, such as making love, sports, dancing, enjoying a summer sunset, or playing with your children. If you are "somewhere else" while making love (perhaps recalling past lovemaking or the movie you saw earlier that evening, or wondering about what you are going to do after making love or where to go on your vacation), then you are going to be relatively unaware of the smells, sounds, and sensations that you are *presently* experiencing. Similarly, if while playing tennis you are thinking about the ball you just hit, you may miss your opponent's returning shot. In order to place yourself advantageously for the return of the next shot, you must be evaluating in an *ongoing* way what your opponent and the ball are doing *right now*.

The phenomenon of not being where you are in time is exemplified by a woman we know who is so lost in remembering her past that she is all but oblivious to her present experience. At the ballet, for instance, she will pay almost no attention to, nor betray any interest in, what is going on up on the stage. Instead, she ruminates about the things she has done in the past. Furthermore, any attempt to talk with her about the ballet she is now attending elicits only a moment of blank staring, from which she recovers by turning the conversation to something from her past. Weeks later, however, she will remember the ballet performance and speak fondly of how beautiful it was and what a wonderful time she had, recounting at length (though vaguely) this now-past experience while yet another present experience is taking place, and being missed. How much better would it be, however, to have not only the memory of the experience, but to have the experience itself as well?

Future

"Go on now, George!"

"You got it by heart. You can do it yourself."

"No, you. I forget some a' the things. Tell about how it's gonna be."

"O.K. Someday—we're gonna get the jack together and we're gonna have a little house and a couple of acres an' a cow and some pigs and—"

"An' live off the fatta the lan'," Lennie shouted. *"An' have rabbits. Go on, George! Tell about what we're gonna have in the garden and about the rabbits in the cages and about the rain in the winter and the stove, and how thick the cream is on the milk like you can hardly cut it. Tell about that, George."*

John Steinbeck
Of Mice and Men

Even though our memories of the past may be faulty, we nevertheless respond to the remembered past as though it were factual and invariant. The present is similarly a case of things being perceived as they "are" (within the limits of one's perceptual skill and filters, of course). The contemplated future has no such inherent or necessary boundaries. You know what happened on your last birthday (to the extent of your ability to recall memories), and you know what is going on now (to the extent that you are able to perceive). Both your memories of the past and your perceptions of the present are verifiable by cross-checking with the memories and perceptions of others, by appealing to records such as photographs and tape recordings, and by monitoring measuring devices such as thermometers, light meters, and tuning forks. But with what records and instruments do you verify the future? You can now decide just exactly what will happen on your next birthday, but the accuracy of that divination of the future can not be verified until that birthday has past. And once it has past, you will probably note that your best laid plans did go astray, even if only in minor details. The future is about things that have not yet happened and is therefore inherently indeterminate. This makes the future a source of speculation and flexibility. The past and present are determined. The future is not.

This is not to say that we do not try to make our futures certain. One of the largest industries in the world—insurance—rests upon actuarial assessments of the future. The fact that insurance companies are so successful and lucrative is certainly a testament to their ability to predict what accidents, illnesses, and liabilities the future holds for their subscribers. But these are statistical predictions characterizing large groups of people. Actuaries may determine that each policyholder has a 1 in 10 chance of being in an automobile accident, but if you happen to be the one who has the accident, it becomes a 1 in 1 chance.

Of course, out of necessity and utility (and perhaps fear) we often attempt to imbue the future with the same certainty we experience when regarding the past and present. Based on the past, we make predictions that the chair will hold us, that the sun will rise, and that we will be hungry again. But we do not *know* that any of those things will be so—only that they have been so in the past. Consider the possibility of floating up from your chair a few moments from now. You scoff. You never have risen unaided before. You're right—it's extremely unlikely. But that is *not* the same as saying it is impossible. History is filled with examples of individuals who, in defiance of the better judgment of their contemporaries, dreamed of and made real things that had been considered impossible. Those scoffing contemporaries knew that the world was flat, that man could not fly, could not have evolved, could not exceed the speed of sound, could not go to the moon.

As long as the future remains (or is perceived as being) open-ended, there is "possibility," and where there is possibility there is "hope." Why is it that when a couple quarrel for the first or even the twentieth time they do not immediately go out and get a divorce? Why doesn't someone who has just lost her true love immediately step to the ledge and jump? Why does a runner who loses a race go back to the starting blocks, rather than hang up his running shoes forever? The reason, of course, is that these people all have hope that what has just become the past is not necessarily the future. They still have hope that the future contains what they have not yet been able to attain. The couple is fighting now, but perhaps better understanding will come of it. The woman has lost her true love, but perhaps someone else will come along. The runner has lost this race, but perhaps he will win the next. Of course, arguing couples do divorce, bereft lovers do jump, and second-place runners do turn in their cleats. But these things occur when people have lost hope: when the couple is convinced that they will *never* be able to reconcile, when the young lady believes there will *never* be another such love, and when the runner thinks that he will *never* be the one to break the tape. Hope turns to hopelessness when the future is perceived as being as unchangeable as the past.

Lacking the certainty of the past and present, the future becomes an arena for speculation. The future is something to wonder about and make calculations about. For instance, a husband might imagine that his wife is going to leave him. He might also imagine that she is never going to leave him. Neither imagining is real until and unless something happens to put into effect one of those futures. Until then, they remain only possibilities. Of course, some individuals respond to their own imaginings as though they were actually happening, or had already happened. The husband who imagines his wife eventually leaving him might feel hurt or angry *now*. Similarly, imagining that he and his wife will live together happily for the rest of their lives might make him feel warm and secure *now*. In either case, the man is responding to a possible future as though it *is* reality. (Remember the old joke about the man with the flat tire who, while walking to a nearby farmhouse to borrow a jack, imagines the farmer being reluctant, then difficult, and finally insulting? When the man finally reaches the farmhouse he walks up to the farmer, shouts, "Keep your damn jack!", and angrily stomps off.)

As the husband of the previous example demonstrated, the future can be either fearful or attractive depending on what you imagine is waiting for you. Those who find the future either frightening or frighteningly veiled often turn to tarot cards, astrology, and psychic readers in an attempt to make the future as certain as the past. In the San Francisco Bay Area there is a "psychic" who comes on the radio to tell callers about their future. Every caller is upset or unsure about the future or some present decision that bears on the future. Their purpose in calling is revealed in a comment made by nearly every caller, which can be paraphrased as, ". . . and I was hoping that you could say something encouraging about this." The psychic's response is essentially the same to every caller. She tells them that things will work out fine, or (if it is a decision) to "take the tall one." Almost without exception the callers sigh with relief once their uncertainty has been banished.

Most of us believe that there is a cause-and-effect relationship between the past and present and the future, such that the future is dependent upon what we do now. That is, once something has happened, we can take the patterns that emerge and draw conclusions about what caused what to happen. We can then use those conclusions to project the future as a result of our present actions. What this contingency relationship between now and the future means is that our present experience and behavior are to a great extent controlled by the future. Once we accept that what is done now will influence what follows (and that it matters what follows), it becomes appropriate to attempt to predict the consequences of situations and behaviors. The basis of this prediction is information regarding patterns in the past or present, but it is still the imagined future which may determine one's behavior in the present.[7]

In this way, the future becomes synonymous with *planning*, which is one of the most important uses of the future. Planning makes it possible to arrange to meet someone at a certain time and place, run production lines, put up buildings with a minimum of wasted time and materials, decide what to study and when, and arrange a nice weekend for the family. We can also avoid unpleasant consequences, for example by deciding to take a warm coat when we realize that the evening is likely to become cold. And planning is the basis for delaying gratification, as when we forgo eating a roast duck until the sauce has been prepared. Having a future made up of experiences and events that are a consequence of the present, we try to avoid the wages of sin by following the Ten Commandments, we use birth control, we put ourselves and our children through years of education, we save money, nuts, bolts, and string, we make investments to provide retirement income, we exercise and eat right to stay healthy, and so on.

This same ability to consider plans can also be debilitating. Guised as the irresolute Dane, Shakespeare said it best:

To be or not to be—that is the question.
Whether 'tis nobler in the mind to suffer
The slings and arrows of outrageous fortune,
Or to take arms against a sea of troubles
And by opposing end them. . . .
. . . Thus conscience does make cowards of us all,
And thus the native hue of resolution
Is sicklied o'er with the pale cast of thought,
And enterprises of great pitch and moment
With this regard their currents turn awry
And lose the name of action.

Individuals who consider future possibilities and find only unpleasant consequences may become immobilized in the present, afraid to do anything that might propel them into one of the fearful futures they have conjured up for themselves. On the other hand, futures conceived out of purely wonderful consequences can become the basis for ongoing dissatisfaction with a present that never quite fulfills the promise that is envisioned.

In each of these instances the futures that are being considered are skewed by the experiences of the past and present. For instance, an acquaintance of ours has a pattern of imagining an apparently wonderful possibility for himself, but then fails to evaluate that shining Grail with respect to the feasibility of attaining it (given his present circumstances) and its suitability (given his personal history). Thus he imagines himself a great painter and immediately goes out to arm himself with the best in brushes and canvas, neglecting completely the fact that he has no history of visual artistry and no notion about what is involved in terms of time and commitment to learn. His mistake is not in dreaming, but in failing to *appropriately* and *usefully* relate his dreams to the present and to the past. While the future is the source of possibilities, it is in the behaviors of the present that a dream will or will not be made a reality.

PART II

The Method

3 The Distinctions

Everything that we do, we do in the present. When you remember an event, the process of remembering that event is occurring now, and whatever you re-experience of that event you are experiencing now. "It" happened in the past, but your reaccessing of representations of it is happening now. Similarly, imagining what you will do tomorrow may create for you intense internal sights, sounds, and feelings, but they are all perceptions that you are having now. Even so, experientially and subjectively, we identify the past, present, and future as being distinct from one another.

Of what relevance are those time distinctions to human experience and behavior? There is nothing new about the observation that people adjust, alter, and evaluate information when determining how to respond within a particular context. Aside from wired-in responses such as a handshake, we do a great deal of processing of incoming information in an attempt to determine the best or most appropriate response. Any context for which you do not have a preset response will provide an example of this processing. Selecting a movie, considering whether or not to help a stranded motorist, evaluating a charity's plea for a contribution, responding to a friend's offer of just one more drink for the road, and playing chess are all examples of contexts in which you are likely to engage in *internal processing*. By "internal processing" we mean the internal manipulation and evaluation of the variables involved in a particular context. For example, do the following exercises.

1 Without paper and pencil, divide 1/2 by 1/3.

2 Decide now what you will wear tomorrow.

Unless you frequently deal with numbers, it has probably been a long time since you were called upon to divide one fraction by another. If you go over what you did to answer the problem, you will probably notice that you had to recall how to divide fractions, then performed the operation while keeping track of the process through internal pictures and talking to yourself either internally or aloud, and perhaps through body feelings and sensations as well. Having computed an answer, perhaps you then further considered whether or not it was the *right* answer. This accessing of memories, representation and manipulation of information, tests, and evaluations and so on are all examples of internal processes. In the second example, in which you decided what to wear tomorrow, you may have accessed information about what the weather has been and is likely to be, what you will be doing, who you will be with, what you have to wear, and then made a decision with respect to some or all of those variables. In this case you were accessing the relevant information, which you then submitted to some kind of internal processing that resulted in reaching a decision about what to wear tomorrow.

Time frames are an important part of our internal processes, playing a pervasive and influential role in determining our personal experiences and in directing our behavioral responses. This will become obvious to you if you think about some decision and notice what time frames you considered and how you used them. The task of deciding what to wear tomorrow provides an example. On what basis do you make your decision? Is it based on what tomorrow's weather or activities are likely to be (that is, the future)? Is it based on what appeals to you now as you look through or imagine your wardrobe (that is, the present)? Or is it based on what you are accustomed to wearing (that is, the past)? Or is it based on some combination of such considerations? Regardless of the content of your considerations about what to wear tomorrow, you will find that those considerations will take you at various times and in various ways into the past, the present, and/or the future. It is our observation, however, that the effect of time categories on experience and behavior is much more pervasive, subtler, and more individually characteristic than is indicated by such simple examples. For instance, consider this slightly more involved example.

As you walk down the street you make (perhaps unconscious) judgments about changes in the surfaces you are walking on, adjusting your stride as necessary. As you look ahead you notice people coming and either move aside or specifically *don't* move aside. You notice the light ahead and, figuring that you will not get to the corner before the light turns red, you slow down. Meanwhile, as you walk, you are thinking about how well things are going and, in accordance with such assessments, you stand tall, smiling jauntily. Then you recall that you have a report due tomorrow morning that you have not even begun and, as you think about what will probably happen if you fail to deliver that report, you stare down at the sidewalk, your shoulders hunched, sighing. But having realized that you will be castigated if you don't get that report done, you shift into high gear and start planning just what you have to do to come through. When you realize that your plan will indeed work, you feel relieved.

Each of the emotions and behavioral responses described in the preceeding example is the manifest result of some internal processing. The slowing of your gait is the manifestation of determining that at your present pace the light will turn red before you reach the corner. If you had not noticed the light (and so had formed no opinion about it), or if your assessment had been that you could beat the red light if you hurried a little, your response would have been different. Similarly, shifting into planning how you will get the report done is the manifest result of the assessment that not having the report will result in castigation. Again, if you had not considered and assessed the consequences, or if your assessment had been that you could get away with not doing the report, your response would have been something other than shifting into planning how to get the report done on time. The same can be said of all of the responses described above, as well as of most of any individual's ongoing responses. In short, behavior is often the result of the particular internal processing in which an individual engages within a particular context. Change those internal processes and you will in some way change that person's responses within that context.[1]

Operative Formats

In detecting the internal processes that create our experiences and lead to our behaviors, we have identified seven distinct processes that are significant in determining an individual's experience and behavior at a given moment in time. The specific set of these variables that an individual is using within a particular context is the *operative format*. In choosing the terminology "operative format" we wish to convey the notion that the variables we are using in this method are not necessarily sequential with respect to one another, but are more usefully characterized as being *simultaneously inter-acting*.

The following description of the seven variables is a representation of the several parts of a simultaneously functioning whole. In describing an engine drive train, for example, we could say that the piston moves up and down, turning the crank shaft, which turns the drive shaft, which turns the wheels. Because of the nature of verbal descriptions, this may create the impression that the events described are sequential. This is not the case, however, since when any one of the drive train elements is moving, *all* of the elements are moving. Similarly, the processes we are about to describe are all operating at the same time, simultaneously influencing one another and the individual's ongoing experience. It is only the sequential nature of a verbal or written presentation that makes it necessary to describe these processes as independent entities.

Notation

Perhaps you remember from childhood those little "moving picture" books. As you thumbed the stack of drawings, just as you would riffle a deck of cards, the little characters came alive and played out their antics before your eyes. But when you inspected those drawings one at a time, the animation of the characters was not apparent. Information that is spread out over too much time and space loses much of its coherence and impact; it is the near-simultaneous representation of those drawings that makes their patterns of movement discernable. As we go along we will develop a system of notation for the EMPRINT method. The purpose of the notation is to provide a way of keeping track of relevant information, to provide a shorthand representation that exposes at a glance the experiential and behavioral significance of that information, and to provide a common language for the representation of the operative formats that characterize an individual in a particular context.

Here is the overall form of the notation as it will be developed.

OUTCOME				Activity
Reference Category	■	Test Category	■	Compelling Category
Cause-Effect				

Subject of Evaluation

Within this overall form, the distinctions that comprise the organizing principle—the *past, present, and future* —will be notated as:

Past	Pa
Present	Pr
Future	F

How the distinctions appear within the overall form will become clear as we introduce and explain the Reference, Test, and Compelling Categories. We will continue to expand the notation in a manner that allows you to grasp the material fully at each step of the way.

Again, we do not mean to imply by the linear representation of notation that there is a necessary sequence to the processes represented. One's responses and behaviors are ongoing manifestations of the simultaneous interaction of the variables we are about to describe.

Outcomes, Activities, and Subjects of Evaluation

OUTCOME				Activity
Reference Category	■	Test Category	■	Compelling Category
Cause-Effect				

Subject of Evaluation

The significance of the method described here is that it includes the variables that underlie the manifestation of individual skills. The application of this method results in a comprehensive description of internal processing capable of providing insight into the origin of skills, as well as providing the basis for replicating those skills in others.

Those behaviors or experiences that we want to understand or replicate are referred to as the *outcome*. Keeping your desk in order, dancing, using criticism constructively, giving good lectures, and being able to decide on a career are all examples of outcomes that someone might want to understand and acquire.

As you can see if you consider these outcomes, each seems relatively more or less complex than the others. This complexity has to do with the fact that some outcomes are the result of other, more discrete "sub-outcomes" that we call *activities*. For instance, the behavior of *keeping a desk in order* is the aggregate outcome of engaging in the activities of "recognizing that the desk needs cleaning," "deciding when to clean it," "getting motivated to clean it," "deciding where to put things," and so on. Similarly, *using criticism constructively* involves at least the activities of "recognizing criticism," "judging the merits of the criticism," and "planning how to incorporate that criticism into future actions." Constructively using criticism may also involve the activities of "making a commitment to respond differently" and "recognizing that I *am* doing things differently."

Each activity requires at least one evaluation. "Recognizing that the desk needs cleaning" requires evaluating just how messy the desk is; and "deciding when to clean it" requires evaluating at least your available time and energy. "Recognizing criticism" requires evaluating whether or not a statement is critical; "judging the merits of the criticism" requires evaluating whether or not a criticism is appropriate; and "planning how to incorporate that criticism" requires evaluating the relative merits of various possible changes in your behavior or circumstances. Thus, underlying the manifestation of every outcome is one or more activities; and each activity requires at least one evaluation, and sometimes several. Because each separate evaluation has its own set of variables, *each evaluation is expressed as a separate operative format.*

So, evaluations lead to behavior. For instance, if you do not evaluate whether or not your desk is clean then you are not likely to engage in the other activities of deciding when to clean it, cleaning it, and so on. Similarly, if you do not recognize when a statement contains criticism you are not likely to evaluate how to adjust your actions in the future in response to that statement, and thus are not going to put that criticism to constructive use. An evaluation is always at the heart of the set of internal processes underlying the operation of an activity.

Just as the outcome may be the result of several activities, an activity may be made up of more than one evaluation. The subject of each evaluation, together with the concomitant set of internal processing variables, makes up an operative format. For example, the activity of "deciding about what personal changes to make" may involve evaluating both *personal strengths* and *needs*, each requiring a distinctive operative format, and both in the service of making "the decision." Using another context as an example, for one person the activity of deciding what to do with her weekend might involve only one operative format, in which she evaluates what she could do that she has enjoyed before.

PLANNING
WEEKEND   Deciding
_____

(Variables)

_____
What I could do that
I've enjoyed before

For another person, deciding what to do with his weekend may involve several operative formats involving evaluations of what he could do that he has enjoyed before, what he wants his experience to be during the weekend (exciting, relaxing, sensual, etc.), and what he could do that would be new and interesting.

PLANNING   PLANNING
WEEKEND   Deciding   WEEKEND   Deciding
_____   _____

(Variables)   (Variables)

_____   _____
What I could do that   What I want my
I've enjoyed before   experience to be

PLANNING
WEEKEND   Deciding
_____

(Variables)

_____
What I could do
new, interesting

Obviously, the differences in the operative formats in which these two people engage will manifest as significant differences in their decision-making behavior and what they end up doing with their weekends. The woman who engages in the one operative format that evaluates what she could do that she has enjoyed before will end up repeating familiar pastimes each weekend. The man whose decision-making activity involves several operative formats evaluating not only past pleasures that could be pursued again, but possible new interests and considerations about what he wants his experience to be, will certainly lead himself to weekend pastimes that will be more varied than those enjoyed by the woman. And, as a function of the "what I want my experience to be" evaluation, some of those weekends will probably be more satisfying.

Operative formats may operate either sequentially or simultaneously. As you no doubt recognize from your own experience, sometimes you complete one evaluation before going on to the next, while in other situations you are making two or more evaluations simultaneously, with the progress of each affecting the others in an ongoing way. The man deciding about his weekend, for instance, could have his operative formats organized as sequential steps in which he *first* determines what he wants his experience to be this weekend, *then* uses that information to assess and choose from his past experiences those pastimes that fit that experience, *then* uses the results of those two evaluations as the basis for evaluating other possible things he could do that would give him that experience and yet be different than what he has done before. In this example, each operative format "feeds forward" to the next.

On the other hand, he might have these operative formats organized simultaneously, so that he is assessing the experience he wants to have, what he has done, and what he could do all at the same time. In this case, each format feeds both forward and backward to the others. Organized simultaneously, it is more likely that, in response to his evaluations of favorite pastimes and new possibilities, he will make ongoing adjustments in his assessment of what he wants his experience to be during the weekend. For example, he feels that he wants to have an exciting weekend and, as he thinks about exciting things to do, it occurs to him to hike in the woods, which he does not really consider exciting but it *is* appealing and so he considers that maybe he would rather have a quiet, contemplative weekend, and so on.

We want to stress that the method we are presenting does not prescribe what is best or most appropriate. It is, instead, a way of usefully describing an individual's internal processes with regard to a particular behavior. Thus, even though deciding what to wear is for most people a simple outcome involving only one operative format, for others deciding what to wear might be accomplished only after going through a complex set of distinct operative formats (such as evaluating past outfits, considering new combinations, assessing what you presently need, deciding what you will be doing today, considering what responses you want to get from others, and so on). And even though deciding upon a career may be for most people a complex outcome involving many activities and operative formats, there are some people for whom such a decision may involve only one activity and operative format— for example, the person who watches a TV documentary about stunt acting, imagines himself as a stuntman, and decides, "That'd be great! I'm going to be a stuntman." The goal in applying the method, then, is not to identify the "right" way to do something, but to understand how a particular individual does what he or she does, and to understand how to replicate a desirable outcome.

There are several advantages to making the distinction between an outcome and the activities that comprise that outcome. Perhaps the most obvious advantage is that it alerts you to the possibility that an outcome behavior to which you are aspiring may in fact be the manifestation of several distinct sub-outcomes (activities). A good example is the outcome of *quitting smoking*. Most people treat that outcome as a single activity—the activity of quitting smoking. Consequently, most people approach the outcome of quitting by trying to avoid cigarettes: by throwing them away, going somewhere where they can't be had, or ignoring them. For the many people we have interviewed who have successfully quit, however, the outcome of quitting smoking was made up of a particular set of activities. These included deciding to quit, making the commitment to quit, planning how to go about it, rehearsing and presetting responses to temptations, appreciating progress and change, and so on. Most of these activities are left out of trying to quit smoking by many people simply because they do not know to include them. That is, perceiving the outcome of quitting smoking as *the* behavior to manifest, it does not occur to these people to consider that attaining their outcome is more appropriately the result of engaging in a set of the more discrete sub-outcomes we call activities.

Another advantage of making the distinction between an outcome and its underlying activities, and between an activity and its underlying operative formats, is that it makes it possible to be more effective and efficient in gathering information. If your intention is to understand how someone successfully manifests a particular outcome then you would probably want to know about all of the various activities (and all of the operative formats) that person relies on in that context. This is especially true if you have no knowledge of the requisite underlying pieces and no previous experience in attaining that particular outcome. The more in the dark you are, the less you can afford to take for granted. If you want to enjoy the same kind of success, you need to be thorough. That could translate into a lot of information gathering, but you really do need to have all of the pieces fully specified. Given your intention, in fact, stopping short of gathering the information about all of the underlying activities and all of their respective operative formats would make much of your previous effort irrelevant.

If, however, you are interested in understanding how you or someone else is *un*successful in a particular context (as a therapist would be, or a teacher with a failing student, or a person puzzling out his problems with relationships) then you would probably not need to gather all of the information about every one of the activities used in the problem context. Rather, you would probably need to specify only those particular activities that this person is either missing, or possesses in a form that is not adequate to achieve the desired results.

For example, you may observe that a friend has made the decision to quit smoking, and knows how to do it, but is missing the underlying activity of "making a commitment." Recognizing this in your friend, you know that you don't need to focus your assistance on the areas of making a decision or figuring out how to go about the actual quitting itself. She has already been successful with those two steps. You need to help her focus on the specific activity of making a commitment. Another friend might have already made a commitment as part of quitting smoking, but subsequently found that "it didn't work." That is, whatever he is doing within his operative format for making a commitment is not sufficient for making a commitment to quit smoking. For example, he might have made his commitment to satisfy his family and friends, which is normally enough to get him to do something, but is not compelling enough in the case of smoking. This then would be the specific operative format you would want to find out about, understand, and help him change.

Breaking an outcome down into underlying activities is also a key to efficiency in acquiring the ability to manifest in yourself outcomes that others are already successful at, but at which you have been only *partially* successful. Sticking with our cigarette example, suppose that you smoke and have tried many times to quit. You could find someone who has successfully quit smoking and learn in great detail from that person just how to go about it. However, you might not need to know *everything* about how that person quit smoking. It may be that what you need are the activities of "commitment" and "appreciation," in which case you need to find out about only those particular activities from the person you are modeling. Knowing this will not only save you time, it will also give you the opportunity to appreciate the number of requisite behaviors at which you are already accomplished.

The distinctions of outcome, activity, and operative format, and their relationships to one another, are covered in more detail in Chapter 9. The following explorations will help personalize these distinctions, making them more immediately relevant to you. We strongly recommend that you spend some time working with the ideas and questions presented in the explorations offered here and in the next four chapters. You will gain a better grasp of the method and, we hope, some useful insights into yourself and those around you.

Explorations

Understanding Yourself Here are a few outlines of the sequences of operative formats that we have found characteristic of people who are particularly good at exercising regularly, managing stress, keeping their relationships fulfilling, or taking care of themselves nutritionally. The outcome is in CAPITALS, the activities are in **boldface,** and operative formats for activities that involve more than one evaluation are in *italics.*

EXERCISE

Motivation to engage in exercise

Planning how best to go about exercising

Doing the exercising, evaluating both:
Following the plan as designed
Following the plan in a way that monitors well-being (strain on heart, muscles, bones, etc.)

Committing to maintaining exercise plan

STRESS
MANAGEMENT

Recognizing level of emotional well-being

Deciding what to do about lack of well-being

Committing to taking care of oneself

Doing what is necessary

Recognizing whether or not the actions taken have brought you to a desired level of well-being

KEEPING
RELATIONSHIP
FULFILLING

Recognizing threat to well-being of relationship

Formulating what to do about threat:
What patterns have led to threat
What response will remove the threat

Responding to the threat

Recognizing whether or not your actions have removed the threat and brought the relationship back to a state of mutual fulfillment

EATING
PROPERLY

Committing to taking care of oneself

Gathering information about nutrition

Selecting appropriate diet

Implementing diet
By selecting foods consistent with diet
By monitoring how much is eaten

We have used the EMPRINT method to move many individuals from inappropriate activities and operative formats to those more useful for achieving the above outcomes. For instance, Robert was often *motivated* to start an exercise program. That is, he wanted to exercise, but he never got around to actually doing anything about it. There was always something demanding his attention: the kids, the bills, the chair with the broken leg, the flowers wilting from lack of water, the new project at work. Robert waited for exercise to happen to him. That changed, however, when we taught him to adopt an operative format for planning. Once he had a way to evaluate and accommodate exercise preferences, nearby facilities, the weather, other commitments, and available time, he was able to use his motivation to propel him into action.

If you have difficulty *maintaining* an exercise program once you have started, the problem may be in your activity of *commitment*. What does your commitment revolve around? Is it only to be able to eventually fit into a certain outfit you want to wear on a special occasion, or to look good during an upcoming vacation? If your commitment to exercise does not include a commitment to a long and healthy life that will be achieved through your physical efforts, you are probably going to leave the sweat behind when the vacation is over or new temptations appear. We are always careful to direct an individual to consider a life-long time frame when making a commitment to exercise. This helps avoid the on-again off-again syndrome, as well as the last-minute big push that can easily result in discouragement or injuries.

Compare the activites you engage in for the above contexts to those listed above. Keep in mind that the ones we have listed are not *the* way to act in these contexts, but are the ones that we have most often found in people who are successful in accomplishing these outcomes. Do the operative formats in which you engage lead to successful behavior in these contexts? How are the sequences of activities in which you engage for these contexts different from those we have listed? If you were to engage in the activites we have listed here, do you think you would achieve the outcomes?

4 Test Category

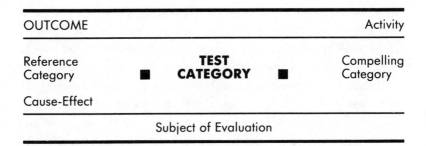

OUTCOME				Activity
Reference Category	■	**TEST CATEGORY**	■	Compelling Category
Cause-Effect				

Subject of Evaluation

Time Frame

Human beings are much more than mere storage sites for information. We evaluate as well. We confirm, decide, ascertain, criticize, estimate, rate, assess, distinguish, discriminate, suppose, believe, deduce, and conclude. In short, we judge input, regardless of whether that input is internally or externally generated. Consciously or not, we constantly pass judgment on our perceptions and thoughts. For example, what went on in your head when you read the previous sentence? In it we made a claim about human experience: "We constantly pass judgment on our perceptions and thoughts."

When you read that statement, did you agree? Disagree? Decide that you did not know enough yet to decide? If you had any response at all to the claim that people are constantly judging input, that response was itself an evaluation (or the manifestation of an evaluation) of the claim; or if not the claim itself, then perhaps our brashness in making it.

As we stated in the previous section, an evaluation, or test, is at the heart of any operative format underlying an activity. To a great extent all of our experiences and behaviors are the ongoing manifestions of those tests. Such tests can be as mundane, unconscious, and circumscribed as those used in writing the letter "A." Unconsciously you judge the "A" that you have just written by referring to and matching its form with your stored experience of what an "A" is supposed to look like. That you normally make this test becomes apparent (that is, conscious) only when you happen to make an "A" that fails the test and is judged illegible, usually compelling you to respond by correcting the "A." Assessing how to respond to a marriage proposal is different in the greater number of tests that must be considered, and in the fact that most of those tests are not as easily resolved as that used to determine the legibility of a letter "A."

There is, in addition, another important way in which the tests involved in evaluating legible handwriting differ from, say, evaluating a marriage proposal. Unless you are creating a new character font, the test for correctness of the letter "A" will be its conformance with past examples. You recall information from your past in order to make a test about the present: Does the letter "A" I have just penned match the letter "A's" I have seen in the past? The tests that are considered in evaluating a marriage proposal, however, are likely to involve not only the present, but the past and future as well. Tests *about the past* may involve such evaluations as, "Has anyone else treated me as well as he has?" "Has she treated me like my mother used to?" "Was I glad the last time I said 'yes' or 'no' to a marriage proposal?" "Have I been able to be live happily with others before?" The time frame for each of these tests is the past. Using this example, several distinctions can be made in the notation at this point. The outcome is "responding to a proposal." One underlying activity is "assessing," and one of the things being assessed (the subject of the evaluation) is "other relationships." This particular operative format begins to take shape as follows.

RESPONDING TO PROPOSAL			Assessing
		Pa	
Reference Category	■	■	Compelling Category
Cause-Effect			

Other relationships

Examples of tests *about the present* include, "Is he sincere?" "Am I excited?" "Am I happy?" "Are we happy?" "Does she treat me well?" The time frame of each of these tests is the present.

RESPONDING TO PROPOSAL			Assessing
		Pr	
Reference Category	■	■	Compelling Category
Cause-Effect			

This relationship

The time frame of the future might include such tests as, "Will we still be happy ten years from now?" "How will things be different if I say 'yes' or 'no'?" "What will he think if I decide to wait awhile?" "Will we continue to treat each other well?"

RESPONDING TO PROPOSAL			Assessing
		F	
Reference Category	■	■	Compelling Category
Cause-Effect			

How this relationship might change

Notice that in terms of the content of what is being evaluated, some of the examples given here for future tests are the same as those given for the past tests: for instance "happiness" and "treated well." The content of what you are evaluating is independent of the time frame within which you make that evaluation. In other words, there is nothing about happiness that inherently makes it something to be evaluated with respect to the past, present, or future. Rather, it may be evaluated with respect to any one (or all) of those time frames.

A test, then, is simply an evaluation, and virtually anything that impinges upon an individual's world will be subject to some kind of evaluation at some level of internal processing. Candidates for evaluation include such countless (often unconscious and "automatic") minutiae as saying a word properly, recognizing a "yield" sign, and knowing whether the ground in front of you will or will not support your weight. Beyond these are evaluations about what to say and how to say it, where to go, how to get there, when to leave, what movie to see, how to respond to a friend who has just criticized or complimented you, whether or not to marry, what is important in your life, and on and on. A half hour of attention to your internal experience will convince you that your ongoing experience of, and responses to, the world are guided by many layers of simultaneous and sequential evaluations.

Furthermore, if you attend to the time frame of those tests you will also discover that they are characteristically evaluations of the past, present, or future. This distinction is significant in that *a past test about a particular input will have a different experiential and behavioral result than will a present or a future test about that same input.*

Suppose, for example, that you are forty-five years old and have spent the last twenty-five years drifting from one unfulfilling, poorly paying job to another, and that you went through two ugly divorces along the way. Recently, however, you have landed a secure, well-paying job, you work with a colleague whom you find attractive, and your boss has promised that eventually you will be promoted into doing what you have always wanted to do. Now suppose that something prompts you to evaluate your life in terms of success. If that evaluation is of the past then you will probably conclude that you have been a failure and feel disheartened (twenty-five years of drifting). If instead that evaluation is of the present then you may conclude that you are doing pretty well (not great, but OK), and feel relieved (you have a pretty good job).

But if your evaluation is of the future then you might conclude that you are doing great, and feel hopeful and encouraged (promotions, perhaps marriage). In each case the world stays the same, but your response to that world is markedly affected by the time frame of the tests you make about it.

Of course, our example presents the simplest of situations. Combinations of evaluations, such as of the past and present, past and future, present and future, or past, present, and future, are all possible ways to use the time frames in a particular context. Someone using a combination of time frames to make an evaluation will have a qualitatively different response than will someone who is using only one of the time frames to make the same evaluation, and different combinations of time frames will also lead to different responses.

Another important point about time frames is the notion of *appropriateness*. Certain test time frames are more appropriate for attaining certain outcomes than are others. Thus, while it's certainly possible to engage in past or future tests while making love, present tests are more appropriate if your desired outcome is to enjoy the sensory stimulation of lovemaking. Similarly, if you are asked to commit yourself to an involved and lengthy project you can make a present test regarding your available time, but it would be more appropriate to make a future test regarding the time that you *will have* available. And the person who does not make past tests with regard to both successes and failures will learn little from them.[1]

As noted above, our mullings (and thus our operative formats) are not necessarily limited to one time frame per assessment. In many situations it is appropriate to make tests that encompass all three time frames. In considering marriage, for example, it's important to consider not only the fact that you are presently happy and in love with your partner, but also your history with that person, as well as what you anticipate your future with that person will be. Clearly, the most appropriate combination of time frames for making evaluations depends upon the context in which they are being applied. We have found, however, that for certain contexts, one or another of the time frames is either inherently or practically most appropriate.

Past Tests In general, tests regarding the past are most appropriate for extracting new information from previous experiences. Most of us look back on unsatisfying conversations and unpleasant interactions and reassess how we could have better acquitted ourselves in those situations. You spend the drive home from a job interview reviewing it in your head, belatedly inserting all of the charm, witty remarks, and cogent points that you failed to use during the actual interview. Or perhaps you rehash an argument with a friend or lover, figuring out how you could have approached the situation so as to have both avoided the argument and attended to your needs. Or maybe the time frame is much broader and you are looking back over the span of a lifetime, considering what you would have done differently and how, and what you would not have changed for all the world. In each case you are evaluating the past as it was and as it could have been, and perhaps even forming the basis for important learnings and changes for your future.

For some people the past is not so much a storehouse of learning experiences as it is a lengthy indictment of failures and proclamations of successes. For these individuals, the past is to be evaluated only in terms of what was, rather than what could have been. Like Colonel Cathcart in *Catch-22*, they look back on their experiences and evaluate which were the black eyes and which were the feathers in their caps. As long as they have more feathers than black eyes (or are able to somehow ignore the black eyes) they can feel content. But if the list is heavy on the black eyes (or if they are given more weight than the feathers) then these people feel discontent with themselves and the world.

Present Tests Tests about the present are generally most appropriate for those situations that require attention to ongoing feedback, such as rock climbing or playing a sport. In addition there are a great many experiences that do not necessarily require a present test, but that are greatly enhanced by evaluations about the present. For instance, a lawyer we knew who was involved in a "big stakes" settlement negotiation was having a terrible time getting any cooperation, let alone concessions, from the opposing side. This lawyer was always very well prepared ahead of time in terms of what he wanted and just how he would approach the negotiation; and as he negotiated he carefully followed his plan. After enduring the opposing counsel's stony contempt for several hours he would retire to develop a new plan, based on what he had read and heard from others about negotiation tactics. But when he returned to the bargaining table to try out the new plan, he would again falter, flail, and fail.

What this lawyer was neglecting to do was to make *ongoing evaluations* about how the opposing counsel were responding to his presentation. He was blindly following his prepared plan, rather than adjusting it to the responses of the other lawyers. He was like an actor reciting lines in a play and then waiting for his fellow actors to respond with their scripted lines. Consequently he did not recognize when his approach was eliciting cooperative, favorable responses, and when he was eliciting antagonism. Lacking ongoing evaluations of the others' responses, the lawyer did not have the feedback he needed to decide whether to continue what he was doing or to change his approach.

Sex is another experience that is enhanced by present testing. Despite the fact that making love is inherently a sensual experience, many people become preoccupied with past and future tests while making love. For instance, rather than attending to how you and your partner are currently enjoying the ways in which you are stimulating each other, you might be engaged in making evaluations such as, "I wonder if she minded my asking her to do that?" and "Did he like that as much as he used to?" Although these assessments may be important, they are not about the present and do not enhance the current giving and receiving of pleasure. Or you might find yourself supplanting your present sensory experience with evaluations about the future while making love. You may be making future tests about what love-making position you ultimately want to be in, or even what you will do when you are finished making love, rather than attending to the pleasures of the position you are in and what you are doing now.

Future Tests   As the time frame of alterability, the experiential domains of the future are *possibility, planning,* and *commitment.* Since plans and commitments are concerned with your future behavior and experiences, they are most appropriately evaluated with respect to the future. This is not always done, however. Some people make commitments based not upon a future test, but upon the present. A common example is the person who is very much in love with her partner and so decides to get married without first giving some compelling thought to what it will be like to be with this person ten, twenty, and forty years down the line. Similarly, many people habitually find themselves overwhelmed with "things" they have promised to do because when it comes time to make a commitment ("Could you write up this report for me?"), the decision is based on present tests ("This seems very important to him"), rather than upon future tests about time, energy, other commitments, and so on.

Similarly, a person who decides to quit smoking as the result of some current compellingly awful experience such as wheezing up a flight of stairs, a terrible coughing fit, a doctor's finding of spots on the lung—that is, a present test—is likely to resume smoking soon. It won't be long before the physical and emotional discomfort suffered while withdrawing from cigarettes constitute a very unpleasant present that cries out for relief. If this person uses a present test in this situation, the current need for relief (which can be had by merely lighting up a cigarette) easily outweighs the commitment that was made in response to another unpleasant experience that is *not currently making its presence felt.*

Had the commitment to quit smoking been based upon a sufficiently compelling future test, it is much more likely that this person would be able to endure and overrule the discomforts of the present. The balance is tipped by the weight of an extremely uncomfortable future (and/or an extremely gratifying future in terms of health, pride, freedom, etc.) as weighed against present discomfort.

To stop smoking, as for virtually all contexts in which behavior needs to be organized along certain lines *over time,* future tests help structure a continuity of behavior that is not possible using present tests. While present tests will orient and *re*orient you in an ongoing way with each subtle change in your environment, the future can be held constant, allowing you to orient to it consistently. People who achieve career goals such as position, prestige, and high compensation use the future in this way. Their unwavering orientation to future benefits keeps them engaged in the work at hand, even if it is difficult or tedious. Imagine how your career would proceed if you did *not* use future tests, if you worked only on what you wanted to, when you wanted to, without consideration of consequences. If your work competed with all other immediate pleasurable possibilities for your attention, how would it fare?

We have found that this difference in test time frame is one of the most important differences between people who are able to make successful commitments to health-related outcomes (such as dieting, exercise, quitting smoking, quitting drugs), and those whose commitments are short-lived and continually frustrated. Those who are able to maintain such commitments invariably employ future tests, while those that are not successful at maintaining such commitments almost always employ present tests. For those who use present tests in these situations, often the only effective approach is to sufficiently control the environment by reducing or eliminating the temptations of the present, so that the environment compels them to fulfill their commitment. Hence the popularity of retreats where alcohol is not available, "fat farms" that serve only low calorie foods, the standing date to go to aerobics class with a friend, and so on.

The time frame of the test that you use in a particular context, then, can make a tremendous, even crucial, difference in your experience and behavior. The test time frame may even be crucial in terms of being competent or satisfied within a particular context. If the examples we have chosen of situations and their most appropriate test time frames seem obvious, it is because most of us agree in general about what is important to evaluate in each one of those contexts. Most of us agree that it is important to learn from past experiences how to improve oneself, that sensual experience is important when making love, and that it is important to preserve one's health. As we will see in the next section, however, it's also true that two people responding in the same context may have very different ideas about what is important to evaluate in that context.

Explorations

Understanding Yourself Find examples of times in your past when you made a commitment to others but failed to follow through on the commitment. What was important to you *at the time you made the commitment?*

It's likely that you were making a present test when you made the commitment (you wanted the other person to feel happy; it seemed like a good idea at the time; it was an interesting challenge), rather than making tests about the future time when you were actually going to have to fulfill the commitment.

Understanding Others Look around and you will find people who don't buy insurance, or who don't save money, or invest, or who use drugs inappropriately. Most of these people are primarily making tests about fulfillment or well-being in the *present*. Those who do buy insurance, save, invest, or avoid substance abuse are those who are making future tests with regard to their fulfillment or well-being in these contexts.

Acquisition Successful investing requires *future tests* regarding what will or could happen (fluctuations in the market, political changes, money supply, interest rates, etc.). People who invest using only a past test are usually not successful. For instance, when inflation is high, such commodities as gold, silver, and real estate are a better bet than are investments tied to fixed interest rates, such as bonds, certificates of deposit, etc. When inflation is low, the opposite is generally true. Several years ago when inflation was running high, people (appropriately) started buying gold and silver. Those who operate only from past tests, however, continued to buy and hold onto the metals even after the inflation situation had changed, and ended up losing a great deal of their money.

Similarly, the real estate broker who shows you charts about how property values have increased is giving you information that is basically unreliable with regard to assessing the property as an investment. Property values may have been driven up by speculation, the creation of new jobs in the area (which may be over now or even about to decline), previous availability of sewer and water services (which are now strained), low interest rates and plentiful financing (which are about to dry up), and so on. The investment value of the property will be found in its *future*, not in its past or present.

Operative formats that include future tests are particularly appropriate for people who lack the aptitude for saving and investing. Usually such individuals do value financial security, but they assess it with regard to their *present* ability to earn enough to pay the monthly bills. Because they consider only their past or current earnings, which may be barely enough to pay the rent and indulge in a few small luxuries, the possibility of saving or investing is usually dismissed. We have these people consider the future, first by imagining being too old to work, and not having any savings to draw upon, and then assessing their financial security in light of this bleak future. Usually the impact of this future test is enough to install the required motivation to learn how to begin budgeting, saving, and investing.

Test Category: Criteria

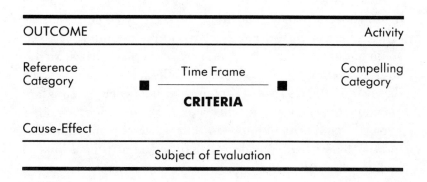

As described in the previous section, the purpose of a test function is to evaluate internal and external experience. But evaluate with respect to what? In order for an evaluation to be made, there must exist some representation of what constitutes a satisfactory or unsatisfactory result. Suppose that we ask you to evaluate the following automobile:

Ford Mustang

Obviously, we have left out something important in our instructions. With respect to what are you to evaluate Ford Mustangs? The results of your evaluation will depend upon the answer to that question. If the yardstick by which Mustangs are to be measured is that of size, then the result of your test will be that the Mustang is a small car. Change the criterion to class and you will determine that Mustangs have little class status among adults, but are considered by some teenagers to be very classy. Criteria such as price, availability, dependability, economy, performance, and cultural implications will all lead you to very different evaluations of the same automobile.

Criteria are the standards by which we evaluate our experiences and the world around us. When Joan says, "What makes him so appealing as a friend is his good sense of humor, and I like the fact that he has a lot of interests," she is revealing to us that the criteria she uses in picking friends are "sense of humor" and "wide range of interests." It may be irrelevant to her, even *unnoticed* by her, that a friend is physically unattractive or stunningly beautiful, rolling in dough or dirt poor, has similar interests or very different interests, and so on. These are other distinctions that can be made about a person, and they are used by some people as criteria for friendship, but they are not important to *Joan* and so do not occur to her as criteria by which to assess a friendship. (Of course, it may be that in another context, those same distinctions that are of no interest to her where friends are concerned become significant criteria. For instance, the other person's "similarity of interests" might become important criteria to Joan when considering that person as a housemate.)

An analogy from Hermann Hesse's *Steppenwolf* is most apt in describing the significance of criteria.

Man designs for himself a garden with a hundred kinds of trees, a thousand kinds of flowers, a hundred kinds of fruits and vegetables. Suppose, then, that the gardener of this garden knew no other distinction than between edible and inedible, nine-tenths of this garden would be useless to him. He would pull up the most enchanting flowers and hew down the noblest trees and even regard them with a loathing and envious eye.

It is necessary to know the criteria being used in a test of the past, present, or future in order to make sense of the results of that test. Knowing that two friends of yours both make tests in the future does not tell you what the results of their tests will be when you ask them if they want to go parachuting. If, however, you also know that one of those friends makes future tests using a highly valued criterion of "familiarity," and that the other values "novelty" as a criterion, you have a basis for understanding, and even predicting, the choices these two people will make. It is the criteria that inform you that the first person is likely to decline the offer (unless he has done something similar to parachuting before) and that the second person is likely to accept (unless she has jumped so often that it is no longer a novel experience for her).

Whether or not a specific criterion is satisfied, however, the outcome of a person's evaluations may depend upon the results of other evaluations of other criteria. For example, the first individual described above may have a criterion about not appearing fearful that is to him *more highly valued* (stronger, more important) than that of familiarity, and so accept the offer to go parachuting even though it is unfamiliar. The second person, on the other hand, may have a criterion regarding safety that is more highly valued than novelty, and therefore decline the offer. Whatever these two people decide, you can be sure that their decisions about parachuting will be made in relation to some criteria. Knowledge of the criteria that each of them uses to evaluate this kind of invitation enables you to make sense of their decision, as well as predict future responses accurately.

Our goal in being able to model the variables underlying subjective experiences and behavior is to both understand and be able to replicate in ourselves or in others those same experiences and behaviors. Toward that end, it is of tremendous value to know, for example, that a talented and successful city planner makes future tests when considering zoning changes. But what is he considering in those future evaluations? Ecology? Economic growth? Safety? Beauty? Quality of life? Profit? Preservation? Function? Knowing that the city planner makes future tests is not enough information to allow us to understand the choices he makes by applying those future evaluations—let alone be able to reproduce those choices. We must also know the criteria that that person is applying to his evaluations of those futures. In other words, we must know on what basis things are being attended to, sought after, valued, or avoided in the future.

In each case, the criteria represent some standard or highly valued quality that must be satisfied, or not satisfied, before a decision can be reached and a response made. *Criteria tell us on what* qualitative basis *a test is being made, and the time frame tells us* when *that person is concerned about those criteria being satisfied.* For example, if a woman's criterion for acceptance of her lover's marriage proposal is "sincerity," she could make past tests of sincerity ("Has he been sincere with me before now?"), present tests of sincerity ("Is he sincere?"), or future tests of sincerity ("Will he still be sincere about our marriage ten years from now?").

A person's ultimate response as a result of the application of a particular criterion to a particular time frame is a function of the *interaction* of those two variables, rather than anything inherent in that criterion or time frame. For instance, in the earlier example of the forty-five-year-old drifter who has finally landed a secure job, the criterion that he used in his evaluations of his past, present, and future was that of "success." His evaluation of his life with respect to success varied depending upon the time frame to which he applied that criterion. (In our notation, criteria are listed beneath the test category since the criteria determine just what it is that a person is testing for or about.)

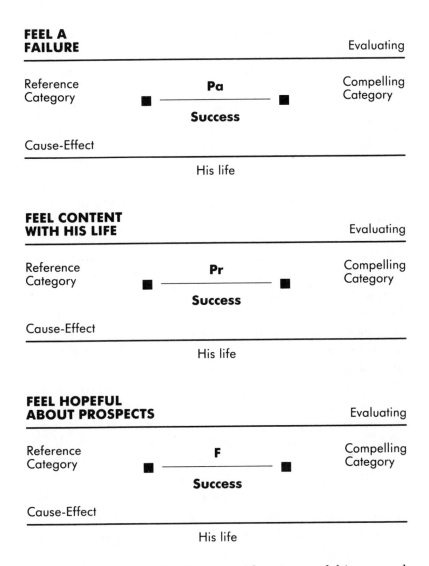

**FEEL A
FAILURE**   Evaluating

Reference   **Pa**   Compelling
Category   ■ —————————— ■   Category
                               Success

Cause-Effect

His life

**FEEL CONTENT
WITH HIS LIFE**   Evaluating

Reference   **Pr**   Compelling
Category   ■ —————————— ■   Category
                               Success

Cause-Effect

His life

**FEEL HOPEFUL
ABOUT PROSPECTS**   Evaluating

Reference   **F**   Compelling
Category   ■ —————————— ■   Category
                               Success

Cause-Effect

His life

In each case the significance of his personal history and present circumstances changes as the criterion of success is applied in turn to his past, present, and future. Thus an individual's response within a particular context is a function of the interaction of his or her personal history, the criteria that person is using, and the time frame to which those criteria are applied.

In modeling a person's experience and behavior, then, it is important to identify the particular criteria that seem to make the difference in generating evaluations. In the parachuting example, the first person may use the criteria of "familiarity" and of "appearing fearful" (as well as many others); but if it is the prospect of appearing fearful that largely determines his responses, then that is the criterion that is important to note in terms of understanding, predicting, and reproducing his internal processes.

Since criteria are not inherent in the situation but vary from person to person, and because criteria make a profound difference in terms of experience and behavior, the question arises as to whether a particular criterion is worthwhile and feasible in relation to a particular situation.[2] For instance, suppose that you are at the supermarket with your four-year-old daughter and she decides to help you by picking out some apples. Not yet wise in the ways of physics and greengrocers, she grabs for the apple that is closest at hand—which happens to be on the bottom of the stack. The result is a pippin avalanche. When you whip around at the rumbling sound and see your daughter standing there amid the rolling apples, how do you respond?

The answer to that will depend upon the criteria you use. We have all seen similar incidents in the supermarket, and the parental response is usually to get angry, yell at or spank the kid, and warn the urchin to keep its hands to itself. The criteria that these parents are applying have to do with decorum ("You've embarrassed me!"), efficiency ("We don't have time for that now!"), and control ("Do as you're told!"). There is nothing inherently wrong with decorum, efficiency, and control as criteria. However, these criteria are destined to be sorely tested when applied to four year olds. So the question arises as to whether a criterion is appropriate in terms of the feasibility of its being fulfilled. One of the most common examples of a criterion that is inappropriate in terms of feasibility can be found in individuals who expect perfection of themselves or others. Practically speaking, anyone using perfection as a criterion, either generally or in a specific context, is often going to be disappointed in his own performance, or that of others. He will have a very different response to a less-than-perfect performance than will someone using the criterion of "learning," or "doing my best."

Beyond the question of feasibility of fulfillment lies the

question of whether or not a criterion is *worthwhile*. Even if you could maintain decorum, efficiency, and control when out on a shopping expedition with your four-year-old, are those criteria worth holding onto when she upsets the apple cart? As a parent, your responsibility is the physical, emotional, and intellectual nurturing of your child. It may be that in this situation the criteria of decorum, efficiency, and control are not in accord with the greater outcome of nurturance. If in this situation you applied (as most important) the criterion of "education" or "nurturing," your response would probably be to help pick up the apples as you explained to your child about the best way to take apples from the stack (with overtones of irritation or good humor, depending on the other criteria being used at the same time).

Consider whether or not the following criteria are worthwhile in the context of giving a party. You want your guests to have fun and enjoy themselves. Suppose you also have the criteria that things be "done on time" and that all guests "participate fully" in the activities you have planned. These second two criteria may not be worth maintaining because they may not be compatible with the criteria of fun and enjoyment. Different people have different rhythms, arriving at different times, finishing drinks, meals, and conversations at different times, warming up to strangers and activities at different rates, and so on. Also, not everyone enjoys the same activities. While some partygoers may enjoy talking, others may prefer to sit alone on the balcony, or listen to music, or play games. Trying to keep the party's activities on time and everyone participating in those activities is likely to infringe upon the fun and enjoyment of some of your guests.

To take another example, many couples value being right more highly than they value being happy. These people end up arguing over such normally inconsequential things as how long it really took to get to mother's, whether she said "rare" or "medium rare," and whether or not he blew it by buying a TV without a remote control. Or there are those people who go shopping wearing glasses tinted with the criterion of "want" instead of "need," and end up making the credit card companies very happy.

The choices you make in life can be understood only in

light of the criteria that you are using, since it is your criteria that determine what you make choices *about*. Furthermore, because criteria are so pervasive and affecting in terms of attentions, perceptions, judgments, and behaviors, your success within any context is profoundly affected by the feasibility and "worthwhileness" of the criteria you use. To say that a criterion has been identified is not to say that it has been specified, however. Just as criteria can vary from person to person and context to context, so can the meanings of each of those criteria vary. Following this section's explorations, we will turn to the specification of meaning.

Explorations

Understanding Yourself   What attracts you to a person as a possible friend? (Interesting, good sense of humor, easy to talk with.)

What attracts you to a person as a possible mate? (Kind, considerate, attractive, someone I can take care of.)

Why did you buy your particular car? (Economical, comfortable, racy.)

Why did you buy your particular stereo system? (Good bass response, nice dials, state of the art.)

Understanding Others   Why would anyone live in:

New York City? (Fast tempo, action, variety, intellectual stimulation.)

The country? (Fresh air, serenity, privacy, natural.)

A condominium? (No upkeep, efficient, tax advantages, less expensive.)

A foreign country? (Exotic, strange, learning situation, test own limits, tax evasion.)

Find people who do like living in these places and ask what they like about them—that is, what personally important criteria these places fulfill.

Acquisition   People who are consistently successful at maintaining their relationships place a high value on the criterion of fulfillment of self *and others*.

People who are consistently successful at completing tasks generally place a high value on the criterion of responsibility, rather than just what's fun to do.

People who consistently take care of their health use criteria regarding feeling healthy and eating foods that are nutritious, while those who do not take care of their health usually place a high value on the criteria sweet, rich, filling, feeling full, etc. in the context of eating.

We have resolved many bitter arguments between married couples and business partners by identifying their conflicting criteria. In the midst of strife the parties in conflict are seldom aware of what really lies at the heart of their disagreement, and in the heat of battle it is easy for each to believe that his or her partner must be somehow inherently flawed. However, once such partners realize that their problems stem from the fact that each is evaluating the situation through a differently colored filter, and that both in their own way are fighting for attainment of their *mutual* outcomes, it is easy to bring them into alignment by having them adopt a mutually acceptable set of criteria.

Inappropriate criteria are often the cause of problems for managers in high-tech industries. We have worked with several managers who were technical engineers before being promoted to management positions. In each case we were asked to help solve "people" problems in the manager's department. It was easy to tell that these managers were using criteria appropriate for working with obedient and efficient machines and passive blueprints. People, however, want to understand *why* they are being asked to carry out instructions and what role they are playing in the overall scheme of things. People function better when they receive respect, courtesy, and all manner of such seemingly irrelevant and time-consuming indulgences. There's no need to drop the criterion of efficiency, but it needs to be supplemented with criteria about whether or not the subordinate has understood the manager's communication, feels appreciated, feels respected, and so on. After adopting new criteria, the managers began to see "syntax error" whenever they neglected these considerations in an inter-action. Many of the managers we have helped in this way have called or written us to let us know that their personal and family relations have improved as well.

Test Category: Criterial Equivalence

OUTCOME		Activity
Reference Category	Time Frame ■ ————————— ■ Criteria ≡ **CEq**	Compelling Category
Cause-Effect		
	Subject of Evaluation	

Some of the criteria that we noted in the previous section include familiarity, novelty, safety, appearing fearful, sincerity, and success—but do we know what any of those words mean to the individuals who use them? The answer to that question is both yes and no. Yes, we all share general definitions of those words, and therefore assume that we know what kind of experience a person means when he or she uses them. But the answer is also no in that, although two people may be talking about the same *kind* of experience—love, for instance—they are not at all necessarily in agreement about what love *is*. One person knows he is loved when his mate hangs on his every word and wants to be with him always. Another person, however, may know that she is loved when her mate does not bother her with fawning attention, and is happy to see her off on her own. Such specification of criteria we call *criterial equivalence*.

Criteria are labels for certain experiential distinctions that we make. But just as the title of a book is not the book itself, a criterion is not the experiences for which it is a label. For instance, in the context of a relationship, Joe's criterion of "compatibility" is only a word, a verbal icon, that has meaning only in terms of the experiences and perceptions Joe has for which "compatible" is a label. That is, what Joe *means* by "compatible" is *having the same interests*, the *same sense of humor*, and the *same needs* as he does; and how Joe knows that someone is compatible with him is that that person has the same interests, sense of humor, and needs as he does.

The distinction between criterion and criterial equivalence may be clearer if you consider a situation in which you are given a criterion to use without any explanation of what that criterion means in terms of perceptions, experience, and behavior. Suppose, for instance, that you are an aspiring screenwriter, and a Hollywood producer has told you to come back with a "high concept" idea for a script. He will apply— and expects you to apply—the criterion of "high concept" to the material you offer him, but what does "high concept" mean? Should it involve tall buildings? Cost a lot of money? Be esoteric? Topical? Drug related? Not until the criterion of high concept is specified can you begin to use it to evaluate your story ideas. (High concept, by the way, means placing a star in a situation appealing to 14 to 24 year-olds.)[3]

Criterial equivalence, then, specifies what you see, hear, and/or feel that lets you know that a criterion of yours *has been*, *is being*, or *will be* fulfilled. As an example, take a moment to answer the following questions. How do you know when . . .

A friend of yours is happy?
You have made a social mistake?
Someone likes you?
You like someone?
You understand something?

The answer to each of these questions is a criterial equivalence of yours. Suppose that the answer to the first question was, "I know a friend of mine is happy when he is smiling." The criterial equivalence here is between happy and smiling (happy $\equiv$ smiling). Not everyone will share your criterial equivalences, however. Someone else might know that a friend is happy by the lilting sound of that person's voice and the ease with which she moves. Another person knows a friend is happy only when the friend says that it is so. And yet another person knows that a friend is happy when *she* feels at ease around the friend.

We generally operate as though others share our criterial equivalences—a circumstance that precipitates more mis-understandings, arguments, and conflicts than any other sin-gle agent. Each of us has our own criterial equivalences, which may or may not coincide with those used by our spouse, friends, associates, government, etc.

Different criterial equivalences for the same criterion can dramatically affect one's perceptions and responses within a particular context. The forty-five-year-old ex-drifter de-scribed earlier evaluated his past, present, and future with respect to the criterion of "success." The criterial equiva-lence that he used for success was *moving toward goals.* In other words, he knows that he is being successful when he is doing something that is taking him toward what he wants to achieve. Given his criterial equivalence and the fact that his personal history includes few examples of actually moving toward what he wants to be doing, it is almost inevitable that when using a past test in evaluating his life he would consider himself a failure and feel disheartened.

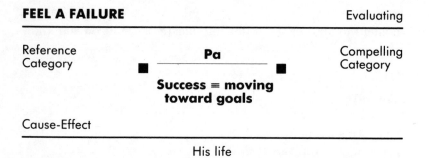

FEEL A FAILURE   Evaluating

Reference   **Pa**   Compelling
Category   ■ ——————————————— ■   Category
                        **Success ≡ moving
                            toward goals**

Cause-Effect

His life

Again we want to emphasize that one's behavior is not the result of any one variable, but of the simultaneous interaction of all the variables. The ex-drifter's feeling that his life has been a failure is not inherent in his criterial equivalence for success, but rather is a function of the interaction of that criterial equivalence, his memories of the past, the time frame of his test, and so on. As we saw earlier, using that same criterion and its criterial equivalence but changing the test time frame to the present or the future can dramatically change his perspective on his life.

Of course, changing the criterial equivalence itself can also dramatically affect one's behavioral responses. Suppose that the drifter's criterial equivalence for success is *learning from mistakes*. Looking back on that same past through the filter of this alternative criterial equivalence would undoubtedly lead him to a different assessment of his life. Perhaps his personal history is filled with mistakes that he has managed to learn from, in which case his past-test view of his life might be considerably more satisfying.

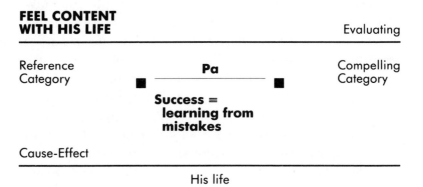

Thus the same personal history scrutinized through the lens of a different criterial equivalence can appear very different. Similarly, one's perception of the present and future will vary depending on the criterial equivalences through which they are experienced and viewed. For instance, if the man in our example had *independently wealthy by age 40* as his criterial equivalence for success, then he is likely to evaluate his life as a failure in the past, present, or future time frames.

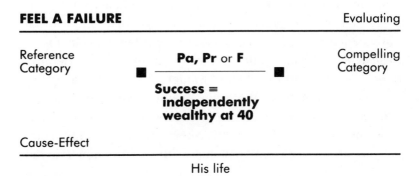

This feeling of failure contrasts sharply with the present relief and future encouragement engendered by the criterial equivalence of "success equals moving toward goals." Knowing an individual's criterial equivalences within a particular context, then, is essential to understanding that person's internal processes and responses within that context.

Politics provides daily examples of the impact that differing criterial equivalences can have upon perceptions and behavior. Richard Nixon did not and does not perceive that his behavior while president qualifies him as a crook. On the contrary, he perceives himself as a patriot. For many Americans, however, his behavior *does* match their criterial equivalence of a crook. Similarly, although in some cases actual differences in criteria do exist between the two major parties (for instance, in 1984, regarding the issue of abortion, the Republican party supported "pro-life" and the Democratic party supported "pro-choice"), more often than not the wrangling is over just what is the *right* criterial equivalence for criteria that they actually share—for instance, what constitutes strength, opportunity, national security, justice, and so on. Indeed, much of what the Supreme Court does is to pass judgment upon the specific and applied meaning of the words used to specify our Constitution and laws. For instance, the 1954 *Brown vs. Board of Education* ruling specified what constituted equal education. Criterial equivalences are the subjectively established standards by which we evaluate our world. Clearly, it is a mistake to assume that your criterial equivalences are inherent in the criteria they describe and, therefore, shared by everyone.

Closer to home, a criterion for which we have discovered a common difference in criterial equivalence among individuals is that of "competence." For many people, the criterial equivalence for competence is that they *already know how to do something*. People who operate out of this criterial equivalence usually find that there is much in the world at which they are incompetent. We know of other individuals whose criterial equivalence for competence is *capable of learning*. These people generally perceive themselves to be quite competent, since there are a great many things they cannot do but that they *could* learn to do if they needed or wanted to. Similarly, while for many people "security" is a highly valued criterion, those for whom security means *knowing what will happen* will have very different ongoing experiences and behaviors than will those for whom security means *knowing I can handle whatever comes along.*

The criterion of "attractiveness" provides a good example of the importance of considering the contextual appropriateness of criterial equivalences. There are many people for whom an attractive person is one who fulfills certain external qualities, such as the man who finds slender blondes with bright blue eyes attractive, or the woman who favors tall, dark men. People using criterial equivalences that are largely limited to such external visual qualifications are often disappointed once the relationship progresses beyond the initial rose-colored glasses stage. A person may be wonderful to look at, but there has to be more to sustain an intimate interaction over time. Therefore, including in your criterial equivalence for attractiveness qualities that to you are important aspects of personality will help ensure that you are attracted to people whose personal qualities are likely to sustain the relationship over time.

Explorations

Understanding Yourself   How do you know when something that you have acquired is "good"? (For example, costs a lot of money; brings me pleasure.)

How do you know when you are successful at doing something? (When you understand; when you are making progress; when you have completed the entire task; when you have completed the entire task on time and with no mistakes.)

Your answers to the above questions will provide you with your criterial equivalences for "good" (at least as far as things that you own are concerned) and "successful." Think of something that you have that you do not consider good, then think of how you could change your criterial equivalence so that you would consider what you have to be good. Think of an example of a failure of yours, then consider how you could change your criterial equivalence for "successful" so that the incident becomes an example of a success.

Understanding Others A married couple may both have "security" as an important criterion, but if to the wife security means *producing income*, while to the husband security means *having the ability to make money*, they could easily end up at odds with one another since it may be that he will not feel compelled to actually be *earning* money.

Think of someone who believes himself to possess a quality that you do not see in him at all (for example, he thinks he is generous, but you find him stingy). What criterial equivalence might he have for generosity that would account for him believing that he has that quality? If you can, ask him how he knows when someone is demonstrating that quality.

Acquisition Most nurturing, satisfied parents share the same criterial equivalence for "smart," which is that smart means *the ability to improve—that my child can do something now that he or she recently could not do.* Parents who view their children through the lens of this criterial equivalence are treated to daily examples of their child's "smartness," leading to important and pleasurable reinforcing interactions between them and their children.

Teachers often fail to inform their students of the criteria and criterial equivalences they are using to evaluate whether or not a student is doing well in class. Thus the student is either left without known standards he can trust and attempt to fulfill, or forced to assume that the standards are the same as for a previous teacher. Either way, both the student and the teacher are at a disadvantage. The teachers who have attended our workshops and have subsequently incorporated a message about their criteria and criterial equivalences into their presentations have consistently reported improvement in student performance.

It is no secret that many people have over-eating and weight problems. Of course, prescribing a modification in one variable is not a panacea; but we *have* helped people change their eating behaviors—changes that led to weight loss and maintenance—by simply changing their criterial equivalence for being finished with a meal from "feeling stuffed" to "no longer feeling hungry."[4]

Some people have an unwitting knack for being unhappy with the person they love. Often the unexpected accomplice is the criterial equivalence they use to determine if the other person loves them. A couple we worked with provides an example. Shirley knew that her husband Bert loved her if he gave her everything she wanted. She constantly made demands and often felt unloved, and he had exhausted his money as well any feelings of generosity. Meanwhile, Bert knew that Shirley loved him when she did things for him that he knew she really did not want to do. Understandably, she spent a lot of time resenting him for callously imposing upon her. Their criterial equivalences obviously needed changing to ones that would lead to mutual satisfaction.

The easiest way of accomplishing this is for each person to find something that the other already does naturally as an expression of the desired feeling (in this case love) and use that as the criterial equivalence. For instance, by asking a few questions we discovered that Bert felt loving toward Shirley when he took care of things around the house—he felt that he was taking care of the house out of love for her. We then taught Shirley how to make this the way she knew she was loved by him. Shirley felt loving toward Bert when she was sharing her most intimate thoughts and feelings, so we helped him recognize this behavior as being loved. This worked well. She demanded less, and the demands she did make were less emotionally charged. He no longer felt compelled to ask her to do something she did not want to do—a great improvement for both of them.

Test Category: Representational Systems

OUTCOME			Activity
Reference Category	Time Frame ■ ——————— Criteria ≡ CEq	**(Rep sys.)** ■	Compelling Category
Cause-Effect			
	Subject of Evaluation		

In order to make a test or evaluation, you must have some kind of representation of what is to be evaluated, and that representation must be related to sensory experience. If we ask you to decide, "Which is brighter, the red of *blood* or the red of *candy apples*?", you can make that judgment because you have stored as reference experiences pictures of what blood and candy apples look like. Those pictures (or, as we prefer to call them, *internal images*) are the internal representations you use to make the comparison. Unless they have been told the necessary information, people who are blind from birth would not be able to answer this question because they would not have the representations of the colors we are talking about upon which to base a judgment.

Consider this question: "Which is the brighter color, *bice* or *smalt*?" Even though those are actual color designations you are probably unfamiliar with them and therefore have no representations (internal images) of them to evaluate. When you look up the definitions of those two colors, your dictionary will give you at least the illusion of knowing what those colors look like by using descriptive words for which you *do* have stored pictures. It is not words that are referenced and evaluated, but sensory-based experiences.

In addition to internal images, you can represent sensations and emotions (the blind person might have a representation for whether bice *feels* warmer than smalt), and you can hear, remember, and concoct inside your head the sounds of symphonies and conversations. In fact, we have the ability to represent internally each of our five sensory systems: visual, auditory, kinesthetic (sensation/emotional), olfactory, and gustatory. These are the stuff of which experience is made; they are called the *representational systems*.

Representational systems are tremendously important in understanding virtually any human endeavor, for it is through them that we experience the world. The representational systems of sight, sound, sensations, emotions, taste, and smell are the cloth from which our internal experiences are cut, the clay from which they are formed. Every experiential moment of your life is the combination of your representations of what you see, hear, feel, taste, and smell, both internally and externally, at that moment.

In terms of the EMPRINT method, the importance of representational systems is that *they indicate in which sensory system(s) a person needs his criterion fulfilled*—that is, through which of the five sensory systems the person is evaluating criteria: how things look, feel, sound, smell, and/or taste. For example, while one person knows that he has drawn a good picture by how it *looks*, another knows by how she *feels* when looking at her art, and yet another person has to *hear* the comments of others in order to know whether or not he has drawn a good picture. Similarly, for many of us who learned to spell phonically, words are spelled rite if the spelling of them *sounds* right, while for the truly good speller a word does or does not *look* right.

The role of representational systems is particularly significant to the criterion of "attractiveness." For many people, the criterial equivalence of attractiveness is fulfilled by primarily visual characteristics (a fact that is not lost upon America's advertising agencies). For one man an attractive woman is one who is slender, tanned, and blond, while for another an attractive woman has big breasts, green eyes, and red hair. Women too may have very specific visually based criterial equivalences, such as big and fair, with clear blue eyes; or wiry and dark, with high cheek bones. We know one person for whom slender, well-proportioned fingers and hands are an important visual criterial equivalence for attractiveness.

To some, auditory and kinesthetic qualities are important in fulfilling the criterial equivalence for attractiveness. A woman's melodic voice may thrill one man, while another man will take no notice whatsoever—not because he is tone deaf, but because he does not value the experience and so has not developed through selective attention the ability to recognize and appreciate tonal differences. One woman will find it attractive that a man talks a great deal, dominating the conversation, while another woman will consider that same man a bore and seek someone who is more moderate, or even quiet. The texture or warmth of skin, strength, size, weight, firmness or gentleness of touch, are examples of some of the kinesthetic characteristics that may go into making up an individual's criterial equivalence for attractiveness.

Another example in which representational systems figure prominently is that of deciding whether or not someone is telling the truth. Some people recognize that they are being lied to when they *see* that the other fellow is not looking at them as he speaks, or that he is fidgeting and biting his lip. Others attend to tone of voice, knowing a lie when they *hear* a statement uttered in a hesitant, quavering voice, or an earnest reply that nevertheless sounds forced. Still others may rely on their own feelings in assessing the truthfulness of a companion, *feeling* that the other person is not telling the truth. In each of these examples, the criterial equivalence for lying is largely represented in either visual, auditory, or kinesthetic terms. (Remember, there is nothing inherent about most distinctions that makes the use of any one representational system the "right" system to use. There are people who find it difficult to maintain eye contact but who can nevertheless be depended upon for honesty, and there are those who naturally speak lies in the most matter-of-fact tones.)

The owner of a music store specializing in fine stringed instruments gave us an excellent example of the significance to the individual of representational systems in making evaluations. Here is a condensation of our conversation with him about people who come into his store to buy violin bows:

Of course, if they know anything about the great bow makers, such as Tourte or Sartori, they'll steer toward those first, but once they get a bow in their hands you find that they're after different things in a bow. Some people come in to look at my bows and end up buying one that they think is beautiful to look at. They like the color of the wood. They'll look at the hair and like the fact that it is clean from frog to tip. If they like the bow but the hair looks dirty, they always get the bow re-haired as part of the deal.

Other folks will hold the bow and feel the balance, and they'll flex it with their hands or on the violin itself to test the tension and responsiveness of the bow. If it responds the way they like, they don't usually care how it looks.

You'd be surprised how many people will buy a bow without even playing on the instrument with it. The ones who know what they're doing, though, insist on trying out the bow on an instrument or two. They need to hear the tones the bow is capable of producing, how it sustains a note at different pressures, and so on.

Representational systems play a significant role in the fulfillment of the criteria of each of the three types of buyers described above. The first group evaluates bows with respect to their *visual* (v) beauty and cleanliness. The second group makes *kinesthetic* (k) tests of such criteria as balance, tension, and responsiveness. And the third group makes *auditory* (a) assessments of the bow's ability to produce and sustain tones. When the representational system used plays a significant role in fulfilling a person's criteria, it is notated beside the test category time frame.

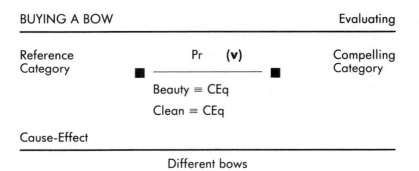

BUYING A BOW   Evaluating

Reference   Pr   (v)   Compelling
Category   ■ ─────────── ■   Category
                            Beauty ≡ CEq
                            Clean ≡ CEq

Cause-Effect

Different bows

BUYING A BOW		Evaluating

Reference Category	Pr **(k)** ■ —————————— ■ Balance ≡ CEq Tension ≡ CEq Responsiveness ≡ CEq	Compelling Category

Cause-Effect

Different bows

BUYING A BOW		Evaluating

Reference Category	Pr **(a)** ■ —————————— ■ Tone ≡ CEq Sustain notes ≡ CEq	Compelling Category

Cause-Effect

Different bows

Although some people may select or reject bows on the basis of having their criteria fulfilled within only one representational system, individuals often base their selections on evaluations made within two or more of the representational systems. For instance, you might select your bow on the basis of both the tones it produces (a) and its beauty (v). Furthermore, tests of these criteria may be hierarchically arranged so that you first select those bows that meet your criteria for sounding good, then select which of those most closely satisfies your notions of beauty.

We should also point out that most criteria are not inherently fulfilled by either one representational system or another. For instance, although "beauty" is listed as a visually fulfilled criterion in the example above, for some people the beauty of a bow might be a function of how it feels or sounds, rather than how it looks. Similarly, for some "tension" might be a visually tested criterion ("I know that it has the right tension by looking at the curve of the bow when it's barely tightened"), or an auditorily tested criterion ("The tension I'm listening for is an interplay of fullness of tone and a certain raspiness").

As with all of the distinctions presented here, representational system distinctions provide a basis for understanding behavior, as well as the possibility of greater flexibility of experience and behavior. Thus the representational system distinction helps us understand how a person can buy a poorly made, poor-sounding violin bow and yet be satisfied with his purchase: that is, his criteria for a good bow need to be visually fulfilled (beautiful wood, ivory and hair still white, dazzling mother-of-pearl inlay on the frog).

The possibility of greater flexibility comes from recognizing that we can be cognizant of and, when necessary, deliberate about the representational systems we are using. It's certainly appropriate to use visually fulfilled criteria in buying a ribbon bow for a birthday present, but applying that same representational system alone to the purchase of an instrument bow is not. A visually oriented person seeking a new bow for his violin needs only to be educated as to the distinctions that can be made about bows in terms of their responsiveness and the varying tones they can produce in order to have new and better choices available when buying a bow.

As we mentioned previously, in most cases there is no inherently right or wrong sensory representation for an evaluation. However, one representational system may be more or less appropriate than another depending on the context in which it is being used. A surgeon, for example, may be severely hampered in judgment and responses if she makes feeling-based (emotional) tests while operating. Such tests create the possibility of bringing to her consciousness feelings about cutting into another human being, being responsible for another person's life, empathizing with the patient's pain, and so on. Such tests are more appropriate for watching a movie or being with a lover, as those are contexts in which having conscious access to feelings is important and appropriate. The surgeon is better off making visually based tests while operating, providing herself with information about the depth of incisions, the health of tissues, the vital signs of the patient, and the possibilities of life or death, without involving her emotions.

We want to stress, however, that the appropriateness of a particular representational system depends upon the context. For instance, individuals whose professional lives place a necessary premium on visually based tests (such as the surgeon described above) may find themselves described as cold or unfeeling by their friends and lovers if they are unable to include emotional feeling-based tests in the context of their private lives.[5]

Explorations

Understanding Yourself

"You say you love me, but you don't show it."
"I've never seen you do it so it can't be true."
"I know I can do it if I can see myself do it."

These examples express some of the ways in which people represent the fulfillment of their criteria in terms of the sensory systems involved. All of the examples are visual: *show* you love me; *see* you do it; *see* myself do it. Is it the same for you? Do you need evidence you can see to know that someone loves you, to know what is true, and to know what you can do? If not, what representational system information do you need?

Understanding Others   How is it possible that a certain woman has a closet full of beautiful shoes, but invariably picks the tennis shoes to wear? It's probably because she buys shoes that *look* good, but when it comes time to wear them, she picks those that *feel* good.

Acquisition   Certain endeavors require that you be able to make fine discriminations within one or another of the representational systems. If you want to play music then you need to learn to hear intervals in your head and match those intervals to what you hear on the outside. Sports require that you develop your kinesthetic representations of how certain movements feel. Painting requires developing the ability to make visual discriminations regarding proportions, line, color, balance, and so on.

In our clinical work, we have helped many clients overcome sexual impotence by changing from making visual tests of whether or not they will be able to perform, to kinesthetic tests of the present sensations and emotions that naturally lead to sexual arousal.[6] We have taught new mothers how to make appropriate auditory tests for determining the meaning of a baby's cry: I'm wet, I'm tired, I'm hungry, I'm lonely, I'm in pain, and so on. We have even used representational system information to aid a friend who was struggling in his attempt to learn auto mechanics. He would study the manuals and poke around an obviously sick engine until everything looked fine. Unfortunately, after starting it up he would discover that whatever it was that he had fixed, it was not what was ailing the motor. So we modeled a master mechanic and discovered that auditory testing is very important in working on engines. We then transferred to our friend this ability to make fine diagnostic distinctions from the humm, purr, roar, rattle, putter, and sputter of an engine.

5 Reference Category

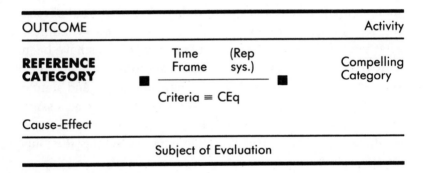

OUTCOME			Activity
REFERENCE CATEGORY ■	Time Frame	(Rep sys.)	Compelling Category
	Criteria ≡ CEq		
Cause-Effect			
	Subject of Evaluation		

All evaluations depend on the referencing of information. For instance, deciding what book to take with you on vacation may require that you consider what you have previously read, what you presently have in your library, intriguing books you have heard about recently, your vacation surroundings, and so on. All of these are sources of information to which you may refer when deciding what book to select.

Evaluations do not occur in a vacuum, but instead depend on the accessing of necessary information. Furthermore, your evaluations will be shaped by what kinds of reference sources you use. The person who decides on a book using only his "present library" as a reference will probably make a different selection than if he also included in his deliberations "what's out in the bookstores." The books in the bookstore are available to him, but unless he uses "what's out in the book-stores" as one of his references it probably will not occur to him to go to the bookstore and find them. As an example, take a moment to complete the following exercise.

- Select a restaurant to go to tonight.
- Pick a close friend to join you.
- Decide when to meet your friend.
- Determine what is important about dining with friends.

Reviewing your internal processes as you made these assessments, you will notice that in order to make the required judgments you referred to all kinds of information, such as what restaurants you have been to, what kind of food you feel like eating, who your friends are, their schedules, what kind of food they like, what your experiences have been with friendship, and so on. These are relatively complex evaluations. But even such a seemingly automatic and simple response as shaking hands with someone requires accessing the reference information that there is someone's hand there to shake. (In this case, the reference is seeing the outstretched hand.)

The *reference category*, then, specifies those experiences, sensations, memories, imaginings, perceptions, and other sources of information one uses in making an evaluation. In other words, if you are going to make an evaluation, you must have some input to evaluate. The reference category specifies where you are getting those inputs from. Many distinctions can be made about kinds of references, but these three that we have found to be most influential and pervasive are *time frame* (past, present, or future), *authenticity* (actual or constructed), and *emotional involvement* (personal or informational). First we will define and present examples of each of these three distinctions, then describe some contexts in which each is appropriately and inappropriately used as a reference. The presentation of the distinctions is followed by a description of the unique characteristics of each of the ten kinds of references that can be differentiated as a result of different combinations of the distinctions.

Time Frames

Whenever you turn to the past for information, you are using a *past reference*. Examples of past references include your memory of finding the gift you had really been hoping for under the Christmas tree, remembering the spelling of "Phoenician," and imagining the torment your father must have gone through when he punished you for locking your sister in the hamper. In each case the information or experience you are referring to is from your past.

In many contexts, operating from past references is both sufficient and efficient. The significance of the words you just read, how to change a flat tire, when to stop ordering cocktails, and recognizing your mate's recurring responses, are all contexts in which having past references saves you the task of figuring out how to respond each time those contexts come up.

When you attend to information that is available to you in your current environment (both internal and external), you are using *present references*. Examples of present references include experiencing the flush of a sudden infatuation, noticing that the flower bed is dry, and imagining how you appear at the moment to others. In each of these instances, the information is being drawn from your present, ongoing experiences and perceptions. In general, any context that involves sensory experience or demands quick responses is an appropriate context in which to use present references. Dancing, making love, playing tennis, enjoying a meal, and working as a physician are all examples of contexts in which present references are essential.

Whenever you imagine something that is yet to happen, you are using *future references*. Examples of future references include imagining being confident at tomorrow's interview, knowing what groceries you will need for the coming week, and imagining how you will look and feel after a year of taking care of yourself. Future references are generally appropriate, if not essential, in contexts that involve planning, commitments, or consequences. Examples of such contexts include planning a party, planning an education, planning a career, buying a house, making a commitment to marriage, and deciding to have a child.

If you are evaluating the past it is appropriate to have at least some past references to evaluate, if you are evaluating the present it is appropriate to have at least some present references to evaluate, and if you are evaluating the future it is appropriate to have at least some future references to evaluate. Without some input from the present, trying to assess whether or not your mate is enjoying dinner is certainly *not* going to be a reflection of what *is* going on, but is much more likely to be a reflection of some past experiences or future imaginings. (Thus a husband may assume that his wife is enjoying her "favorite" dish and not notice that she is poking at it tentatively, sighing, and making faces.) Similarly, you are not likely to make a very relevent test if you do not use a past reference when trying to assess whether or not you performed well last week.

Authenticity: Actual and Constructed References

Stuart was returning home from a particularly frustrating day at work. He wanted an evening that was very different from the day he had just had. By the time he opened the door he was already in high spirits thinking about the fun and romantic evening he planned to have with his lady, Anna. When he finally found Anna she was sitting on a chair in the backyard, sighing as she traced slow circles in the grass with her toes. Her face was puffy and streaked with dried tears. Stuart had seen those slow circles and heard those sighs before and, as he remembered those previous instances, the same feelings of concern and compassion that he had felt then once again welled up inside him. Realizing the inappropriateness of his plans, he set them aside, knelt beside Anna, took her hand, kissed it, and waited quietly for her to tell him about the injustices of her day.

In this example, Stuart makes and responds to a *present* test regarding Anna's emotional state. That test is based upon Stuart noticing Anna's present appearance and behavior, and on his memories of having seen her in such a state at various times in the past. Stuart's present test is based on *actual* reference experiences. That is, Stuart is actually looking at and listening to Anna (a *present actual* reference) and his memories of her being depressed in the past are memories of actual incidents (a *past actual* reference). The combination of these two references provides Stuart with the experiential basis he needs to recognize that Anna is upset about some injustice.

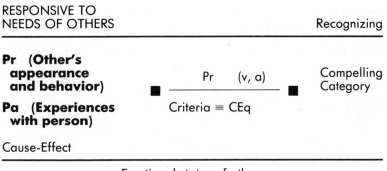

RESPONSIVE TO NEEDS OF OTHERS		Recognizing
Pr (Other's appearance and behavior) **Pa (Experiences with person)**	■ $\dfrac{\text{Pr} \quad (v, a)}{\text{Criteria} \equiv \text{CEq}}$ ■	Compelling Category
Cause-Effect		

Emotional states of others

If Stuart had not noticed Anna's behavior, or if he had not recalled previous similar experiences, he would not have recognized the significance of her behavior and probably would not have responded in the way he did. Even with the most well-defined criteria in hand, making an evaluation without relevant references is like trying to carve a marble sculpture without the marble. If you are going to make an evaluation you not only need a standard (criterion) to apply, but you have to have something to apply that standard to. In this instance Stuart used actual experience as the basis for his evaluations. Actual experience, however, is not the only basis people draw on for their evaluations. Consider the following example.

Preston and his wife are deciding where to go for their vacation and have agreed that they should go somewhere they have not been before. When his wife suggests Arizona, Preston remembers movies he has seen about the desert and then imagines what it will be like, viewing the stark landscape through squinting eyes and feeling the heat sap his strength. "No way," he says. Her next suggestion is New York City. Preston has heard and read a lot about big cities and imagines what it will be like to watch hordes of people scuttling beneath the skyscrapers, hearing horns honking, the jostling, frenetic pace. "No way," he says. On her third attempt, his wife suggests buying a tent and camping gear and heading for the Sierras. Recalling idyllic stories told to him by friends of the great outdoors, Preston once again imagines what it will be like to be there, this time seeing the brown of the fallen pine needles, the green of the trees, and the seamless blue of the sky. He hears a stream, a breeze, and feels airy and relaxed. "Yeah, I want to go there," he sighs.

Preston's decision about where to go for his vacation involves two operative formats, and is largely based upon *constructed*, rather than actual, experiences. That is, they are experiences that he has never actually had, but has created in his imagination. In the first operative format Preston evaluates what each possible vacation spot will be like. By piecing together snippets of past actual references (from movies, books, word of mouth) about the desert, New York, and the mountains, he is able to construct for himself the experience of what it will be like to be in each of those places. Of course, never having actually been to any of those places, he may be ignorant of important aspects, such as mosquitos buzzing away the solitude of the Sierras. Regardless of whether or not his future imaginings are accurate, however, Preston uses them as data in evaluating where to vacation.

Where did these imagined experiences come from? In considering each of the vacation choices Preston created a future, but it is clear that the nature of that future (that is, the experiences he imagines having in the desert, New York, and the mountains) is determined by the past references he has regarding those places. At some point he had seen in a movie, or had been told, or had read that deserts are hot and dry. Using his reference experiences for being hot and thirsty, Preston was able to imagine what it would be like to be in the desert. If no one had ever told him that deserts are hot and dry, but had instead informed him that they are places of balmy evenings and quiet solitude, Preston would have created a visit to the desert based upon whatever reference experiences he may have had in relation to "balmy evenings" and "quiet solitude." (Had Preston's wife suggested Naini Tal for their vacation, he would have been unable to do anything but ask for more information since he is utterly unfamiliar with Naini Tal, and so does not know which of his personal reference experiences to access in evaluating it as a choice.) Preston's use of constructed references is notated with a subscript "c." (Actual references have no subscript.)

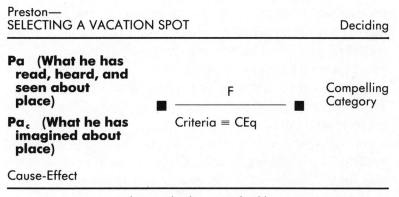

Preston—
SELECTING A VACATION SPOT   Deciding

**Pa (What he has
read, heard, and
seen about
place)**   F   Compelling
                                        ■ ———————————— ■   Category
**Pa$_c$ (What he has   Criteria = CEq
imagined about
place)**

Cause-Effect

What each place will be like

Once Preston has used his past references to construct imagined future experiences (what it will be like to be in New York, the desert, and the Sierras), those three imagined future experiences then become *future constructed references* to be used in the second operative format in the selection process. In this next operative format Preston evaluates each imagined vacation possibility with respect to the kind of vacation he wants to have (that is, with respect to the criteria he wants to satisfy).

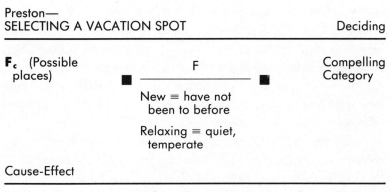

Preston—
SELECTING A VACATION SPOT   Deciding

F$_c$ (Possible   F   Compelling
places)   ■ ———————————— ■   Category
                               New = have not
                                 been to before

                               Relaxing = quiet,
                                 temperate

Cause-Effect

Where I want to go

Thus the results of one operative format may show up as a reference in another operative format. This sharing of results may be simultaneous (as in the example with Preston), so that "What it will be like to be in the desert" is evaluated concurrently with his evaluation of "Do I want to go to there?" The results of one operative format may also be sequentially passed on as a reference to another operative format. Had Preston been operating sequentially, he would have first imagined what it would be like to be in the desert without considering it in relation to his upcoming vacation.

All future references are constructed. You can recall actual experiences that you have had, and you can notice what is going on around and in you right now. But, at least in our present stage of conceptual and scientific evolution, the "arrow of time" prevents us from actually going into the future or of having memories of *actual* future experiences. The future, then, cannot act as a source of actual reference experiences since we can't be in it or have memories of it.[1] We can, however, make a future test in order to *imagine* what the future will be like. That imagining then becomes a constructed future reference that can be used in other operative formats. A future reference is created automatically each time a future test is made.

In addition to the future, constructed experiences may be created in the present or created and recalled from the past. For example, if in planning how to present yourself in an upcoming job interview you call upon as references how you would have liked previous interviews to have gone, then you are using *past constructed* references. In that case you are using reference experiences from your past that you have changed to something other than what they were—recalling how you forthrightly offered your qualifications, rather than recalling the stammering and sweating that you actually did, for instance. Similarly, imagining that you are playing tennis like your instructor as you sit watching her play is an example of a *present constructed* reference.

In making the distinction between actual and constructed references we are relying on the notion of "consensual reality." Elwood P. Dowd's rabbit, Harvey, was "actual" to him, but not a part of consensual reality and so (as cold as it may seem) an example of a *present constructed* reference.

There is a distinctive class of constructed references that is so affecting and prevalent that it warrants special notice— what we call *vicarious* reference experiences, which are constructed references about the experiences of others. You could, for example, imagine what it would have been like to have been your father while he was punishing you for some childhood transgression (Pa_c). Or you can imagine what it is like to be your father now as he watches your own children commit that same offense (Pr_c). These incidents actually occurred, but you still don't have your *father's* experience. Both of these vicarious reference experiences are constructed out of pieces of past and/or present references that give you a *notion* of your father's experience.

Books, the silver screen, television, and radio are all frequent sources of vicarious experience. In identifying with fictional characters we are able to vicariously live the lives of others by constructing what it must be like to be them. In the darkness of the theater, when Paul Newman sinks the final ball to beat Minnesota Fats, a hundred arms hold the cue; in reaching out and touching Elliot, E.T. touched millions of brows; the night it finally "happens" for Claudette Colbert and Clark Gable, the blanket barrier comes down for us all, and each of us is finally alone with either Claudette or Clark. Books such as Upton Sinclair's *The Jungle* have provided such compelling vicarious reference experiences (in this case, what it is like to work in a slaughterhouse) that they have led to movements, protests, and legislation. Radio used to transport and transform millions of listeners into lawmen, sleuths, and superheroes. And in airing such dramas as *Roots* and *The Day After*, television has in an evening provided millions of people with vicarious reference experiences for what it is like to be snatched from your home and family, and whipped and cowed into slavery, or to face the immediate aftermath of a nuclear war.

The fact that a reference is constructed does not necessarily mean that it is less affecting than an actual reference. We often create for ourselves pasts, presents, and futures that are imbued with the same *subjective* authenticity that we normally accord our actual experiences of the past and present. For instance, you probably know someone who typically constructs a future possibility (a date, a job offer, a lottery prize, etc.) and then responds to that constructed future as though it is a "sure thing." (We'll go into this subject further in the chapter on the Compelling Category.) In general, however, if an actual reference experience is available, then it is preferable to constructed experiences for several reasons.

■ Actual reference experiences are richer in terms of sensations, perceptions, environmental responses, and so on;

■ They are more accurate in terms of the sensations, preceptions, behaviors, and responses that are characteristic of the experience;

■ They are often more subjectively compelling because they "really happened."

Constructed reference experiences are more appropriate for those contexts in which personal experience is not available, such as stepping into someone else's experience to broaden your own, or using your imagination to explore unfamiliar contexts.

Emotional Involvement: Personal and Informational References

In the above example, when Stuart came home and saw Anna, he not only recalled past experiences of Anna looking, sounding, and feeling in that same way, but he in some measure *reexperienced how he felt at those times* as well. The time you stuck a screwdriver into a live electrical outlet, the day you became class president, and the morning you spent wandering around a strange city, are all examples of actual reference experiences. If in recalling those experiences you recall not only the information about what happened, but the sensations or emotions of the experience as well, then that memory constitutes a past *personal* reference experience. (Throughout the rest of this book, a reference is assumed to be actual unless it is specifically designated as being constructed.)

Thus, feeling your arm tighten or jerk back, or feeling again pain and fear when you recall sticking that screwdriver into the outlet constitutes a past personal reference. Feeling once again the pride or pleasure or anxiety you felt when elected class president is another example.

Personal references may also be from the present and future, and they may be constructed as well as actual. Being aware of how you feel as you stroll along in the evening, observing the twilight colors, smelling the evening smells, and feeling the cool air on your face, is an example of a *present personal* reference. Imagining what it feels like to be the man with the cane who is shuffling by constitutes a *present constructed personal* reference. Preston's constructed notions of New York, the desert, and the mountains were more than mere pictures and sound. He also *felt* what and how he would feel in each of those places and thus was using *future constructed personal* references when choosing his vacation spot. (Personal references are notated with a superscript "p" following the time frame of the reference.)

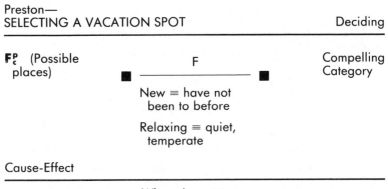

Preston—
SELECTING A VACATION SPOT — Deciding

F_c^p (Possible places) — F — Compelling Category

New ≡ have not been to before

Relaxing ≡ quiet, temperate

Cause-Effect

Where I want to go

It is often the case, however, that we recall, witness, and imagine experiences without feeling the sensations and emotions that are inherent in those experiences. For example, you might recall nearly getting flattened by a car while riding your bike, but not feel any of the fear (or exhilaration) you felt at the time of the incident. You could, in fact, recall that you were very frightened when it happened without actually re-experiencing the fear itself. In this case, the memory of the narrow escape is strictly data, devoid of the sensory and emotional content that was *of* the experience. We term such references *informational*. The example just given is, then, a past *informational* reference. (Informational references are notated with a superscript "i"—for example, Pa^i.)

The difference between informational and personal references was exemplified during a discussion among the authors about the planet Saturn. For LCB, Saturn was just a picture in her head—a picture to which she could refer when necessary. DG's experience, however, was of *being* at Saturn. He would imagine being in space some distance from Saturn, watching through his own eyes as its immense storms swirled across its face and feeling what he would feel were he actually in such close proximity to the glowing gas giant. Out of pieces of other references, DG has constructed a personal experience of being near Saturn, while for LCB the picture of Saturn remains a piece of data that is unconnected with her ongoing sensations or feelings. *Informational references, then, are those references that do not include sensations or emotions that are of the experience being referenced.*

Like personal references, informational references may be from the past, present, or future, and may be either actual or constructed.

■ The bicycle incident mentioned above is an example of a *past informational* reference.

■ To look back on your childhood and dispassionately imagine what would have happened had you been hit by that car is an example of a *past constructed informational* reference.

■ Watching someone dance, noting their rhythms and movements without responding kinesthetically or emotionally yourself to those rhythms and movements, is an example of a *present informational* reference.

■ If you imagine what that dancer is thinking and feeling without getting caught up in those thoughts and feelings yourself, that is a *present constructed informational* reference.

■ To imagine being desperately ill twenty years from now as the result of smoking, but without feeling the attendant discomfort or desperation as you imagine that future, is an example of a *future constructed informational* reference.

Informational references are most appropriate for those contexts in which you do not want or need a sensation-based reference: for instance, knowing the value of "pi," or how to convert Fahrenheit to Celsius, or how a worm is attached to a hook, or—for some people—what Saturn is like.

By combining the distinctions of time frame, authenticity, and emotional involvement into different constellations we can differentiate ten types of reference experiences:

Past, Actual, Personal
Past, Actual, Informational
Past, Constructed, Personal
Past, Constructed, Informational
Present, Actual, Personal
Present, Actual, Informational
Present, Constructed, Personal
Present, Constructed, Informational
Future, Constructed, Personal
Future, Constructed, Informational

Each of these references is singular in terms of what it contributes to experience and to an evaluation. That is, each type of reference will contribute a different influence to the outcome of an operative format. In the chapters that follow we will describe the special role played by each of the references in interaction with the other variables in an operative format. Your ability to understand and replicate another person's aptitudes will often depend on specifying and adopting the kinds of references they are using. It is worth the effort, therefore, to explore and become familiar with all the references. In the following summary, the unique characteristics of each of the ten types of references are described.

Summary of the References

Pa^P (past actual personal reference) Recalling actual occurrences from your past, including the reexperiencing of sensations or emotions connected with those occurrences.

Past actual personal references are appropriate for reexperiencing something from your past for the purpose of finding examples of experiences you might want to repeat (your deter-mination, for instance, when you hiked out of a snow storm); finding unpleasant experiences that you want to use as goads or warning reminders (that time you let things slide and thereby let others down); or for reminiscing (what it was like to fall in love with your mate).

Pa^i (past actual informational reference)   Recalling ac-tual occurrences from your past, without reexperiencing the sensations or emotions connected with those occurrences.

Past actual informational references are appropriate for gath-ering information from uselessly unpleasant past occurrences (recalling what you did when your son went into convulsions), or for gathering information from past occurrences for which the attendant sensations and emotions are at the moment irrelevant (the steps in planting a tree; where your friend lives; what you have done in the past to straighten a bent nail).

Pa$_c^p$ (past constructed personal reference)   Recalling an imagined occurrence, including sensations or emotions that might have been part of such an occurrence.

Past constructed personal references are appropriate for en-riching the range of experience available to you from your past by changing your personal history to either make it more satisfying (how you were elected class president and were therefore respected by your classmates—when in fact you never even ran for the office), or to generate other pasts from which to learn (constructing past trials and triumphs to bolster your present courage for some challenge you want to face).

Pa$_c^i$ (past constructed informational reference)   Re-calling an imagined occurrence without experiencing the sen-sations or emotions that might have been part of such an occurrence.

Past constructed informational references are appropriate for enriching the range of experience available to you from your past by changing your personal history, but without the sensations and emotions of that imagined past affecting your current state (imagining what it would have been like to have been crippled as a child; or to have had immigrant parents; or to have bought that corner lot).

Pr^p (present actual personal reference) Having an emotional involvement when attending to what you can currently see, hear, taste, smell, and feel going on around and in you.

Present actual personal references are appropriate for those contexts in which you want or need ongoing feedback regarding your sensations and emotions (making love; jogging; watching your child ride his bike for the first time without training wheels; learning to play a musical instrument).

Pr^i (present actual informational reference) Attending to what you can currently see, hear, taste, smell, and feel going on around and in you *without* experiencing an attendant emotional involvement.

Present actual informational references are appropriate for those situations in which you want or need ongoing feedback but for which your sensations or emotions would be either uselessly unpleasant (while performing surgery; while listening to your work be criticized) or irrelevent (typing a paper; fixing the car).

Pr$_c^p$ (present constructed personal reference) Imagining something occurring now and experiencing the sensations and emotions that belong to what is being imagined.

Present constructed personal references are appropriate for those times when you want to attend to the ongoing internal experiences of others, either for empathy (therapist gathering information from a client; listening to your child describe the trouble she is having at school), or for vicarious experience (watching a movie; imagining you are hitting the ball, feeling yourself make the movements, as you watch your tennis teacher demonstrate a stroke).

Pr$_c^i$ (present constructed informational reference) Imagining something occurring now without experiencing the sensations or emotions that belong to what is being imagined.

Present constructed informational references are appropriate for attending to the ongoing emotions of others, but in a detached way, providing what is commonly referred to as "perspective" (a physician gathering information from a patient; an attorney trying to settle a lawsuit; a family therapist working to understand the dynamics of a family's interactions), and for generating experiences for which sensations and emotions are irrelevant (looking at a building and "seeing through" the skin of the building to imagine how it is constructed; imagining the furniture in the room rearranged).

F_c^p (future constructed personal reference) Imagining what something will be like while experiencing the sensations or emotions of the imagined event.

Future constructed personal references are appropriate for those situations in which what you do now will have a direct bearing on how you or others will feel in the future (when considering stopping smoking, feeling what it would be like to have emphysema or what it would feel like to be sixty and healthy; when deciding about whether or not to marry, considering what it will be like to be with your mate through the years; while shopping for Christmas presents, imagining how you or your friends will feel when they open the presents you are buying for them).

F_c^i (future constructed informational reference) Imagining what something will be like without experiencing the sensations or emotions that belong to what is being imagined.

Future constructed informational references are appropriate for those contexts in which you want or need to consider possibilities and plans that are either best made without sensations or emotions (making investments; buying life insurance; figuring out how to face someone who scares you), or for which sensations and emotions are irrelevant (figuring out how to go about building the extra bedroom).

The appropriate uses described for the various references do not necessarily coincide with how a particular individual *does* use these references. We all know someone who reminisces about things that never happened (past constructed personal references), as well as people who torture themselves with the unpleasant feelings dredged up when recalling their trials and tribulations (past actual personal references). The medical or dental student who empathizes with the pain and fear of her patients (present constructed personal references) will have a very different experience of her training than the student who either imagines what is going on inside the patient without being personally affected by the patient's suffering (present constructed informational references), or simply does not imagine what is going on inside the patient (either present actual personal, or present actual informational references). One person may buy a lottery ticket and become ecstatic thinking about what he will do with the money, and later feel robbed because his number was not picked (future constructed personal reference), while another person thinks about the possibility of cancer, emphysema, and heart disease as she lights up another cigarette (future constructed informational reference).

These last two examples of individuals using certain references in less than appropriate contexts highlight an important *functional* aspect of references. In part, the significance of these various kinds of past, present, and future references lies in how subjectively compelling each of them is. For many people, reading and hearing about the carcinogenic dangers of cigarettes remains an *informational reference* and consequently not very compelling. They know the facts as well as anyone else, but the danger of the carcinogens in the smoke rings they blow is no more a part of their *personal* experience than is the fact of rings around Saturn. Responses change dramatically, however (though perhaps not enough to quit smoking—see Cameron-Bandler, Gordon, and Lebeau, 1985), when the dangers of carcinogens become a *constructed personal* reference in which one feels the discomfort of wheezing and gasping, feels the fear upon learning that the diagnosis is cancer, feels the pain of burning lungs and operations, and so on. Obviously, even more compelling is actually having had the experience of learning you had cancer, of the disability and the pain (becoming, then, an *actual personal* reference).

In summary, all evaluations (and therefore all responses and behaviors) are based and depend upon the information that is referred to in order to make that evaluation. The reference category specifies whether the information referred to is from your past, present, or future, whether those references are actual (actually occurred) or constructed (created, imagined), and whether those references are personal (that is, evocative of the emotions or sensations that are *of* the experience) or are informational (devoid of emotions or sensations that are *of* the experience).

Of course, knowing the references used by someone in manifesting a behavior that you would like to replicate does not provide you with that person's personal history. For example, the person who is excellent at negotiating uses certain sequences of operative formats, each of which includes certain tests, criteria, criterial equivalences, and references. The one thing that we cannot readily replicate in our exemplar's operative format is his personal history in relation to negotiating. This personal history contains a wealth of relevant information that appears in his evaluations primarily as references (also in a more codified form as cause-effects, discussed in the next chapter). We can replicate the *kind* of references he uses, but we cannot replicate the personal history that provides the content for those references.

Thus the usefulness of replicating the kind of references an exemplar uses at first seems fruitless, until we recognize that, to a great extent, *the exemplar's personal history in relation to a specific context is a function of the kinds of references he has been using.* The particular references he has been using have consistently guided the exemplar's attentions and experiences along certain lines. For instance, the lawyer who was making no headway in his settlement negotiations did not use a present reference with respect to the ongoing responses of opposing counsel—one of the references that we have found to be characteristic of all good negotiators. Having used present references over the years, these individuals have discovered things about the responses of an opponent in a negotiation that the person who does not use a present reference will be blind to. This blindness, however, is neither hereditary nor is it necessarily permanent. By using the same references as the exemplar, you too will be oriented toward those experiential and informational sources that are appropriate for success in that particular context, and at the same time, you will be accumulating a personal history that will increasingly contribute to your success.

Explorations

Understanding Yourself   The particular references you use can dramatically affect your responses. For instance, consider the context of attempting to save a troubled relationship. If the only references you are using are "things that I have already done that haven't worked," then your evaluations are likely to soon lead you to feeling *hopeless*. If instead your references are of "things I haven't tried yet," then your evaluations are more likely to lead to responses such as *curious, engaged,* and *hopeful.* If you add as a reference "how fulfilling your relationship could be in the future once the present difficulties are resolved," you are likely to remain *motivated* and perhaps even *committed*.

Find something in your life that you have given up on. What references are you using when you evaluate that situation? Now find something in your life that is difficult but that you are nevertheless still engaged in. What are the references you are using? When you use these kinds of references to evaluate the first situation do you still feel like giving up? What kinds of references would you need to use in order to again pursue what you have given up on? What references can you use to keep engaged?

Understanding Others   Find someone who is holding a grudge, and ask him about the references he is using (for example, "What do you think of when you think of that person?"). You will probably find that he is primarily using past actual personal references of the awful thing that person did, and no present references regarding how that person is different today, and no future references of that person being different in the future.

Acquisition   Some people are adept at consistently accomplishing what they set out to do. Once they establish a goal, that goal remains a reference in *all related operative formats*. This ensures that the goal is there to influence their behavior in all contexts that are relevant to attaining the goal.

Pick a goal for yourself, such as financial security, or being attractive. Now specify how you would know that you had achieved your goal. Make an exhaustive list of situations that are related to your goal (for financial security: shopping, incurring and paying bills, making career plans, etc.). Go through the list and, imagining being in each of those contexts, insert your goal as a reference in each situation. For example, if your goal is to reduce the amount of stress in your life and to enjoy more leisure time, make sure you consider that information in your evaluations as you decide whether or not to make another long-term, time-consuming commitment to a project.

You may find constructed personal references particularly useful if you tend to make most decisions based only on what you have actually done or experienced in the past. The set of references consisting of what you have actually done, while valuable, provides a relatively limited set of experiences upon which to draw. By creating references in all of the time frames, taking constructive advantage of your own history as well as of the experiences of others, you expand your range of possible responses to different situations. We have developed several formats for creating constructed personal references, the use of which always results in increased flexibility and creativity in achieving personal and professional outcomes (see Cameron-Bandler, Gordon, and Lebeau, 1985).

Some people can be fooled by other people—over and over again. They have a hard time predicting how others will respond, even people they know well. We have worked with many such people. By directing them to their past actual references, we assist them in discovering the behavioral patterns that have been manifested by their family, friends, and colleagues. This "researching and cataloging" results in a coherence through time and is far more useful than what they typically do, which is to listen to what people are *saying* about themselves (present actual reference) and then forget to attend to what those people have actually *done* (past actual reference). We teach them to store examples and detect patterns, which can then be used to understand and predict the responses of their friends and associates.

Future references are a storehouse of knowledge for what is possible. When we are assessing a person's capacity for creativity, we always check to make sure that person is using future references. If they are missing, we install their use for those endeavors that require creativity. Future references are not the cause of creativity, but without them the creative process is more like a trial and error approach.

6 Cause-Effect

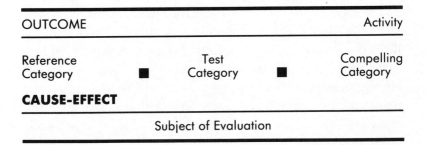

OUTCOME   Activity

Reference   ■   Test   ■   Compelling
Category   Category   Category

CAUSE-EFFECT

                         Subject of Evaluation

Suppose that after several unsuccessful hours of standing out on the road hitchhiking with your thumb sticking out you wave and flail your arms at the next car that approaches you—and it stops to pick you up. When you next find yourself by the road trying to hitch a ride, what method do you use to induce a motorist to stop? You could reason from your previous try that the flailing of your arms *caused* the motorist to stop and pick you up. If such a cause-effect relationship between arm-flailing and being picked up holds true for most motorists, then you have discovered a technique worth repeating when you need a ride in the future.

Different individuals will have different responses to their success at hitchhiking. Some will be sure it was the arm-waving that caused the motorist to stop, and will use that approach again the next time they need to hitch. Others will not be sure whether it was the arm-waving itself that was responsible for getting the motorist to stop, or whether it was a combination of the arm-waving and the kind of person the motorist was, or whether it was merely a coincidence. The next occasion for hitchhiking is likely to find this person using the standard thumb approach, while periodically experimenting with arm-waving in an effort to find out if there is justification for establishing a causal relationship between the two methods. Still another person may not even consider that there was a contingent relationship between the arm-waving and being picked up, or consider it and be sure that it was merely a coincidence. Either way, this person will probably stick with the standard thumb approach.

These examples do not exhaust the possible responses, but they do illustrate the point we wish to make, which is that the causal relationships you perceive will affect your experience and behavior in a particular context. Such cause-effect relationships are created whenever an individual comes to believe that some particular circumstance necessarily leads to some other particular circumstance. In other words, a cause-effect relationship is a *contingent* relationship between occurrences as, for example, when a person believes that spending money *leads to* contentment. In the world of experience, however, there is little that is etched in stone, and so there are other people who believe that the way to hitch a ride on the contentment express is *through* asceticism, or *through* being loved. Furthermore, each of these cause-effect relationships leading to contentment will engender its own unique experiences and behaviors in those who subscribe to them. For example, the person who believes in the cause-effect between spending money and contentment will, when discontent, feel motivated to go on a buying spree, while the person who has tied contentment to asceticism will feel motivated to simplify his life, perhaps by getting rid of possessions.

In addition to the particular subjects believed to be causally linked, a cause-effect relationship is also characterized by the time frames it presupposes. Whenever an individual believes in and expresses a cause-effect relationship, both the cause and the effect of that relationship will be perceived as occurring within certain time frames. Take as an example the cause-effect, "eating properly will make me healthy." In addition to the contingent relationship between eating and health that is being expressed here, this contingent relationship is also being perceived in terms of the present having an impact on the future: eating properly *will make* me healthy (notated as: eating properly $\rightarrow$ healthy; $Pr \rightarrow F$). This same contingent relationship between eating and health can be perceived in terms of other time frames as well.

I was healthy because I ate properly.	$Pa \rightarrow Pa$
I am healthy because I have always eaten properly.	$Pa \rightarrow Pr$
Because I ate properly as a youngster, I will be healthy in my old age.	$Pa \rightarrow F$
Eating properly makes me healthy.	$Pr \rightarrow Pr$
Eating properly will make me healthy.	$Pr \rightarrow F$
When I start eating properly, I will become healthy.	$F \rightarrow F$
Because of some awful health problems I had, I now eat properly, which will eventually make me healthy.	$Pa \rightarrow Pr \rightarrow F$

Cause-effect relationships, then, may be drawn between any of the time frames. Thus you can perceive the past causing effects in the present ($Pa \rightarrow Pr$), the past causing effects in the future ($Pa \rightarrow F$), the present causing effects in the future ($Pr \rightarrow F$), the past causing effects in the present which in turn cause effects in the future ($Pa \rightarrow Pr \rightarrow F$), and so on. An individual who says, "I don't feel good about myself because my father never believed in me," is operating out of a cause-effect relationship in which the past ("father never believed in me") is responsible for (*the cause of*) the present ("I don't feel good about myself") ($Pa \rightarrow Pr$). People who are concerned about conserving natural resources are demonstrating a belief in the cause-effect relationship that present resource utilization *will determine* future resource availability ($Pr \rightarrow F$).

Although most contingent relationships can be expressed with respect to any of the time frame patterns listed above, which one you use can have a marked effect on the role that cause-effect plays in influencing your subjective experience and behavior. If you review the cause-effect examples given above, reading each as though it were true for you and pausing after each one to reflect upon how each cause-effect affects your perceptions, you will find that there is a subjective difference in each of them even though the content remains the same for all the examples. Because of how we regard and respond to the past, present, and future, each of the above cause-effect patterns is subjectively and functionally unique, and therefore the pattern used does make a difference. The time frames to which you assign the content of causal relationships can be significant.

Past-to-Past (Pa → Pa)

When you turn to your past (however immediate or remote) in order to determine how one occurrence caused another, you are generating past-to-past cause-effects. You may look back and realize that your friend had agreed to go to the party with you *because* you made it sound like fun. Or that *the reason* you did well in math was that the teacher encouraged you. Or that you have been lonely as an adult *because* your parents never taught you to be close to others. Or that the enactment of civil rights legislation *was accelerated by* the civil rights movement.

Past-to-past cause-effects provide a wealth of information about what has worked and what has not worked. Our pasts are very rich in actions and reactions, and some of those reactions are ones we would like to repeat, while others are ones we want to avoid repeating. In sifting through the ashes of the past we are often able to discover what (we think) made it possible for one flame to burn brightly, while another merely sputtered. One result of such discoveries is the subjective experience of *understanding*. Understanding is often enough to satisfy us, to create a sense of relief and comforting acceptance.

Another result of the discovery of past contingent relationships is the *behavioral information* inherent in the cause-effect itself. You can use that information to adjust your behavior in the future. For instance, having recognized that failing to call your wife when you were late made her feel unloved (I didn't call → she felt unloved; Pa → Pa), you can use that cause-effect as the basis for changing your behavior in the future—for instance, by calling her to let her know when you will be home. Similarly, after failing an exam a student may look back at those exams on which he has done well, and realize that in those cases he made it a point to seek out the teacher for personal answers to his questions (asked teacher questions $\rightarrow$ did well in the class; Pa $\rightarrow$ Pa). Knowing this, he can put that cause-effect into effect by seeking out the teacher with his questions.

Typically, there is nothing inherent in the past-to-past cause-effect that takes it beyond the point of being merely an observation on the causal connection between past occurrences. That's fine if all you want is an understanding of how things came to pass. If, however, you are facing unpleasant outcomes that you do not want to repeat, past-to-past cause-effects can become a form of torture. If the would-be scholar in the example above went no further than discovering the various reasons for his failures, he would merely be tightening the bonds that he creates with each addition to his growing list of personal deficiencies. When on the rack of "failure," each new discovery of an example of "how it failed" becomes just another turn of the screw unless the past-to-past cause-effects are somehow used as the basis for appropriately reorganizing present or future behavior. If he is to do well consistently in the future, it is not enough for the student to recognize that there was a cause-effect relationship between his asking questions and doing well in classes. That cause-effect must become the basis for appropriate changes in his present and future behavior, or he will again fail, and again end up wishing that he had asked questions when he had the chance.

Past-to-Present (Pa $\rightarrow$ Pr)

Causal connections can be made between the past and the present, informing us about how things have come to be the way they are. The occurrences of the past are perceived as having had an effect that persists to the present. The subject matter being considered in connection with the present may be broad and encompassing ("I am a *lonely person* because I never learned to make friends"), or it may be narrow in focus

("I am *lonely tonight* because I didn't make arrangements to meet with my friends"), depending upon the subjective experience of the individual at that moment. In either case, something current is perceived as being a consequence of something that has gone on before.

Like past-to-past, past-to-present cause-effects provide understanding, which can be an end in itself. It may simply be nice to know that you take care of your tools because your grandfather taught you to respect them when you were a kid, or that the reason you resent your older brother is that he never acknowledged you when you were a little girl. Also like past-to-past, past-to-present cause-effects provide information about what to do or not to do in the present and future to move either toward or away from certain outcomes. Thus, recognizing that you feel good as the result of having exercised during the past week, you can use that past-to-present cause-effect relationship between exercise and feeling good as a basis for making a commitment to continue exercising.

For many people, past-to-present cause-effects regarding their shortcomings can create a great deal of motivational inertia when it comes to doing something about those shortcomings. These active descriptions of contingencies often quickly decay into stagnant justifications for the present state of affairs. If trudging through your past has taken you only as far as the disheartening discovery that you do not have a good job *because* you never had a good education, then you are stuck. "That's just the way it is," you might say. And worse, that is the way it will probably continue to be—until and unless you use that discovery to fashion a behavioral rope with which to pull yourself into the future you want for yourself (in this case, perhaps getting a good education at an adult night school or technical institute).

Past-to-Future (Pa → F)

The threads we have spun in the past can reach beyond that past and even the present to bind the future. In those instances, certain future occurrences are perceived to be the direct consequences of things that have happened in the past.

"Because I had musical parents I will be able to learn an instrument." "I will never be able to make a good living because I never got a good education." "Only people who grew up in the city will be able to understand our situation here." "Since my parents got along well, I will probably get along well with my wife when I get married." In each of these examples, what is possible or probable in the future is determined by what has been true in the past.

Of course, the subjective impact of past-to-future cause-effects goes beyond indicating what is possible or probable, often becoming more like a pronouncement about what *will* be. The causal certainty of the past can have the effect of prescribing the future. The way you were (or "it" has been) determines how you (or "it") will be. In this way the past can provide the reassurance and justification of history for those futures that you want to maintain for yourself. During hard times it is reassuring and encouraging to know that you will get through your present trials because you have gotten through trials before (gotten through before → will get through again; Pa → F). Similarly, it is gratifying and reinforcing to perceive that because you praised your children's achievements and educated them when they failed they will grow up eager to try things (praise success, educate failure → eager to try; Pa → F).

Past-to-future cause-effects can be reassuring and appropriate provided that the future they describe is one that you want and that is worth having. If it is instead an unpleasant and disabling future, the cause-effect can become a set of blinders that keeps you on a narrow road while the opportunities and choices to either side go unnoticed. The resigned acceptance of a future hobbled by the past often prevents any possibility of action in the present intended to change that limiting cause-effect. Thus the person who wishes for a good living (but is "forever" prevented from having one by his lack of education) applies only for jobs that do not require education, and does not even consider signing up for night school. If a past-to-future cause-effect that dictates an unwanted future is to be appropriate, it must be used as the basis for additional operative formats that result in plans and commitments to more appropriate and satisfying behavior.

Present-to-Present (Pr → Pr)

Present-to-present cause-effects specify contingent relationships between ongoing occurrences. Unlike the other causal patterns, present-to-present cause-effects presuppose the *simultaneous* occurrence of the cause and its effect. For example, "Watching the sunset makes me happy." Or, "When I treat others respectfully, they respect me." Or, "I am learning more because I am taking chances." In each instance, two things are currently going on (remembering that what is "current" is subjective and varies by context), and the occurrence of one is perceived to be contingent upon the occurrence of the other.

Present-to-present cause-effects can provide understanding of what *is* causing what to occur. Perhaps you are curious about what draws you outside each evening for a glance up at the night sky. Then one day you realize that facing the evening stars or clouds makes you feel alive—and now you understand what propels you out the door each night before bed. Once recognized, you have the opportunity to take the cause-effect beyond the passive service of understanding and actively employ it when you desire the outcome it produces. If you are feeling disconnected and emotionally adrift, you now have the choice of deliberately going outside to face the evening sky and thereby change your mood, rather than sulking around the house wondering about the cause of your malaise and trying to wish it away.

Present-to-Future (Pr → F)

When you perceive that a particular occurrence in the present will necessarily lead to certain future occurrences, you are generating a present-to-future cause-effect relationship between those occurrences. Examples include, "Exercising will make me healthier" (exercise → healthier; Pr → F); "Our being together on my birthday today will make being at work tomorrow easier" (being together → work easier; Pr → F); "Thinking highly of myself will make others think better of me as well" (think highly of self → others think better of me; Pr → F). In each case a particular future is believed to be contingent upon the occurrence of certain behaviors and circumstances in the present.

The significance of present-to-future cause-effects is that they can specify what needs to be done now in order to either avoid something awful or to achieve something wonderful in the future. This makes present-to-future cause-effect relationships particularly important for initiating and maintaining the pursuit of long-term goals, such as developing a career, developing a good game of tennis, developing a better world, and anything that has to do with one's health. For instance, believing that smoking will ultimately lead to dire consequences for one's health is usually an important prerequisite to quitting smoking (in terms of both making the decision to quit and maintaining abstinence from cigarettes). Another example is the black South African priest who recently initiated a program of getting black and white families to have dinner together once a month, believing that personal interaction will eventually lead to tolerance and understanding.

In dealing with present-to-future cause-effects, however, it is important to remember that they concern consequences in the *future*, which is a brew that will change as each new ingredient is added. Once the pronouncement of a present-to-future cause-effect has been made, one may blindly submit to it, forgetting that, in the inimitable words of Yogi Berra, "It isn't over until it's over." Of course, keeping your present recipe for the future the same is fine as long as the future you are now brewing is one that you want. If it's not, however, and you accept it as immutable, then you are left with nothing to do but wait for the inevitable, wishing that it would not be, and perhaps stewing over what to do about it when it happens.

For instance, you might hear someone say, "As an overweight, overstressed executive I will probably get ulcers and heart disease—maybe even cancer." That sounds final. This person may wonder how much time he has left and how he will pay the hospital bills, praying that he squeaks by a few more years without any serious ailments. More appropriate, however, would be to use that cause-effect as the stimulus to engage in planning how to *change* his present behavior (in this case, overeating and the way he responds to stress) in order to avoid that dreadful future.

Future-to-Future (F → F)

If what we have done and are doing affects the future then, of course, so will what we do in the future affect the future. In recognizing or generating such contingent relationships between two or more future occurrences we are establishing future-to-future cause-effects. For example, "When inflation returns it will cause great hardship for many people" (inflation → hardship; F → F); "If she grows tired of me she will go looking for others" (tired of me → go looking for others; F → F); "If I start painting the house tomorrow it will make dad very happy" (painting the house → dad happy; F → F). In each example, it is perceived that some *future* behavior or circumstance will necessarily lead to some other future behavior or circumstance.

The future-to-future crystal ball can be a wonderful instrument, opening a window on the possibilities of the future. Once you have leaped from the present into the crystalline refractions of the future you are relatively free to consider what you want to consider, without those considerations necessarily being dulled by the shades of the past and present. Wishing to advance yourself professionally, you can imagine all manner of things that you might do to improve your state, and then speculate about the results. For instance, "If I get a higher educational degree, I will get greater respect from my colleagues and more referrals"; "Writing articles—or even a book—would bring wider attention and speaking engagements"; "I could move to Los Angeles where the competition would force me to do my best." Those cause-effects that seem in accord with your outcome can then be adopted as beliefs worth fostering.

Future-to-future cause-effects, then, are speculations about what might happen, and what the effects might be. Sometimes that little qualifier, "might," is forgotten, however, and the individual starts responding to the cause-effect as though it is actually happening in the *present*. For example, the man who believes that if his wife gets tired of him she will go looking for others might start trying to discover if his wife is indeed tired of him. If he can unearth even a small shred of evidence that his wife is tired of him, his cause-effect may lead him to imagine a future in which she is involved with someone else. He might respond *in the present* to his own imagining by feeling hurt, jealous, outraged, and so on. (As shown in the following example, cause-effects are notated below the references.)

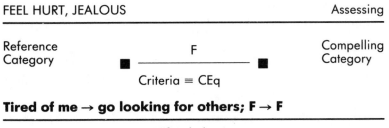

FEEL HURT, JEALOUS		Assessing
Reference Category	F	Compelling Category
	Criteria ≡ CEq	

Tired of me → go looking for others; F → F

Wife's behavior

All of this emotional fire is fueled by the future-to-future cause-effect, which is something that has not really happened. Furthermore, the search for evidence is justified only if there actually *is* a cause-effect relationship between his wife being tired of him and her looking for other men. He has forgotten that *he* generated that cause-effect and that it may not at all reflect how she would respond to being tired of him. (Perhaps it would cause her to simply withdraw from him, or perhaps it would cause her to try to draw him out more.) Since future-to-future cause-effects can be generated without the experiential influence of the past or present, it is inappropriate to use them as the basis for action unless the validity of that cause-effect is supported by appropriate past or present references. If a particular future-to-future cause-effect is, in your experience, valid, and it portends a future that you would rather avoid, then it should lead to another operative format in which you figure out what to do about changing that future.

Past-to-Present-to-Future (Pa → Pr → F)

Cause-effects may be represented and stored as contingent occurrences that span all three time frames. For example,

"Because I was abused as a child I'm confused now about relationships and probably will be a poor parent" (abused → confused about relationships → poor parent; Pa → Pr → F); "The way he asked his question makes me curious, so I will have to find out more about him" (way he asked → curious → find out more; Pa → Pr → F); "I know a lot about the business because of what my boss taught me, so I will do well when I'm out on my own" (boss taught → know a lot → do well on own; Pa → Pr → F). The common pattern in all of these examples is that something that happened in the past caused something to be the case in the present, which in turn will cause something to occur in the future.

The subjective experience of the chain that is forged when past, present, and future are linked is one of continuity and inevitability. The continuity is a function of having all three time frames represented "at once," and the inevitability is a function of the seeming lack of choice in the present and future "because" of the determined past and present. This makes past-to-present-to-future cause-effects particularly appropriate for maintaining behaviors that you want to persist over time. For example, a teacher told us, "The preparation I have done determines the quality of my lecture, which will in turn determine the quality of my student's experience" (preparation → quality of lecture → student's experience; Pa → Pr → F). Assuming that this teacher values his student's experience, this particular cause-effect will probably be instrumental in ensuring that he continues to prepare well for his lectures.

The same chain of continuity and inevitability that makes this cause-effect pattern useful for maintaining desirable behaviors can make it inappropriate when it is in the service of behaviors that you *don't* want, shackling you to a future that you would rather avoid. For a person who believes, "I yell at my wife because my parents always yelled at each other, so I'll probably end up with marriage problems too" (parents yelled → I yell → marriage problems), this particular situation is all locked up. It is apparent to this person that the links in the chain have been fired, forged, and quenched. But sometimes these links may be more like the rings a magician uses, banging them together to show they are solid and locked, then twisting them apart to remind us not to take too much for granted. Past-to-present-to-future cause-effects that seem to bind you to unwanted behaviors and an unattractive future should be used as the impetus for gathering information, then deciding and planning how to change your behavior and, thereby, your future.

The Influence of Cause-Effects

To cast cause-effect in a sharper, more revealing light, we submit the important possibility of *not* forming a cause-effect. Consider the following example.

An eighth-grader we know, named Nate, took violin lessons at school and thus immediately became part of the grade school orchestra. These were group lessons, of course, lasting only about forty minutes a day, three or four days a week. On the rare occasions Nate did take his violin home to practice, he would invariably find something else more pressing to do that evening. The culmination of the efforts of the class was a concert. Nate wanted to do well; he wanted to make his parents proud. Unfortunately, two bars into the piece the little black notes began to run together and the boy was hopelessly lost. He felt humiliated, and the patronizing encouragement of his parents afterwards served only to confirm that he had reason to feel humiliated . . . but Nate had learned his lesson.

What was the lesson that Nate learned? We might expect him to realize that his poor performance was the result of his lack of experience, or instruction, or practice, or motivation, or a combination of those factors. But none of these possibilities even occurred to him. What Nate learned from this experience was that he possessed no musical talent. Instead of generating a cause-effect in response to his debut, he responded to the experience as though it were the fulfillment of a *criterial equivalence* for "no musical talent" and so simply "recognized" that he is not a musically inclined person. In other words, he used his failure as the basis for affixing the stamp of "musically inept" upon his self-concept, rather than perceiving the cause-effect relationship between the small amount of instruction he had received, his neglect of practicing, and his current inability to play the instrument.

Even the most dismal and well-substantiated cause-effects presuppose the possibility of change (since, if the causal relationship is to be believed, changing the cause would necessarily result in a change in the effect). But the acausal form of Nate's recognizing an *inherent* attribute in himself offers no hope of change. Cause-effect at least supplies a possible point of intervention (the cause), if indeed Nate wants to learn to play the violin. In this case it is the causal influence of practicing that must be addressed if Nate is to change his performance.

The particular time frames within which the cause-effect is perceived may also make a difference. All cause-effects provide understanding, but they are useful in terms of change only to the extent that they are used as grounds for assembling other operative formats that lead to behavioral changes (for example, making decisions, planning, gathering information, making commitments, motivation, and so on).

Beyond these common grounds there are other, often significant differences. For Nate, past-to-past, past-to-present, or past-to-future cause-effects ("I did not perform well because I did not practice"; or "I am not performing well because I did not practice"; or "I will not be able to perform well because I didn't practice") all convey a certain degree of immutability by virtue of the cause belonging to the unchangeable past. If he were to generate present-to-present or present-to-future patterns ("I am not playing well because I am not practicing"; or "I will not be able to perform well because I am not practicing"), he would be using cause-effects that might seem more accessible to intervention. Subjectively and practically, the *ongoing* behavior of the present is more accessible to change than are behaviors of the past. And a future-to-future cause-effect ("I will not be able to perform well if I don't eventually practice") suggests that practicing need not be done now, but can be put off until some unspecified later date.

Recognizing a cause-effect relationship between practice and performance would not in itself ensure that Nate would start practicing and become an accomplished violinist. What it *does* ensure, however, is that he has the opportunity to perceive the quality of his performance as a function of his behavior rather than as a function of his innate self, and so he has the opportunity to take the steps necessary to change his behavior.

Most important is the realization that, regardless of the content or pattern, cause-effects are *created*. This is, to our minds, a staggering realization in terms of the malleability of our experiences and behaviors. As we have demonstrated throughout this book, your internal processes shape your experiences and behaviors *and* your experiences and behaviors shape your internal processes. In swallowing its own tail, our experiential snake feeds on itself and yet finds itself undiminished. In fact, the snake grows stronger as it feeds its self on itself, becoming more and more of what it is. Change comes when the snake is given something different to feed on, which then becomes its (new) self.

This is not to say that all you need to do to make someone into a conservationist is to instill in that person a belief in present-to-future cause-effect relationships. Behavior is a manifestion of cause-effects working in concert with the other variables specified in the operative format. The same belief in present-to-future cause-effects that enables an individual to be a conservationist can also form the foundation for outcomes that are quite different. We have recently had a Secretary of the Interior who (by the standards of various conservation lobbies) demonstrated that he was notoriously anticonservation-minded, if not positively rapacious. It would be a mistake, however, to assume that this man was lacking in appreciation for present-to-future cause-effect relationships. The difference between his perspective and that of the conservationists may have lain not in the time frames of their cause-effects, but in the criteria to which the secretary and the conservationists applied those cause-effect relationships. If, for instance, the secretary's criteria are profit and efficiency, then he would be expected to open up publicly held lands for sale or lease to private concerns. Such a move now, he believes, will lead to greater revenues for the government and the corporate community, and will lead to more efficient management of those lands and of his agency, since he will no longer have those lands to manage—a present-to-future cause-effect.

In fact, some of the most successful conservationist moves have been made by those groups that in some way manage to include and satisfy the criteria of their putative foes, such as by finding ways that a conservation proposal can include the ability to turn a profit. Conservationists who recognize and include in their appeals the criteria of those groups that might otherwise be unsympathetic exemplify the usefulness of being able to make such distinctions as criteria. Similarly, knowing that cause-effects provide us with compelling explanations (and therefore justifications) can provide you with tremendous leverage when trying to free your own or others' experience and behavior from their present moorings, setting them on a new course. These new headings can be taken by either changing those debilitating cause-effects to which you currently subscribe, or by adopting as your own those cause-effect beliefs that underlie those aptitudes that you would like to replicate.[1]

Explorations

Understanding Yourself Why are you reading this book? Do you have a present-to-future cause-effect between "learning" and "having more choice" (learning → choice), or between "reading" and "being able to do it" (reading → able to do it)?

Understanding Others People who are resigned to history repeating itself are generally operating out of past-to-future cause-effects.

Some people believe that hard work will get them where they want to go, based on past-to-present and present-to-future cause-effects. Those who do not generate present-to-future cause-effects, however, typically believe that it is luck that will get them what they want.

Acquisition Parents who are nurturing operate out of a cause-effect between what they do with their kids and how their kids will turn out as adults (what I do with my child → my child's adult character and abilities).

Think about your child and find something that he or she

can do now. Go back through time and find what you did that contributed to the development of that ability in your child. Then consider what that ability will lead the child to as an adult.

Some people are confident that they can eventually accomplish something even though they have failed at it before. Find an example of something at which you have failed. Going back through time, determine what caused you to fail. What could you have done differently, or paid attention to, or said, or thought that could have led to success? Imagine redoing that past, this time doing or saying or thinking in the way that would have brought success. Keep doing this until you have changed that failure into a learning about how better to achieve success in the future.

We have elicited and transferred many operative formats that relate in various ways to ensuring that a person will behave ethically. Although the criteria varied slightly for each person, each operative format contains essential cause-effects between the person's behavior and the consequences of that behavior to others specifically, and to the larger environment in general (all living things, ecosystems, the planet). The cause-effects encompass the belief that actions the person did or did not take in the past contributed to how past events transpired (Pa $\rightarrow$ Pa); that what they have or have not done in the past has helped shape the current situation, and likewise that the situation in the future will in part be a result of what they are doing now (Pa $\rightarrow$ Pr $\rightarrow$ F); that what they are doing now has an immediate effect on others (Pr $\rightarrow$ Pr); and that the actions they take, or fail to take, in the future will in some way alter future events (F $\rightarrow$ F). Similarly, when we want to enhance an individual's self-esteem we direct him to establish and use cause-effects in all of the time frames just mentioned, but between his actions and the benefit that others have received from him, as well as how he has benefited from his own behavior. Adopting these cause-effects leads him to realize *and remember* the significant part he has played in the lives of those around him.

7 Compelling Category

OUTCOME			Activity
Reference Category	■	Test Category ■	**COMPELLING CATEGORY**
Cause-Effect			
		Subject of Evaluation	

When have you done something that you knew was not good for you to do, such as taking a drug, or smoking a cigarette, or eating a piece of pie, or having an affair? When have you not done something that needed doing, such as taking care of the lawn, writing a term paper, or getting the car fixed? When have you not done something that you knew would be good for you, such as relaxing, or taking a course in night school, or turning off the TV? How is it possible that a person will do something they know is not a good idea, or not do something that they know *is* a good idea? To answer this question we must first talk a bit about "reality."

For most of us, establishing what is real as opposed to what is not real borders on being a fundamental drive. We argue about who is "right," what is the "correct" answer, what "really" happened, and on and on. One of the most disturbing things that we can face is a challenge to our perceptions of what is real. Consequently, we have the Scopes "monkey trial," Galileo imprisoned by the Inquisition, angry baseball managers kicking dirt on umpires, and couples in therapy attempting to thrash out just who really is culpable for their problems. Even a psychotic hallucinating voices and visions tries to convince those around him that his six-foot rabbit is real, rather than simply saying, "Oh, you don't see it? Oh well . . .", then shrugging and walking away. Nor do those around him simply shrug it off as a difference in perception and opinion, let alone sincerely ask how the rabbit is doing today.

What is so important about separating what is real from what is not? There are several answers to this question, but the one we are concerned with here has to do with the *need to respond*. We need to know what is real so that we can know what to respond to and how to respond. Is your mate in love with you? Your response to your mate will vary tremendously depending on your answer to that question. Is it true that you are a sensitive person? Is it true that you have been scarred by the past? Is it true that anything is possible in the future? Are the conversations you sometimes have with yourself of your own manufacture, or are you eavesdropping on the spirit world? In each instance, what you believe to be real will profoundly affect your emotions and actions.

Suppose your child comes running out of his room, whimpering and frightened because there is a "monster" in his closet. As an informed adult, you know that there is not a monster in the closet, and so you do not call the police, or lock the door, or grab a kitchen knife and go monster hunting. The monster is not real to you. But there is your little boy, shaking and tearful. The monster *is* real to him, and so he is responding appropriately as far as he is concerned, by being frightened and running to you for help. The point is that we do not respond to what *is* real—we respond to what we *think* is real. For the frightened child, his representation of a monster in his closet is *compelling enough* that he responds to that representation as though it were real. As long as he perceives it as real he must respond to it as such. That is the demand of what we perceive to be real.

This phenomenon is not confined to childhood bogeymen, of course. To William Jennings Bryan, the Biblical account of creation and the spiritual threat of the theory of evolution were so real that he felt compelled to help prosecute John Scopes for teaching Darwinian evolution. When the authors were children, the development of nuclear weapons created in our families (as it did in most families of the fifties) the reality of a nuclear war. Compelled by this very real possibility, we stocked up on canned goods, read literature touting home-made bomb shelters, and practiced diving under our seats at school, one hand shielding our necks, the other our eyes. Despite a continuing exponential growth in nuclear arsenals, however, we subsequently went through a period in which very few people gave nuclear war much thought; or if they did, they did not feel compelled to do anything about it either in terms of political action or of self-preservation. In recent years the possibility of a nuclear holocaust has become real once again to vast numbers of people, who are accordingly scared and motivated to do something about it.

While working with incarcerated juvenile delinquents, one of the authors (DG) was astonished to hear from most of the petty and not-so-petty thieves interviewed variations on the following theme.

DG: Did you think you'd be caught?

J: Naw, I knew they couldn't catch me.

DG: But you *did* get caught. You're here.

J: (Shrugs) Well, I made a mistake on the job, that's all.

DG: Do you think you'll steal again when you get out?

J: Sure. They won't catch *me* again.

What an amazing thing for someone to say who *has been* caught and *is* sitting in jail! How is it possible to believe as this person believes? Do you think that if you go out and rob a store you will not get caught? Probably not. It is probably your perception that there is a very real chance that you would get caught or hurt, and that such a fate is real enough to dissuade you from attempting a robbery. But for most of the juveniles the author interviewed, the possibility of getting caught at committing a robbery was no more real, no more compelling, than the monster in the closet is to an adult.

The point is that differences exist between any two individuals as to what is represented as real. "Real" experiences cannot be ignored; they compel the individual to respond in whatever way he or she has learned is appropriate for that particular reality. Of course, the range of perceptions and beliefs that can be considered real or not real (and therefore worth responding to or not worth responding to) is infinite. One thing that can be distinguished about our individual realities, however, is the particular time frames to which each of us characteristically relegates our realities.

What is compelling in terms of time frame was illustrated during a minor family conflict. Three adults (Ed, Frank, and Iris) were engaged in conversation when Tad, the teenage son of one of them, listlessly walked in and, with a downcast face and whiny voice, asked where he could find the rags he needed to finish washing the car. All three of the adults were familiar with the boy's characteristic lack of self-sufficiency, and were familiar with his pattern of repeatedly asking for assistance until someone ended up doing "it" for him. The adults responded in the following ways.

Frank got red in the face, narrowed his eyes at Tad and angrily said, "I don't want to hear it anymore! Enough is enough!"

Ed asked Tad where he might look first, then, if he did not find the rags there, where he could check next; and failing that, what were still other possible places to find a rag?

And then Iris stood up, took Tad's hand and said, "Don't worry, I'm sure we can find one somewhere."

How can we account for these three very different responses? Frank exploded at Tad's inquiry about a rag. Frank's explanation was that "Tad has always pulled this stunt of whining for help until he gets it," and that he was tired of it and angry about it happening again. In this incident, however, Tad had *not* repeatedly whined for help in finding the rag. This was his first request for a rag, and it remained to be seen whether or not he would actually "pull his stunt" again. Frank's evaluation was about all of those previous times when Tad had abused Frank's experience by wheedling help from him. Thus Frank's behavioral response was to his past test which "revealed" that Tad had always pulled this stunt. For Frank in this instance, then, the past is more compelling than either the present or future.

Upon questioning Ed we found out that he was concerned about Tad becoming an adult who was unable to fend for himself. Ed could see that unless Tad learned to think for himself, he would face many unnecessary difficulties in life. Accordingly, the intention of Ed's behavior was to teach Tad to think in ways that would lead to independent action. For Ed, the helpless future he imagined for Tad was real enough that he felt compelled to respond to that future.

Iris' response was to help Tad find a rag. She told us, "I could see that he was nervous and that he really wanted to know. He felt terrible." Iris said nothing about Tad's history or about what his future might be. Her only concern was "What is going on with Tad right now"—the present. As far as Iris was concerned, Tad was uncomfortable and in need now. And, being capable of doing something about that present reality, she was compelled to help find the rag. Iris can remember the past, of course, but to her it is over and done. She can imagine the future, but to her it is hazy and unpredictable. What is real and compelling to Iris is what is going on around her now—the present.

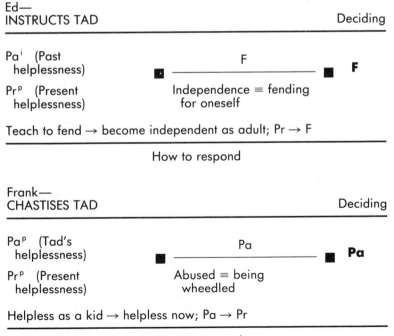

Ed—
INSTRUCTS TAD   Deciding

Pa^i (Past helplessness)   F
                                                                          ■ **F**
Pr^p (Present helplessness)   Independence ≡ fending for oneself

Teach to fend → become independent as adult; Pr → F

How to respond

Frank—
CHASTISES TAD   Deciding

Pa^p (Tad's helplessness)   Pa
                                                                          ■ **Pa**
Pr^p (Present helplessness)   Abused ≡ being wheedled

Helpless as a kid → helpless now; Pa → Pr

How to respond

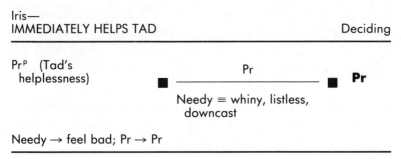

Iris—
IMMEDIATELY HELPS TAD   Deciding

Pr^P (Tad's
  helplessness)

                                        Pr

Needy ≡ whiny, listless,
       downcast

Needy → feel bad; Pr → Pr

How to respond

In each of these three examples, the outcome of the operative format is largely a function of the time frame which that
person finds compellingly real. Both Ed and Frank were just
as aware as Iris was of Tad's present need to find a rag. Their
responses to Tad's need, however, were in Frank's case a
function of evaluations about the past and in Ed's case a
function of evaluations about the future. The *compelling time
frame*, then, is the time frame within a particular operative
format evaluation that *leads to behavior*.

What the compelling time frame tells us for a particular
context is whether it is the past, present, or future that a
person experiences as most real, and thus most demanding of
a behavioral response. However, the actual behavior that the
compelling time frame "demands" will be determined by the
simultaneous impact of the references, tests, criteria, criterial
equivalences, representational systems, and cause-effects
(as well as, perhaps, other operative formats). You may have
noticed that the compelling time frame was not the only difference between the three people in the example just given.
The fact that past references of Tad's helplessness were
informational for Ed but *personal* for Frank, and that each of
the three used different criteria and cause-effects, certainly
has much to do with the differences in behavior that each of
them manifested in response to Tad's request.

To illustrate the effect of the interaction of the distinctions,
let us compare Ed's computations to those of a fictitious person we will call Linda. If Linda is privy to the same examples
of Tad's past and present helplessness and lack of initiative,
and if we change only Ed's cause-effect, from "teaching him
to fend for himself now will make him independent as an

adult" to "not learning independence by age ten makes one helpless as a teenager and helpless as an adult," and leave everything else the same, what will Linda's response be?

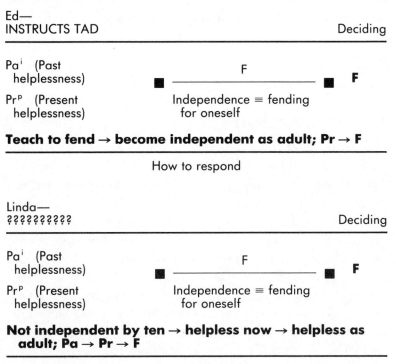

Ed—
INSTRUCTS TAD   Deciding
_____

Pa^i (Past   F
  helplessness)   ■ ———————————————————— ■   **F**

Pr^p (Present   Independence ≡ fending
  helplessness)   for oneself

Teach to fend → become independent as adult; Pr → F
_____

How to respond

Linda—
?????????   Deciding
_____

Pa^i (Past   F
  helplessness)   ■ ———————————————————— ■   **F**

Pr^p (Present   Independence ≡ fending
  helplessness)   for oneself

Not independent by ten → helpless now → helpless as adult; Pa → Pr → F
_____

How to respond

Like Ed, Linda will evaluate the future with respect to Tad's prospects for independence and probably determine that he will not be independent as an adult, *but she will not perceive that there is anything that she or he can do about it* except, perhaps, hope that he will change, or hope that the world will not treat him too harshly. Linda's response might be to sit quietly and feel sorry for Tad, or offer him the information he is asking for (since it won't make any difference in terms of his future), or tell him that she hopes he will someday be able to fend for himself, or any of a hundred other responses. All of those responses, however, will encompass Linda's belief in the importance of a fending-for-oneself kind of independence, the cause-effect belief that the way Tad was as a child determines the way he is now and will be as an adult, and her *compelling* premonition of a future of dependence for Tad. Similarly, if we were to restore to Linda Ed's cause-effect (teach to fend → become independent as adult; $Pr \rightarrow F$) but change her criterial equivalence for independence to "independence ≡ not taking abuse," then she might respond by encouraging Tad to stand up to Frank's assault.

Subordination

Looking back at the examples we have used so far in this section, you will notice that in each operative format the time frame of the test is the same as the compelling time frame. The very fact that a person has felt compelled to respond in some way means that he must have made some test (even if unconsciously) that was in accord with the behavior manifested. For instance, in order to avoid answering with a random yes or no each time you are offered, say, an orange, you must make an evaluation each time as to whether or not you *like* oranges, or if you *want* one now, or if you *will have time* to eat it, or whether or not you answered yes last time and so should answer no this time to "keep things balanced," and so on. Whenever a person is compelled to respond, and when *only one test* is being made in the operative format that generated that response, then the time frame of the test will be the same as the compelling time frame. If it were otherwise, then our responses would be essentially random. And though responses are many other things, they are *not* random.

The exception to the observation that the test and compelling time frames will be the same within a particular operative format occurs when more than one test time frame is being used and the results of the tests being made are somehow incompatible with each other—for example, the present test "I want to go out tonight" and the future test "I will get into hot water if I don't get this work done tonight." The incompatiblility of tests is usually resolved by *subordinating* one of the time frames in favor of another. A familiar example of this process is found in the situation of diners facing the dessert tray at the end of a big meal. Three friends—Arbuckle, Wally, and Eileen—find themselves in just such a situation. After they have finished their main courses, the waiter comes over to their table with the dessert tray and asks them if they care for dessert.

Arbuckle, who is unquestionably overweight (and does not want to be overweight), takes a piece of pie. He knows what overeating has meant in the past, and what overeating will mean in the future, "But," he says, "I want it." Arbuckle has ample reference experiences (both personal and informational) with regard to the effects of overeating. He also is able to evaluate what will happen if he overeats. He knows he will gain weight. But knowing this does not compel him to reject dessert. Arbuckle craves the pie now, and it is that present evaluation that is most compelling for him. To Arbuckle, the past and future are not real in the sense of being compelling, but the present *is* real and, when pitted against the pale realities of the past and future, the present wins hands down. When one time frame is more compelling than another, as in this case, we say that the less compelling time frame is subordinate to the more compelling time frame. In Arbuckle's case, *the future is subordinated in favor of the present.* In other words, when Arbuckle makes conflicting tests about the present and the future, it is the tests regarding the present that will direct his behavior.

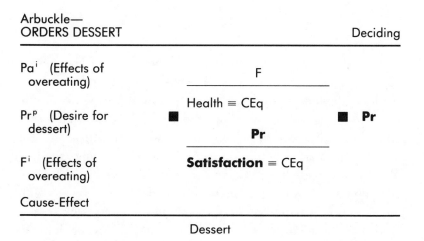

Arbuckle—
ORDERS DESSERT   Deciding

Pa^i (Effects of overeating)   F

Pr^p (Desire for dessert)   Health ≡ CEq   ■   ■ **Pr**

                                              Pr

F^i (Effects of overeating)   **Satisfaction** ≡ CEq

Cause-Effect

                                  Dessert

Wally knows that he would enjoy the pie now, but he turns the dessert down. He says, "Naw, I'll regret it later. I'll wake up in the middle of the night with heartburn if I eat any more." Wally has had heartburn from overeating before, but he does not have heartburn now—he wants the pie now. It looks and smells good, but he imagines waking up in the middle of the night with heartburn, regretting his indulgence; and that possible future is so much more compelling to him than the fact that he is now coveting the pie, that he reluctantly turns down dessert. When Wally makes conflicting tests regarding the present and the future in this situation, it will be the content of the future tests that will generate his behavior. Wally *subordinates the present in favor of the future.*

Wally—
DECLINES DESSERT   Deciding

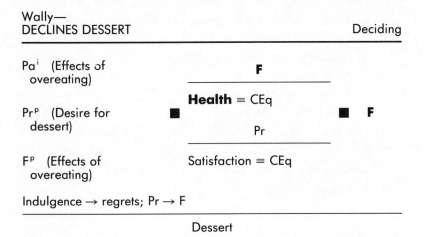

Pa^i (Effects of overeating)

F

Health $\equiv$ CEq

Pr^p (Desire for dessert)   ■   ■ **F**

Pr

F^p (Effects of overeating)

Satisfaction $\equiv$ CEq

Indulgence $\rightarrow$ regrets; Pr $\rightarrow$ F

Dessert

Eileen also is considering eating the pie, but she nevertheless turns it down, saying, "Pie has never agreed with me." Although Eileen's objection may seem similar to Wally's, it is not. Eileen is not turning down the pie because of what *might* happen (as did Wally), but because of what *has happened.* For Eileen, the past is compelling. As far as she is concerned, if the pie has made her ill before, then it will make her ill if she eats it now or any time in the future. Wally tries to reason with her that she was ten years old when she last got sick on pie and that she might now be immune to its effects, or that she might get used to it if she tries it enough times, but his arguments fall on deaf ears, for they are about the unconvincing present and future. Eileen *subordinates the present and future for the past,* and goes without dessert.

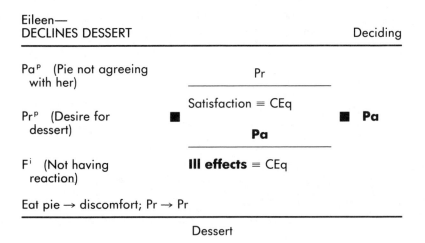

Eileen—
DECLINES DESSERT   Deciding

Pa^p (Pie not agreeing   Pr
    with her)
                                    _____

                                Satisfaction $\equiv$ CEq
Pr^p (Desire for   ■   ■ **Pa**
    dessert)
                                        Pa
                                    _____

F^i (Not having   **III effects** $\equiv$ CEq
    reaction)

Eat pie → discomfort; Pr → Pr

Dessert

The utility of knowing the compelling time frame is obvious in the notation of the computations that Wally, Arbuckle, and Eileen made. In each case conflicting tests are made, and in each case it is the compelling time frame that determines what the choice will be. That is, when a person's computations involve conflicting tests, *the time frame of the compelling category will tell you which of those tests that person will almost certainly subordinate and which of those tests will guide that person's behavior.*

As another example, consider a person who is lying in bed, about to go to sleep, who suddenly remembers that she left the shovel lying out in the garden—and it's supposed to rain tonight. If she is characteristically compelled by the present, it is likely that she will subordinate the unconvincing future for the present and go to sleep. If, on the other hand, she is compelled by the future, she is likely to subordinate the present and get out of bed (even if complaining all the while) and save the shovel from a rusty future.

A very talented graphic artist and designer in Los Angeles offers yet another example of subordination. He was asked to design a line of doodads and gewgaws as part of the marketing of a well-known rock star. This artist does not like that kind of work and was, in fact, embarrassed to talk about it with us. He accepted the assignment, however. He was willing to subordinate his present considerations of what he considers appropriate work in favor of the future possibility of that "high-profile" doodad assignment eventually leading to his being able to do what he wants to do artistically. Given his criteria, if this artist had instead subordinated the future in favor of the present he would probably have turned down the rock star marketing offer. Similarly, a city planner given to subordinating the future is more likely to approve plans that meet current needs. If the city planner is given to subordinating the present, however, she can be counted on to view more favorably those plans that she believes will eventually lead to a "good" city (even if that plan means current hardship) than she will be disposed toward plans that she believes promise to take care of a present problem at the cost of generating a future problem.

Explorations

Understanding Yourself What are some things that you will not let your children do? Very often the restrictions you impose are the result of compelling future representations of dire consequences. For instance, your son asks to ride across town on his bike, you make compelling images of him being hit by a car and paralyzed as a result of a head injury, and say "no way." You are making a future test using the criterion of his well being. This becomes more compelling than your past or present references of your son being a safe and competent bike rider.

Understanding Others For those who squander money, present desire is more compelling than any future representions they may have of having to pay for what they are buying, or of not having money for future needs. They are making compelling present tests.

Those who are chronically late also often find the present more compelling. Thus they frequently subordinate considerations of commitments made in the past, or future consequences of not showing up on time, in favor of what is currently going on.

Someone who will not do business again with a person who has burned him is compelled by the past or future (that is, how that person has burned him, or how that person is likely to burn him again), while all the honesty, sincerity, and explanations that the person can convey in the present are not compelling.

Acquisition   People who are consistently successful at evaluating deals and contracts find representations of future possible problems most compelling (rather than future possible rewards, which lead many people to be seduced by the possibility of gain). The purpose of this compelling future is to identify possible problems in the deal or contract and take care of them now, rather than having to litigate them later on.

Certainly, people who take care of their health (exercising, eating right, avoiding coffee, cigarettes, and drugs) generate and maintain compelling future representations of both the possible benefits and dire consequences of the things they ingest and do. We have developed formats that install such compelling futures in persons undergoing substance abuse treatment programs (see Cameron-Bandler, Gordon, and Lebeau, 1985). While this one variable cannot stand alone to solve such problems, it is absolutely necessary for obtaining long-term results.

For one man we worked with, the problem was that the future was the *only* time frame that was compelling to him. He was attending graduate school, and all of his attention was focused on graduation, which was still a year and a half away. His original motivation for going back to school was to be able, someday, to provide a decent life for his family. Now that future was in sight, and he wanted to reach it as soon as possible. He was compelled to load up on classes during the day and stay up most of every night doing research. However, his tunnel vision into the future also caused him to overlook and disregard pressing family needs—affection for his wife, help with the kids, money for *this* month's rent—that needed taking care of now. He did not need to drop out of school, but he did need to subordinate the future enough to be able to notice and attend to present needs—or there would be no family to come home to on graduation night. We had him imagine and evaluate a future in which his pursuit of a diploma did, indeed, cost him his wife and children. With this future in mind as a reference, and with the accompanying cause-effects in place, the present became and remained a compelling force.

Summary of the Method's Variables

The EMPRINT method is intended to be used both diagnosti cally and for purposes of acquisition. In terms of diagnosis, the method provides a set of variables that can be used to understand the internal processes underlying a person's experience and behavior within any particular context. In terms of acquisition, the method is intended to make it possible for you to identify the internal and external behaviors that others employ to manifest desirable skills, aptitudes, and traits, and then to acquire from those persons the internal processes that result in those behaviors.

An individual's experience and behavior within a particular context are the manifestation of the evaluations he is making. An evaluation is a function of a set of simultaneously interacting variables. This set of interacting variables is called an *operative format.*

The first of these variables is the *test time frame.* This variable identifies which of the three time frames (past, present, and future) you are evaluating. The second variable is *criteria,* which are the standards you apply when making the test. What is being tested, then, is whether or not—or to what extent—your criteria were (past), are being (present), or will be (future) satisfied.

A third variable is *criterial equivalence,* which is the specification of what particular behaviors, perceptions, activities, etc., constitute fulfillment of a criterion. A fourth variable is the *representational system* of the test (*visual, auditory, kines-thetic,* or *olfactory/gustatory*). Often, the fulfillment of a criterial equivalence will occur only in a particular represen-tational system. Together, these four variables constitute the *test category.*

The fifth variable is that of *reference category*, which speci-fies whether you are using the past, present, or future as an experiential basis for your evaluation. References may be either *actual* (from your actual experiences), or *constructed* (created by assembling pieces of experience); and either *personal* (including emotions and sensations that are *of* the experience), or *informational* (merely data, with none of the emotions and sensations that are of the experience). Since it is not possible to have had actual experiences from the future, all future references are constructed.

The sixth variable is the relevant set of *cause-effects*, which specify those contingent relationships that a person believes to be operating within a particular context. Cause-effects are characterized both by their content and by the time frames they presuppose.

The seventh variable specifies which of two or more in-compatible tests you experience as more real, in the sense that it compels a behavioral response from you. This *com-pelling category* time frame determines which of the tests will be expressed behaviorally, and which will, therefore, be *subordinated.*

Taken together, and for every evaluation made, these inter-acting variables constitute an operative format that results in the manifestation of certain experiential and behavioral re-sponses. For a particular individual, the content of the seven variables that make up an operative format will vary de-pending on the particular context being considered.

To help keep track of which operative format is being elicited or discussed, the notation for each operative format includes the *OUTCOME*, *Activity*, and *Subject of Evaluation*. The outcome is the behavior that is ultimately manifested, and an outcome can be the result of one or more activities. Each activity consists of one or more evaluations. For each evaluation, what is being evaluated is the subject of the evaluation.

Notation for the method includes the cause-effects and the reference, test, and compelling categories.

OUTCOME		Activity
Reference Category	■ Test Category ■	Compelling Category
Cause-Effect		
	Subject of Evaluation	

The variables for each category are notated in the following format.

OUTCOME		Activity
Time Frame, Authenticity, emotional involvement	■ $\dfrac{\text{Time Frame (Rep. sys.)}}{\text{Criteria} \equiv \text{CEq}}$ ■	Time Frame
Cause-Effect Content; Time Frames		
	Subject of Evaluation	

8 The Method at Work

Excellence in human beings is not something that is found only among Olympic athletes, Nobel Prize recipients, and Oscar winners. Excellence can also be found in the guy next door who started a diet and stuck to it; in the second grade teacher who is wonderfully adept at getting children to want to learn; in the woman at work who can tell even the tamest of jokes and have you choking with laughter; in Uncle Joe who can fix a chair so it doesn't squeak; and, sometimes in some ways, in you. The fact that people's excellent abilities often go unrecognized, taken for granted by them and by those around them, does not in any way diminish the worthiness of their special abilities.

All of us have areas in our lives in which our abilities are not what we want them to be. And for every one of those areas we can find someone else who is adept at getting the kinds of outcomes we would like to get. As we have demonstrated so far in the presentation of the EMPRINT method, the experiences and behaviors we have at a given moment are the manifestation of certain internal processes—processes that can be described.

The purpose of such a description is to provide a kind of map or model of that person's internal processes with respect to his behavior. We can then use this map to understand how it is possible for that person to do what he does. The kind of maps we are drawing here go beyond understanding, however, providing the essential pieces for *replicating* the kinds

161

of responses another person has in a particular context. That is, by reproducing in yourself the same operative formats used by someone who is your exemplar in a certain situation, you will become capable of manifesting the same kinds of desirable behaviors.

To facilitate the description of the processes, the presentation so far has for the most part related a person's responses to only one of the variables at a time. As significant as each of those variables may be, however, ultimately our experiences and behaviors are the manifestation of *all* of those variables *simultaneously interacting* with one another. It's time now to put all the pieces together. What follows are four examples of "next-door neighbor" kinds of excellence— outcomes that are worth understanding and replicating because of their value in making our lives richer, more satisfying, and more pleasurable. These examples will be presented as sequences of activities and operative formats, with each of those operative formats described and discussed as a simultaneous, interacting process.

Keeping a Sales Force Working Well

As the manager of a branch office of a large brokerage firm, Al is responsible for overseeing the performance of twenty full-time stockbrokers. Al's responsibilities include educating the brokers (using research updates, periodicals, and so on), overseeing their compliance with SEC regulations, and making sure that none of the brokers is "churning" accounts (buying and selling simply to generate commissions). One of Al's most important functions is to maintain motivation in his brokers—a formidable task during dry spells when the market is not producing much business and commissions are drying up.

Al is particularly adept at maintaining motivation among his brokers during such droughts. Dozens of books and hundreds of business seminars have been devoted to the problem of motivation, most of them describing just what to say and do with dispirited staff members, and how to do and say it. Al doesn't favor such shotgun approaches to dealing with his staff, preferring to respond to each of them as individuals and according to their individual needs.

For example, during one dry spell Al became concerned about Bill, a neophyte broker, who sat disconsolately at his desk, chewing on his pencil, looking tired and worried. Considering what he knew about life as a stockbroker, and about Bill in particular, Al decided that for Bill to pull out of his slump, he needed to know three things: that the entire staff was simply enduring one of the market's cycles, and that it would eventually end; that there were nevertheless things that he could and should be doing to better his situation; and that he was a valued and important member of the staff.

With his goals set, Al made plans about the best way to get these three pieces of information across to Bill. He had noticed Bill listening in on office conversations about market cycles, but had observed that what was said made little impression on him. Al realized that it was crucial for Bill to recognize that what he was being told was important, so Al decided that the best approach would be to call Bill into his office, shut the door, tell Bill to sit down, pointedly tell his secretary to hold all calls, and then launch into a description of Bill's present behavior and plight. This would be followed by an affirmation of Bill's worth as a member of the staff and an assurance of Al's confidence in his ability to do well. Al would then provide Bill with a more realistic perspective on the cyclical nature of the stock market, followed by suggestions for things that Bill could do to enhance his client list. Finally, Al would instill an eagerness in Bill to carry out his suggestions.

When the time came to put his plan into action, Al paid close attention to Bill's responses, proceeding to the next step in their interaction only when he was sure that Bill was fully with him. For instance, Al refrained from moving on to explaining market cycles until he was sure that Bill understood that Al regarded him as a capable stockbroker. Al explained to us that if he had been unable to get Bill to respond the way he wanted him to during their conference, he would have sat back and reevaluated his plans, coming up with some modifications. Or if Bill had said something that indicated to Al that he had been wrong in his assessment of what was going on with Bill, then he would have reevaluated what Bill needed—this time, however, starting by asking Bill some questions. For instance, it could have turned out that Bill was already well aware of his worth, competence, and economic facts, but that he was plagued by worries over his home life.

The approach that Al used with Bill was by no means his "standard" approach. Al has no standard approach. As an example of another approach he has used, he described his interaction with another member of the staff who was a veteran of the firm. Despite her ten years as a stockbroker, Fran too had taken to lingering and sighing over her morning coffee, moping about the office, and leaving early. Al could see that Fran was not doing all that she could be to drum up business, and her despairing remarks indicated that for some reason the present dry spell had overwhelmed her, making her forget about the eventual, inevitable upturn.

Although Fran needed some of the same messages that Bill did, Al knew from his past experience with her that the same approach would never work. Instead, Al went to *Fran's* office, asked if she minded some company, then sat down and began to shoot the breeze about things outside of the office context. As the conversation turned to the economy, Al brought up previous dry spells and together they explored the fact that although they seem endless, they always do end. That, Fran agreed, was something to look forward to. From there Al casually turned the conversation to analyzing and swapping stories about what methods seem to work best in drumming up business. Soon Fran was enthusiastically making plans to renew contacts with her old clients, and to establish new ones. This approach would not have worked with Bill, but it was the perfect medicine for Fran.

Most immediately distinctive about Al's approach to supervising his staff is that he uses what he knows about them as the basis for structuring interactions that are appropriate for each of them as individuals, rather than assuming that they will all fall under the spell of some standard approach. As we noted earlier, dozens of prescriptive interactional approaches are being hawked as the cure for motivational problems, as well as other staff/management problems. The very appeal of these approaches—that is, that they are prescriptions for interactions, and so require little time and effort on the part of the manager—is also their limitation. People *are* individuals, and they vary in terms of what they respond to. Al's approach obviously requires more time and effort on his part, but the manifest result of his individually oriented approach is that he fulfills his professional responsibilities in a way and to a degree that is generally recognized as exceptional.

Al's First Step—Identifying What the Person Needs

Within the outcome of "Keeping a sales force working well," Al goes through a sequence of three activities. Each activity has one operative format. The first of these makes it possible for him to *identify what the person needs*. The expectations for staff performance are highly standardized in his profession, so the criteria by which Al evaluates the needs of his staff are usually with respect to whether or not they are "motivated," "committed," and "active" (unless, of course, he sees some indication that a person's office behavior is due to circumstances outside of the office).

Al tests for these criteria in the present; that is, he is initially interested in determining whether or not a person *is* motivated, rather than whether or not they *were* or *will be* motivated. Furthermore, the present is compelling, so that any indications that a person has been or will be motivated are subordinated to the recognition that that person is presently unmotivated. He knows that someone is motivated when he sees that they continue to pursue their goals despite any stumbling blocks. Evidence of commitment is that the person is engaged in business interactions with co-workers (for example discussing the possible effects of recent economic news or asking for tips on how to talk to clients, as opposed to merely complaining or talking about sports or movies). And the criterial equivalence for activeness is that the person is making phone calls, setting up appointments, and so on.

In assessing a staff member's motivation, commitment, and activeness, Al relies on his direct observations of that person's behavior, and what he knows about his or her past behavior (shared personal history, previous job performance, and so on). Underlying Al's evaluations is his belief in a cause-effect between his intervention and the future failure or success of the staff member.

KEEPING SALES FORCE
WORKING WELL   Identifying

Pa^p (Observations of person)	$\dfrac{Pr \quad (v, a)}{\text{Motivated} \equiv \text{pursues beyond "blocks"}}$	Pr

Pa^p (Observations of person)

Pa^i (Circumstances)

Pr^p (Person's behavior)

Pr^i (Person's sales, activities)

$$\blacksquare \; \frac{Pr \quad (v, a)}{} \; \blacksquare \quad Pr$$

Motivated ≡ pursues beyond "blocks"

Committed ≡ engaged in business interactions

Active ≡ makes phone calls, appointments, etc.

My intervention → their success or failure; Pr → F

What person needs

The behavioral outcome of this operative format is that Al determines what, if anything, one of his staff currently needs with respect to motivation, commitment, or activity. The fact that the present test is compelling is important because it precludes the possibility that Al will ignore an employee's current malaise on the basis that he (Al) has determined that that person *will be* motivated, committed, or active in the future. Such subordination of the present for the future would be inappropriate since (1) there is no guarantee that the employee will in fact recover the necessary motivation; (2) in a performance-oriented profession, the longer the employee continues to be unsuccessful the more likely it is that he will develop an unfavorably skewed perception of his own competence, feeding into a spiral of poor performance, poor self-concept, poorer performance, and so on; and (3) if nothing is done to reorient the person, he will probably once again allow his motivation to dissipate when the next drought occurs.

The reference experiences that characterize Al's internal processes at this point help ensure that his assessment of a staff member's needs are based on information that is both direct and substantial. Rather than relying on the second-hand reports of others, he uses his *own* observations as an information source. The employee's past behavior is an important reference here because it provides the experiential background against which his present behavior can be evaluated. And finally, the cause-effect relationship that Al perceives between his intervention and his employee's future performance is essential in terms of motivating Al to engage in this assessment in the first place.

Al's Second Step—Developing a Plan   Once he has decided what a particular staff member needs, Al generates a plan for how best to give that person the needed information. Underlying this activity and operative format is a perceived cause-effect between how he will deliver the information and whether or not his intervention will be effective. The test he makes is about the future, and it involves detailed visual representations in which he assesses various possible ways of interacting with the employee. This assessment is done with respect to the criterion of "effectiveness," which for Al means that the person responds the way he wants him to. The reference base for these future evaluations is his list of needs for this person, and his past experiences with the person.

KEEPING SALES FORCE
WORKING WELL   Planning

Pa^P (Experience
   with person)   F   (v, a)

                              ■ ————————————————— ■ F

Pa^i (Needs: they are   Effective ≡ get this
   important, information,   person to respond the
   behavior)   way I want him to: for
                                  example, that this is
                                  important, that he is
                                  important, reassured
                                  about ability, have
                                  perspective about
                                  cycles, eager to carry
                                  out new behaviors

My delivery → effectiveness; F → F

How to give person what he or she needs

Conspicuously absent from Al's operative format for planning are any past personal or informational references regarding management theories or techniques. With only his outcomes for the person (the information about needs that was generated in the previous operative format) and his personal experiences of that person as his reference base, any plan that Al comes up with is likely to be in accord with the idiosyncracies of that person.

It is also significant that the primary criterion Al uses in evaluating possible interaction choices is that of what will be effective *for this person;* this approach focuses his orientation solely toward accomplishing the outcome. If, instead, Al's criteria included such considerations as easy, familiar, tested, pleasant, businesslike, or brief, his plan selection would be oriented by criteria that were not necessarily in accord with the outcomes he has in mind or the person he has to deal with. For instance, the approach that he used with Bill might have been "familiar" to Al, but it would nevertheless have been a wholly inappropriate approach to use with Fran. By using only "what will be effective" as his criterion, Al frees his planning from unuseful constraints, and further enhances his ability to respond to his staff as individuals. Driving his planning is the cause-effect Al perceives between the form of his delivery and whether or not he succeeds in getting his employee to respond.

Al's Third Step—Implementing the Plan   Having formulated his plan, Al is ready to put it into action. While effecting his plan, Al makes ongoing assessments (present tests) regarding where he and the employee are in the sequence Al has roughed out. As they interact, Al watches and listens closely to the other person's responses to detect whether or not the employee is "with me," and whether or not he (Al) is "progressing" appropriately with respect to the sequence. What keeps Al progressing through the sequence and monitoring the employee's responses is his belief in a cause-effect relationship between the employee going through the planned sequence and his ultimate ability to get what he needs.

KEEPING SALES FORCE
WORKING WELL   Implementing the Plan

Pa^i (Planned
    sequence)

Pr^p (Employee's
    responses)

$$\blacksquare \underline{\hspace{1cm} Pr \quad (v, a) \hspace{1cm}} \blacksquare \quad Pr$$

With me ≡ responding
    the way I want him to

Progress ≡ moving in
    accord with plan

They go through sequence → they will have what they need; $Pr \rightarrow F$

Are we on track

As a result of Al's cause-effect that success depends upon going through the sequence, his orientation during delivery is to follow his plan. Al stays on track. This is facilitated by his present test for progress with a past reference of the planned sequence. Without the criterion of progress and a reference for the plan, Al's interaction with his emloyee would certainly meander; with that criterion and reference he is able to stay on course.

Many managers have the ability to plan interactions with employees, and the ability to stick to those plans, but lack criteria regarding the ongoing responses of the employees, and so march on through the planned sequence without recognizing that they have left their troops (in this case, their employees) far behind. Al avoids this pitfall by including in his present test the criterion of "with me," which ensures that he proceeds *with regard to the ongoing responses of the other person.* The criterion "with me" (or its surrogate, such as "understanding" or "recognition"), then, provides the ongoing feedback that Al needs to know whether or not his employee is, in fact, responding in the way that Al wants him to.

If Al discovers that he is unable to get a person to respond in the way he wants him to, he goes back to his planning operative format to reassess his approach. If he discovers that he was in error about what the person needs, he goes back to his operative format for identifying needs to reassess what to give that person. After he identifies the appropriate needs, he then moves on through the operative formats for planning and implementing, continuing in this way until the employee is once again motivated, committed, and working well.

We use Al's operative formats to instruct managers on how to improve their performance, much to the delight of their subordinates as well as their superiors. But the value of Al's talent is not limited to the world of business. The exceptional teachers we have modeled all demonstrate patterns remarkably similar to Al's. It is not surprising that these teachers are successful at keeping their students motivated to learn.

This sequence of operative formats will work in any situation in which a person needs support and encouragement. In Chapter 12 we explain how to adopt and transfer operative formats. When you finish that chapter, return to this section and put this sequence to work for you. Use it when you want to encourage your child to continue learning a sport or a musical instrument. Use it to rekindle motivation and commitment in a colleague who is struggling under the weight of a big project. Use it with a discouraged friend who is about to give up hope of ever finding a suitable job. Consider it a gift from Al.

Never Repeating Mistakes

As the mother of two, a three-quarter time bookkeeper, wife, and all-around human being, Deborah has her share of opportunities for making mistakes. Like most of us, she has blamed her kids for transgressions that (it turns out) they did not commit, has bought five gallons of paint that looked hideous once it was actually on the walls, has thought that her husband wanted to go out when what he really wanted was to stay home, and has used 1982 tax forms to compute 1984 taxes. In short, Deborah says "Whoops!" and knows the taste of shoe leather as well as any of us. There is a talent that Deborah enjoys, however, that sets her apart from many of us stumblers—she almost never repeats her mistakes.

For example, Deborah and her husband love the desert and wanted to share its beauty with their twelve-year-old son, whose appreciation was usually limited to the newest video-game in town. So they arranged a week-long camping trip in the Sonora Desert. To make the trip more palatable to the boy

Deborah arranged for his best friend to go with them. Unfortunately, the preteen groaning and whining started long before they arrived at their campsite, and it continued unabated (despite good-natured cajoling and unnatural threats) until they arrived back home. Those boys were *bored*, and the trip went down in the family annals as an unmitigated disaster.

However, Deborah did not close the book on this disaster immediately. She recognized the trip as a mistake, and wished she had paid closer attention to her son's obvious reluctance to go along. She spent some time thinking about how she had come to make this mistake in the first place, and eventually realized that she had been paying more attention to her imaginings about how wonderful the trip would be than she had to her son. She then thought about what she could have done at the time that would have led her to give her son's reluctant responses the consideration they deserved. This led to the realization that if she had just taken a moment to remember what it was like to be her boy's age, she would have realized that the trip was not (yet) for him. The last thing she did before putting this trip behind her was to imagine being in the future, once again making plans that included her son. In her words, she did this to practice "stepping into the age-shoes of my kid, and to assess whether or not I can and will do what I need to from now on." She discovered that she could do it, and with another week like the one they had just spent as the alternative, she knew she *would* do it, too. Since then Deborah has made it a point to momentarily step back into being a youngster when making plans that include her son.

There are dozens of other examples. Deborah realized she had made a mistake by inviting her entire family over to her tiny house for Thanksgiving dinner, rather than agreeing to hold the festivities at her parents' home where there was plenty of room and everyone could have been comfortable. Deborah's downfall had been her notion that the only way to have control of the party was to have it at her house, and she resolved that next time she would ask her mother if she could use her house for a family party that *she* (Deborah) would take charge of.

On another occasion Deborah allowed a friend to flatter her into buying a dress that Deborah was actually embarrassed to wear. From this incident she learned to stand by herself before the mirror for a few moments before deciding on a clothing purchase so that she could pay attention to her own preferences. And as yet another example, Deborah once yelled at her son for watching TV rather than doing his homework, only to find out that he had not been assigned any. Her response had come out of her belief that this was just another example of the goldbricking her son had at times been guilty of. But it was not, and thereafter Deborah always asked first before yelling about the homework situation.

Characteristic of all of Deborah's responses is that once she recognizes her mistakes she (1) figures out how she came to make it, then (2) figures out what she could have done in order to have made things turn out more satisfactorily, and finally (3) considers whether or not she is capable of doing what needs to be done next time, and just how motivated she is to do it. This is in constrast to those people who, having made a mistake, neglect to consider what they did that led up to it, and so make that same mistake again and again. Even those of us who do figure out what led to our mistakes are still likely to repeat them because there is no identification of what to do *instead* in that same situation in the future. The closest such individuals come to rectifying their mistake-prone behavior is to promise themselves to never again do what they did. But once in a situation people must respond, and human beings have a tendency to opt for the familiar. Thus, as often as not, the promise is forgotten, and the mistake repeated. As automatic and natural as Deborah's corrective response to having made a mistake seems to be, it is, nevertheless, a computational skill that can be modeled and learned.

Deborah's First Step—Identifying the Mistake   Like everyone else, what starts Deborah considering whether or not she has made a mistake is the realization that some "undesirable" consequence has resulted from something she did. (We put "undesirable" in quotation marks to draw your attention to the fact that what is considered undesirable varies considerably from person to person.) When this happens, she looks back on what happened and what she did, and tries to evaluate whether or not she could have responded in a different and better way. That is, she makes a past test with respect to the criterion of *alternative* responses.

If she finds that she could not have done differently, or that she could have done differently but not better, then she does not perceive what she had done as a mistake. For instance, the time she put a box up on the closet shelf and the shelf collapsed was not a mistake because she could not have known that the wood was rotted and so could not have done differently. The time she faithfully followed the cheesecake recipe and it turned out to be a flop was likewise not a mistake because she could not have followed the recipe any better than she did—although she will use a different recipe in the future.

If, however, she does perceive that she could have acted differently and better, then she deems her behavior a mistake. In making this evaluation she relies not only on her past personal memories of what happened, but on her present personal experience of the unpleasant consequences as well. The important cause-effect that underlies this evaluation of the past is that her behavior somehow caused the unpleasant consequences.

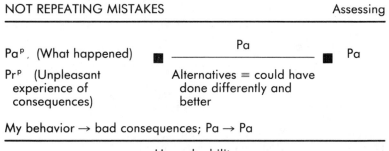

NOT REPEATING MISTAKES   Assessing

Pa^P, (What happened)   ■ ——————— Pa ——————— ■ Pa

Pr^P (Unpleasant   Alternatives ≡ could have
experience of   done differently and
consequences)   better

My behavior → bad consequences; Pa → Pa

Her culpability

We can all think of someone we know who characteristically does not take even this first evaluative step upon discovering that something he did had an unfortunate consequence. It may be that such a person lacks a cause-effect between his behavior and the bad consequences. It may also be that he perceives such a cause-effect, but that he does not evaluate whether or not he could have done otherwise. The result is that such a person may lament what happened, but perceive it as inevitable. The present personal reference that Deborah uses with regard to the unpleasantness of the consequences enables her to maintain her motivation to resolve the situation.

Deborah's Second Step—Identifying the Underlying Cause-Effect Once Deborah has identified what she has done as a mistake, she then initiates an operative format through which she discovers the cause-effect underlying her unfortunate actual behavior in the problem situation. In this operative format she uses a past test with respect to the criterion of understanding, which to her means knowing what led her to behave as she did. Her references include not only past personal references regarding what happened, but past personal references of other similar experiences and past informational references that may have a bearing on understanding what happened. This operative format is fueled by two cause-effects: that a certain set of circumstances led to her behavior; and that understanding how she made the mistake will help her respond differently in the future.

NOT REPEATING MISTAKES   Identifying

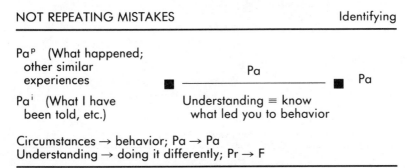

Pa^P (What happened; other similar experiences

Pa^i (What I have been told, etc.)

Pa

Pa

Understanding ≡ know what led you to behavior

Circumstances → behavior; Pa → Pa
Understanding → doing it differently; Pr → F

Cause-effects underlying mistake

Through these evaluations, Deborah identifies what factors were (potentially) under her control in the situation in which she made her mistake. For example, when she was sorting through how she had gotten into the vacation mess with her son, she determined that she had been more attentive to her internal images about the future trip than to her son's present distress. Her preoccupation with her own plans, then, was a causal factor in making the mistake. The importance of this step is two-fold. First, it provides important information regarding relevant causal behaviors that will be used in the subsequent operative formats. Second, the simple recognition that her behaviors "caused" the mistake helps ensure that she perceives the outcome of that situation as a matter of choice, rather than as an example of something that is preordained by the world or by her "nature."

For the person who knows that he has made a mistake but who does not recognize how his behaviors were causally related to that mistake, the most common response is to use that mistake as the basis for building a criterial equivalence, or as further proof of an existing criterial equivalence. For instance, without this operative format Deborah might have gleaned from her vacation mistake that she is a "fool," or "dense," or "over-optimistic," or that her son is a "whiner," and so on. The significance of creating criterial equivalences rather than cause-effects is that criterial equivalences presuppose existence—the way things *are*—and so are relatively unchangeable. Cause-effects, on the other hand, presuppose contingency—the way things depend upon one another—and so are potentially changeable.

Deborah's Third Step—Specifying a Preferred Cause-Effect Once she knows what led her to make the mistake, Deborah then figures out how she could have responded in a preferable way. Again, this is a past test with respect to the criterion of understanding, but understanding in this operative format is defined as identifying what would have led her to carry out the preferred alternative behavior. The referential grist for this evaluative mill includes her memories of what happened, the cause-effect underlying her actual behavior, previous similar experiences, and information regarding such situations and responses (from friends, books, and so on). Driving this particular evaluation of the past is a cause-effect relationship between her behavior and consequences, and a cause-effect between understanding what would have worked better and being able to respond differently and better in the future.

NOT REPEATING MISTAKES   Identifying

Pa^P (What happened;
   C → E for actual
   behavior; similar   Pa
   experiences)   ■ ────────────────── ■ Pa
                               Understanding ≡ what
Pa^i (Things heard and   would have led to
   read)   carrying out alternative

My behavior → consequences; Pa → Pa
Understand what would have worked → respond differently; Pr → F

Effects of different behaviors

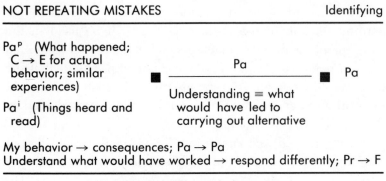

Of course, it's not enough to know what *not* to do. One must also know what *to* do, and this is the information Deborah gets as a result of this operative format. This is the difference between insight and change. Until you know what to do, there is little choice but to repeat mistakes, or hope that the situation does not arise again, or endure more trial and error if it does, and so on. However, knowing what *to* do gives you a great measure of control, and assures you of consistent improvement.

Deborah's Fourth Step—Committing to Be Different
The last activity Deborah engages in to avoid repeating her mistake uses the information and understandings concerning what to avoid and what to do—information and understandings gained through the previous operative formats. Armed with her new understandings, she ventures into the future to test her resolve to be different. Using as references the unfortunate incident itself, what she learned about the cause-effects underlying her mistake, and what she has learned about the cause-effects underlying an alternative and better way of responding in that situation, Deborah imagines the same situation arising again in the future. As she does this she evaluates what it will be like if she makes the same mistake again, and what it will be like if she uses the alterna-

tive behavior. To make the future as realistic as possible, and therefore as compelling as possible, she includes everything she would be seeing, hearing, and feeling. Furthermore, this evaluation is made with respect to the criterion of "stupidity"; and because her criterial equivalence for stupidity is *repeating mistakes*, it is a criterion that is anathema to Deborah's self-concept and is therefore compelling. Thus imagining not using her alternative behavior and risking making the same mistake in the future is repellent to her, and is manifested in her behavior as determination to employ that alternative behavior consistently.

NOT REPEATING MISTAKES   Testing

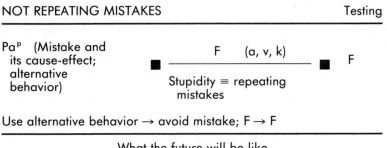

Pa^P (Mistake and
its cause-effect;
alternative
behavior)

F   (a, v, k)

Stupidity ≡ repeating
mistakes

F

Use alternative behavior → avoid mistake; F → F

What the future will be like

Many of us sift through the ashes of our mistakes until we find those abrasive bits of behavior that led to making the mistake. And some of us continue to sift those ashes until we find those behavioral gems that would have made it possible to avoid the mistake. Among those who get as far as uncovering "what I should have done," however, this realization often leads to a moment of remorse and self-recrimination, and a promise to do better next time. Then all is forgotten until the next time the same mistake is repeated. When repeated, however, there is little need to go through the two operative formats for understanding, leaving one free to jump right to remorse and self-recrimination.

Deborah's final operative format, on the other hand, all but ensures that she will be completely committed to fulfilling her intention of changing her behavior. Her criterial equivalence that stupidity means repeating mistakes makes the possibility of her repeating a mistake an example of her stupidity. This would be a judgment that goes against the grain of her self-concept and so is very compelling. It's not enough to just have a future test that allows you to recognize the awful consequences of not using the alternative behavior. Manifesting Deborah's degree of commitment to not repeating a mistake requires that your future test of the consequences of *not* following through be evaluated with respect to criteria that are tied to your self-concept—criteria that, if violated, would also violate your concept of self.

Deborah was one of several persons from whom we elicited the patterns for the talent of not repeating mistakes. We transformed those patterns into a series of instructional sequences that anyone can use to acquire this valuable aptitude. "The EMPRINT Format for Converting Mistakes Into Learnings" has been presented to a variety of groups.[1] It's a big hit with parents. They learn it and then take their children through it to avoid being reduced to repeating the age-old tirade, "If I've told you once I've told you a thousand times. . . ." Children will make mistakes; that's an important part of growing up. But now there is an explicit way to teach them how to use mistakes as an impetus to learn and change. And it seems to us much better to teach your youngster how not to repeat mistakes than to have to hear yourself say, "If I've told you once I've told you a thousand and one times. . . ."

Good Timing

Ben is a successful book agent. One of the things that he is particularly good at is a skill that is little appreciated, less used, and much abused: timing. As the representative of working writers in a crowded and competitive literary market, he sometimes has the difficult job of telling a client that her manuscript has been rejected, is unsalable, or needs to be trimmed by half—plus other minor changes. But while some bearers of bad news worry about their own culpability or discomfort, Ben is more concerned with the feelings of the receiver of the news. Not that he is particularly solicitous of his or her feelings, for he delivers his point without wavering. Rather, he is concerned that the target be there when the point strikes home. Therefore, before speaking he observes whether or not his client is in the most appropriate frame of mind to receive the news.

Ben times his giving not only of bad news, but of good news as well. For instance, he was meeting a publisher for lunch and wanted to pitch to him a great manuscript he had just received from a new client. At lunch Ben noticed that the publisher seemed edgy and angry, so he kept the manuscript in his briefcase. It soon came out that two of the publisher's biggest projects had recently been hacked by the critics. The wounds were mortal and the books had died on the bookstore shelves. The publisher talked about "regrouping" and getting some of his dependable authors back on the best-seller list as soon as possible.

Ben recognized that the publisher was not in the appropriate mood to receive a pitch about an unknown writer, but he also believed that the book in his briefcase was just what the man needed. He rummaged through his memory for what he knew about the publisher—what he cared about, what he responded to—searching for a way to create a "window of receptivity" in him. He recalled that the publisher had always impressed him as someone who was easily caught up in the drama of the failures and successes of the moment, forgetting utterly the endless cycle of pans and plaudits that have passed. Ben commiserated with the publisher, acknowledging to him that Ben knew he only put his efforts behind books that were important to him. They agreed that there was a basis for feeling hurt, disappointed, and discouraged. Ben gently helped the publisher recall that what had sold well and what had fizzled in the past was often unpredictable, and that there were many variables beyond the publisher's control. The publisher relaxed a little. Ben brought up a couple of previous times when the publisher had thought that his business would fail. The publisher chuckled over those memories. Ben pointed out the publisher's many successes, making sure to mention the unknown authors the publisher had supported who, because of that unwavering support through the inevitable ups and downs, became recognized and successful. The publisher couldn't help but feel some pride. Ben stated confidently that the publisher would persevere in the future with projects and authors he cared about, and that the publisher's commitment to what he knew to be worthy would again be a source of satisfaction. Ben continued in this vein until he and the publisher were speculating about the future. Judging that the publisher was at last receptive, Ben brought out the manuscript and they discussed it.

The same skill that Ben shows in timing his business communications is also evident in his interactions with friends and family. One day he received a delightful call from his ex-wife. He intended to tell his present wife about the call, but when he got home he found her depressed and disconsolate. His ex-wife was by no means one of his wife's favorite people, and he judged that to mention the phone call now would only add an edge of threat and indignation to his wife's unhappy mood. Although Ben was able to cheer his wife up as the evening progressed, the ice was still thin and not yet ready for skating, so he kept the telephone call to himself. Ben's wife awoke the next morning with both a smile for Ben and (to Ben, more important) a smile for herself. He could see that her mood of the previous evening had evaporated and that she once again felt good about herself. He told her about the call, and she took it in stride.

It's easy to find examples of people who don't seem to notice the emotional states of others and who, wearing the hobnail boots of ignorance, go stepping (even if inadvertently) on the emotional toes of those around them. Whether they observe the emotional state of their victim and ignore it, or they simply don't notice the emotional states of others at all, the result is the same. The excited teenager is on the way out the door with his first date on his arm when his father stops him to berate him for the lousy job he did on the lawn and to tell him he will have to fix it in the morning. You are expecting guests for dinner and are hard at work on the preparations, running late and frantically ricocheting about the kitchen, when your next door neighbor walks in and sits down for a chat. A friend of yours who has leaned heavily on your friendship recently asks you to set aside your plans for the weekend and help him move. After you've helped him rent, load, and unload the truck, your mood and manner are understandably brusque. Ignoring all your signals, however, your friend now asks if you will help him fix his car next weekend.

Ben's skill goes beyond taking note of the emotional states of others. If the other person is not in an appropriate state to receive the communication that Ben wants to make, he does what he can to help that person change his state to a more appropriate one. This behavioral step is missing from the repertoire of many people who are nevertheless able to recognize when the moods of their companions are auspicious or inauspicious. Without such a step, the only choices are to cast the news upon the current waters and hope that it is well received, or to hold the news back and wait for the emotional weather to change. Instead, Ben takes an approach that is both respectful and strategic, and is therefore worth modeling.

Ben's First Step—Assessing Other's Receptivity   The first of Ben's timing operative formats is initiated when he begins interacting with someone to whom he needs to communicate something of importance. Ben immediately starts making present tests of the other person's receptivity. For Ben the criterion of "receptive" means *being in an emotional state that enables someone to respond appropriately*. Ben makes these evaluations based upon the particular message he wants to deliver, his memories of this person's moods and responses (a past reference which is, for him, informational), his present observations of the other person (a present personal reference), and a future informational reference of how the other person will respond if the communication is well-timed. Compelling Ben's assessments is a powerful set of cause-effects, including "timing makes it possible for others to hear and respond well," "lack of timing can lead to the loss of a communication and the jeopardizing of a relationship," and "timing leads to success."

GOOD TIMING Assessing

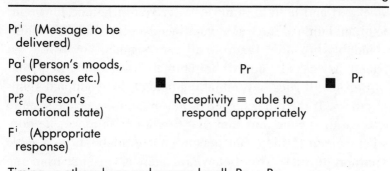

Pr^i (Message to be delivered)

Pa^i (Person's moods, responses, etc.)

Pr_c^p (Person's emotional state)

F^i (Appropriate response)

Pr

Pr

Receptivity ≡ able to respond appropriately

Timing → others hear and respond well; Pr → Pr
Lack of timing → miscommunication, jeopardized relationship; Pr → F
Timing → success; Pr → F

Other's emotional state

All of the cause-effects to which Ben subscribes make it of paramount importance that he search for, and respond to, receptivity in others. Of equal significance, however, is his use of a present test, which makes it possible for him to respond to the other person's *current* state. Those who assess the receptivity of another by using either past tests ("He has always been interested in this before") or future tests ("I'm sure she will be interested in hearing this") run the risk of being woefully out of sync with the person.

In accord with this present test of receptivity are Ben's past and present references, which provide him information about the person with whom he is interacting, rather than orienting him to his *own* emotional state. In this way, neither the enthusiasm that he feels about delivering pleasant news nor the reluctance that he feels about delivering unpleasant news greatly influences his assessments about when to speak. Again, Ben communicates news—pleasant or unpleasant— *only when its recipient is in a frame of mind to best respond to it.*

Ben's Second Step—Generating Ways to Create Receptivity If Ben detects that the present lay of the land is rocky, rather than either plowing forward anyway or waiting for the rocks to dissolve, he does what he can to smooth the way. He calls this "creating a window of receptivity," and it involves his making future tests regarding what he can do and say that will make the other person more receptive. Anything he can do to smooth the way will make him more effective.

In making his plan he relies upon his past experiences of this person, his past experiences with making this particular kind of communication, and the current nature of his interaction with this person. He also keeps in mind the message he needs to deliver. This operative format is fueled by his belief that creating a window of receptivity will make it possible for him to deliver the communication successfully and preserve the relationship.

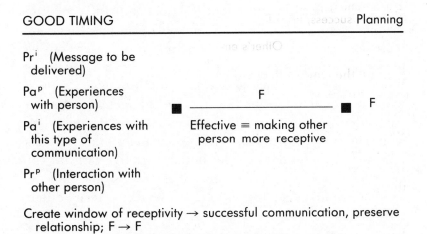

GOOD TIMING · Planning

Pr^i (Message to be delivered)

Pa^p (Experiences with person)

Pa^i (Experiences with this type of communication)

Pr^p (Interaction with other person)

F

F

Effective ≡ making other person more receptive

Create window of receptivity → successful communication, preserve relationship; F → F

Ways to create receptivity

It is significant that Ben uses a future test in his attempt to create a window of receptivity. A present test would be more likely to lead him to simply try various approaches until he hit upon one that was effective. If instead he used a past test, he would probably try again and again the same things that he has done before in similar situations. Ben's future test allows for a richer plan, one that can take into account past experience and present circumstances, as yet untried possibilities, and the possible influences of all three of these information sources.

It is also significant that Ben uses the criterion of being "effective." This addresses the *outcome*, rather than orienting him only toward eliciting a standard set of emotional responses, such as curious, happy, or relaxed, which are emotional states that might or might not be appropriate for the particular news Ben has to deliver. Again, Ben's intention is that the other person be appropriately receptive, which will mean different emotional states depending upon the person and the news.

Ben's Third Step—Monitoring the Interaction While Implementing the Plan Having come up with a way to help the other person become more appropriately receptive, Ben puts his plan into effect. This is not something that he does *to* the other person; rather it is something he does *with* the other person. That is, as he puts his plan into effect and therefore changes how he is interacting with that person, he pays close attention to whether his approach is making things better, worse, or having no effect at all. He wants to know if the direction in which he is steering the interaction is congruent with the other person's inclinations. To do this, Ben makes ongoing present tests with respect to the other person's receptivity, as he does in the initial operative format. The cause-effects to which Ben subscribes are also the same as those in the first operative format. In fact, the primary difference between this operative format and the first is that now he has a plan to which he refers as he interacts.

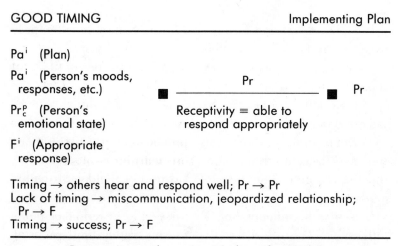

GOOD TIMING   Implementing Plan

Pa^i (Plan)

Pa^i (Person's moods, responses, etc.)

Pr_c^p (Person's emotional state)

F^i (Appropriate response)

Pr

Pr

Receptivity $\equiv$ able to respond appropriately

Timing $\rightarrow$ others hear and respond well; $Pr \rightarrow Pr$
Lack of timing $\rightarrow$ miscommunication, jeopardized relationship; $Pr \rightarrow F$
Timing $\rightarrow$ success; $Pr \rightarrow F$

Progress toward creating window of receptivity

Ben's concern in the continuing interaction is the same as it was when they first sat down together: to be sure that this person is appropriately receptive to the communication that Ben has to deliver. The difference is that now Ben also has a plan against which he can check his progress in affecting the other person's emotional state. If at any point it becomes evident that his plan is not working to achieve his outcome, he reengages his operative format for planning. He then uses the other person's responses as additional information upon which to either modify his plan or to develop a new course of action.

No one likes to have their toes stepped on. And everyone dislikes the taste of shoe leather that accompanies stuffing your foot in your mouth. But it is not enough to simply recognize these truths. That Ben is consistently able to avoid both of these outcomes is a function of how he organizes his internal processes with respect to caring about and noticing the emotional states of others, and doing what he can to make a useful difference in those states. When we interviewed Ben to elicit his operative formats for good timing we discovered, as we often do, that he had other skills that enhanced his knack for timing his messages. For instance, Ben has the ability to discern, with a high degree of accuracy, the emotions that others are experiencing. He is also skillful at *moving* a person from one emotion to another. If you adopted Ben's program for good timing, but found that you also needed to add these other pieces to be effective, you would also want to model the operative formats for these additional skills.

Life-Long Learning

For many people, learning is what you had to do in order to get out of school and into a job or profession. Possibly that job or profession required a little more learning—of skills and the ropes, perhaps. Once that was over one could settle down into a comfortable rut. However, it seems that "ignorance is bliss" is an aphorism that, soon, few will be able to embrace. It is becoming obvious that the increasingly rapid pace of technical and informational evolution will soon make life-long

learning a necessity for anyone who wants to keep professionally and culturally current. This may be bad news for those
who wince at the prospect of nonfiction books, classrooms,
seminars, libraries, and studying, but Sarah will remain
unfazed.

Sarah is a life-long learner. She is constantly acquiring
new information and knowledge that she can use to improve
either herself or the world. The range of her inquiries
stretches from forms of psychotherapy, to cooking healthy
meals, to marketing audiotapes. There are few stones that she
would not turn over, but the sheer number of those stones is
overwhelming, and so Sarah is forced to pick and choose. For
instance, a few years ago Sarah started a small consulting
business for which she keeps her own books (after learning
about bookkeeping, of course). As the business grew and the
computer era dawned, she decided to learn about computers
and buy one to keep her accounts, write correspondence, and
stay capably conversant with the information age. The computer she bought sat for some time untouched, not because
Sarah had lost interest in it, but because the other things she
was studying took precedence. At the time, she was learning
about nutrition, wine, and the stock market. Sarah describes
having before her "a pyramid of learning possibilities that
stretches into the distance." Those subjects that are right
before her are the clearest and most compelling. She pursues
those interests, while the host of other attractive prospects are
currently less well defined and waiting in the wings. The
computer, too, waited in the wings until a phone call from
Sarah's accountant (informing her of records that would soon
be needed) brought the computer to center stage. Reshuffling
her pyramid of learning possibilities, she set about picking
her way through the manuals and books, becoming familiar
with the workings and uses of the computer—a task that was,
for her, exciting and fun.

Although no one would deny that the world provides an
endless stream of things to learn about, many people simply
don't notice them. For example, if the doctor tells such people
that they are not eating properly, they simply ask the doctor
what to eat and not eat. It never occurs to them to learn about
nutrition. These individuals gather information about what to

eat, but have no understanding of why they are not healthy and what systemic difference their eating choices make. Similarly, a great many people spend their whole lives complaining about, praising, and being mystified by the actions of our government and economy without it ever occurring to them to learn about how that government or economy actually functions.

It also happens that some people recognize things worth learning about, but have no way to set priorities for those possibilities. Thus, learning how to write good business letters (which Joe needs to do for his work) is just as compelling a possibility as learning about how to get the best finish on a car paint job, studying the history of philosophy, and finding out why stars come in different colors. These last three areas of exploration are certainly worth pursuing, but are probably not as currently important for Joe as learning how to write those business letters. The person who is not able to set appropriate priorities may end up dissipating his time and energy.

And finally, even for those who are able to set priorities, many find learning to be an onerous task. Often the result is either avoidance of the task, or a begrudging plodding through the necessary steps. It's easy to argue that computers are not everybody's cup of tea, and that the fun and excitement that Sarah enjoyed in learning about them was simply an indication that computers happen to appeal to her. The fact is, though, that once Sarah starts learning about *anything* she is excited and has fun. How is it possible that Sarah has an ever-widening pyramid of possible learnings, pursues them according to their priority, *and* finds the pursuit exciting and fun?

Sarah's First Step—Selecting Learning Possibilities
The cause-effect that initiates Sarah's operative format for selecting what is worth learning is her belief that "learning is the only way to get what I want." It is this cause-effect that impels her to search her world for what to learn. When she becomes aware of a possibility, she evaluates the degree to which learning about that particular thing will allow her to be

more capable, will be interesting, and will be fun. In other words, she evaluates possibilities by making a future test with the criteria of "capable," "interesting," and "fun." Any possibility that fulfills one of these criteria is added to her pyramid of things to be learned. In making these evaluations she maintains a reference of the things she wants and needs, and is particulary attentive to learning possibilities that are available through the people around her.

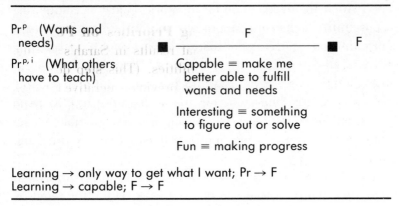

LIFE-LONG LEARNING   Selecting

Pr^p (Wants and needs)

Pr$^{p, i}$ (What others have to teach)

F

F

Capable ≡ make me better able to fulfill wants and needs

Interesting ≡ something to figure out or solve

Fun ≡ making progress

Learning → only way to get what I want; Pr → F
Learning → capable; F → F

What is worth learning

Sarah's three criteria are listed in order of priority, with "capable" being of greatest importance by far. Those learning possibilities that will make her more capable in areas that she values will be placed much nearer the apex of the pyramid than those possibilities that are merely interesting, although of course all three of her criteria are compatible with and enhance the others. For instance, learning about computers is, to Sarah, important to her future capabilities, while learning how the telephone works is merely interesting. Learning about wine is also important to her future capabilities in that she counts it as a necessary element in being able to entertain appropriately, besides being interesting and fun.

It is also significant that her test is about the future, rather than the present or past. Using a present test to identify what to learn about out of the myriad of choices would drastically limit her choices since she would tend to discard those possibilities that were not *currently* significant. When Sarah was told by a doctor that she might be prone to osteoporosis in her old age, she immediately started learning about nutrition, because osteoporosis would impair her capabilities. Had she instead used a present test, she probably would not have felt compelled to learn about nutrition because *her current capability was not in danger.* Many people use past tests when considering what to learn, an evaluation that most often leads them to learn about things they already know something about.

Sarah's Second Step—Setting Priorities on Possibilities

A second operative format results in Sarah's setting priorities on her learning possibilities. (This step does not necessarily immediately follow the previous operative format, but becomes relevant whenever she needs to decide how to use her time and energy for learning.) Again, she makes future tests with respect to a hierarchy of criteria, but in this case the criteria have to do with well-being. At the top of Sarah's list is her child's well-being, next is her personal mental capability, her commitments to others, then her physical health, and so on. Sarah bases this assessment upon what there is to learn about (the pyramid of choices), the current needs of others, and future constructed references of what needs to be done in the relatively near future.

LIFE-LONG LEARNING   Selecting

Pr^P (Learning possibilities)

Pr^P_c (Needs of others)

$F^{i \to p}_c$ (Things to be done)

∎ ——————————— F ——————————— ∎ F

Child's well-being ≡ CEq

Personal mental capability ≡ CEq

Commitments to others ≡ CEq

Own physical health ≡ CEq

Not learning what *needs* to be learned → not do well in life; Pr → F

What to actually start learning

The priorities that Sarah sets for her criteria help her to quickly and consistently separate out those learning possibilities that are about to become significant in terms of the well-being of herself and others (near future) from those learning possibilities that are *relatively* unimportant. The hierarchy allows those learning pursuits that are most relevant to personal, family, and relationship well-being to emerge clearly. People whose criteria are not organized in a clearly defined hierarchy are often either indecisive about what to do, resulting in a lack of action, or flit from one pursuit to another without regard for relevance. (Obviously, criteria will vary from person to person. What is most important to Sarah might be completely irrelevant to someone else. Having a clearly defined hierarchy of criteria, however, will benefit anyone.)

The superscript for Sarah's future reference (i→p) is a representation of the fact that as she views the various commitments in her future, those that are not pressing are informational; they are seen at a distance, lack detail, and are not compelling. As a commitment moves closer to needing to be fulfilled, however, it grows more compelling, until it becomes a personal reference in need of action. The qualitative differences in how she perceives the imminent and remote commitments in her future make it possible for her to feel compelled by those learning possibilities that are pressing, while not feeling overwhelmed by the many commitments that are not yet pressing.

Although similar in content to the cause-effect in the first operative format, the cause-effect in this operative format is significantly different in the orientation it creates for Sarah. In the first operative format ("learning is the only way to get what I want"), the cause-effect is couched in positive terms. That is, it orients her *toward* learning what she needs to learn. In the second operative format ("not learning what needs to be learned will keep me from doing well in life"), the cause-effect orients her *away* from the dire consequences of *not* learning. Thus the cause-effect she uses in discovering things worth learning is, appropriately, inclusive, while the form that the cause-effect takes during the setting of priorities is exclusive—which is appropriate when she is faced with parceling out her limited time and energy among various learning possibilities.

Sarah's Third Step—Learning for Understanding A third striking aspect of Sarah's ability as a life-long learner is the fact that once she is engaged in the process of learning something (no matter how mundane a subject it might seem to others), she experiences excitement and fun. The ongoing evaluation that she makes while learning is that of whether or not she now understands something, which for her means figuring out something new. The referential basis for this ongoing evaluation includes all of her past and present informational and personal experiences that she can usefully bring to bear on what she is learning about, as well as a future reference of already having attained the benefits that come with learning about the particular topic.

LIFE-LONG LEARNING   Learning

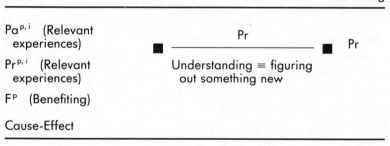

$Pa^{p,\,i}$ (Relevant experiences)

$Pr^{p,\,i}$ (Relevant experiences)

F^{p} (Benefiting)

Cause-Effect

Understanding ≡ figuring out something new

Her progress

Sarah knows she is understanding something when she is figuring out something new. For her, confronting the challenge of a new puzzle is exciting and fun. Thus each time Sarah is engaged in piecing together new information she realizes that she is increasing her understanding, and at the same time she is having fun and feeling excited. She is delighted much of the time; and she is almost always learning. She learns for the joy that learning brings. But she does not get lost in that joy. As she learns she draws upon all of her experiences to help her discover what is new and what is not, and keeps herself directed by keeping that future reference of her outcome before her.

The criterion for learning most often touted is the very one that Sarah uses: understanding. But for most people it is mere lip service. A much more common criterion than "understanding" is one having to do with attaining the outcome itself (such as completion, success, correctness, and so on). Sarah offered a revealing example of the difference between using criteria of completion and using criteria of understanding while keeping the outcome as a reference. She had new business telephone lines installed in her house, but her phones didn't work. When she followed the wires she found a horrifying tangle that somehow tied her several telephones, answering machine, and computer together. Feeling helpless before this web of wires, she decided that she wanted to learn how it all worked. She spent some time following up various strands, reconnecting them, and testing the results. At last she hit upon a combination that worked. She was in business, *but she was still dissatisfied.* "I got it correct, but it bothered me that I didn't understand what made it correct, so when the repairman got there I made him explain it to me—how the phones work . . . it's really amazing!"

In the course of transferring Sarah's aptitude for life-long learning to others, we discovered a common pattern. Sarah has a cause-effect that learning leads to being capable, while those in need of her aptitude often have a criterial equivalence in the general form of "not knowing means I am incapable." By installing Sarah's cause-effect we have been able to break this criterial equivalence, freeing the person to gain knowledge they would never have otherwise pursued. This cause-effect broke the bonds of a criterial equivalence that made being capable a matter of whether or not they *already* knew how, rather than whether or not they could or would learn how.

We do not wish to give the impression from the examples used in this chapter that all outcomes involve three or four operative formats. Some outcomes involve only one activity and one operative format, while others involve a dozen or more. The examples used here were selected to introduce you to some straightforward sets and sequences of operative formats, rather than plunging you into complex and intertwining examples. Fortunately, most of the skills we have modeled have, in fact, been fairly straightforward, involving no more than five or six operative formats.

As we said at the beginning of this chapter, excellence can be found in the people you interact with every day. Sarah, Ben, Deborah, and Al are probably not thought of by their friends and acquaintances as exceptional human beings. In fact, they would probably describe themselves as ordinary people struggling with the ordinary challenges of daily living. We agree that they are, like most of us, ordinary people. But we also recognize that, like each of us, they have certain extraordinary talents.

Fortunately, it is not necessary to revere or even to like the person from whom you want to acquire a particular talent. It is only necessary to recognize his or her particular competence. Unlike previous mentoring relationships that required months or years of contact, the information you need about the operative formats can be gathered in hours. Looking for the extraordinary abilities that reside in ordinary people may not lead you to reverence, but it will help you to develop a greater appreciation for your fellow man—as well as the means to personal and professional achievement.

That some people have the ability to recognize and appreciate otherwise overlooked talents is itself the manifestation of a worthy and valuable aptitude. It is an aptitude that will allow you to take advantage of the extraordinary skills that await your discovery. It is an aptitude that the EMPRINT method can help you develop and apply.

PART III

Making the Method Work for You

9 Selecting an Outcome

In the previous chapters we introduced the organizing principle and set of distinctions that are used in the EMPRINT method. We also introduced the fundamental presupposition upon which the method is built—that if it is possible for someone in the world to enjoy a particular skill or trait, then it is possible for you or anyone else to acquire and manifest that same attribute. But making that possibility a reality requires more than knowledge—it requires knowledgeable action.

The knowledgeable action we are referring to is the action required to specify the operative formats underlying a behavior or experience that you want to make your own or pass on to others, and then putting that information to use. The EMPRINT method is a source of knowledge about how to direct your actions in these useful ways. Because it is a skill *acquisition* process, the EMPRINT method marks out the steps required for *transferring* skills as well as understanding or appreciating them. The method's acquisition process for adding other people's talents to your repertoire of skills requires that you pass through three major stages.

The first of these stages involves determining your outcome, finding at least one person who does well what you want to be able to do, and identifying the activities and operative formats involved in fulfilling that outcome. Once that is done you are ready for the second stage, which involves the elicitation and specification of each of the variables for the operative formats you need. The final stage in this sequence is the installation of those fully specified operative formats into yourself or others.

This chapter offers suggestions and pointers that will aid you in successfully manuevering through the first stage, the stage of determining your outcome and identifying the kinds of activities and operative formats required to attain that outcome. The next two chapters include a set of elicitation and detection techniques that will come in handy in the first stage and that will carry you through the second stage of specifying the variables for the individual operative formats you want to adopt. Then, in Chapter 12, you will be introduced to several examples of installation sequences that you can use (or take others through) to actually adopt operative formats and thereby acquire the skills and traits you desire.

The path through these stages is one we have walked many times. We have explored its meandering side trails and discovered a few hazards that need to be avoided. As we guide you along the path we will point out the hazards, and make sure that you remain on sound footing. Each step you take will not only bring you closer to your chosen destination, it will also reveal one more previously hidden aspect of the journey. At the end of our walk together you will be familiar enough with the terrain to explore the path again on your own.

The Outcome

The most important initial step is to specify exactly the outcome you want to model and the context in which it occurs. To gather information about underlying activities and operative formats without having taken this vital first step is to invite confusion and frustration. Without having established an explicit outcome, you will find yourself gathering information about multiple contexts simultaneously, with no way to sort that information into discrete operative formats. It would be like asking a stranger whether you should turn right or left at the next corner without having first decided where you want to go. Before you take any other steps, know which specific skill you want to acquire or be able to pass on to others.

The fulfillment of this first step begins when you answer the question, "What can others do that I want to be able to do (or want to be able to teach others to do)?" There are people in the world, and you probably know some of them, who typically organize their time and activities so that they are productive, or punctual, or manage to have time left over for leisure. Others are shrewd investors, exercise consistently, or respond to frustrating setbacks with good-natured aplomb and constructive actions, or eat wisely, or arise early, or never over-commit themselves while maintaining productive relationships with others, or pull off successful parties, and on and on. As we have said before, the menu of possible experiences and behaviors is endless.

As illustrated by the examples of possible outcomes listed above, what is defined as a behavior is not limited to those things that we manifest externally. Normally when we speak of behavior we are referring to what we can see and hear a person actually doing. Remember that in the EMPRINT method, however, a behavior is *whatever* a person does. Thus an internal response, such as the emotional response of feeling comfortable and trusting even when being criticised, is a behavior. For this individual in the context of being criticised, then, the behavioral response is to feel comfortable and trusting.

In addition to emotional states, internal behaviors may also encompass cognitive processes. For example, as you evaluate the definition being put forward here—that cognitive processes are internal behaviors—you may search through your personal experiences for information and examples that either match or do not match the definition, you may weigh the evidence, consider the implications of such a definition, and so on. Furthermore, all of this may take place very quickly. Few people looking at you as you sit there making these extensive internal computations and evaluations would recognize that you were doing anything beyond reading a book, but certainly you would not say that you are not doing anything but reading. In fact you would be deeply involved in internal processing behaviors in response to the need to evaluate what you are reading. (By way of contrast, perhaps you can recall times when you have read the words on a page but did not engage in the internal processing that makes those words comprehensible.) Similarly, adding numbers in your head, assessing your own needs or those of others, planning what to do tomorrow or with the rest of your life, making a commitment to change, and motivating yourself to cut the lawn are all examples of internal behaviors. *Thus any external, emotional, or cognitive response to or within a particular context can serve as an appropriate outcome.*

Stating Your Outcome in Positives   Simply identifying a behavior you would like to incorporate in yourself or in others is not a sufficient base from which to begin elicitation and modeling. The behavioral outcome you have selected must first be made *appropriate* for elicitation.

In establishing for yourself an appropriate outcome, it is important that you express that outcome in terms of what you *want*, rather than what you *don't* want. For instance, you do not acquire the ability to not oversleep; you acquire the ability to *arise early*. Rather than not overeating, you acquire the ability to *eat wisely*. Identifying the desired outcome in positive terms—specifying what you want to do, rather than what you want to avoid—is essential for success. It is our experience that those formats that underlie any form of "not doing" are cumbersome at best, are rich in opportunities for confusion regarding appropriate contextualization, and are inappropriate for acquisition.

If an outcome is expressed in the form of not doing or avoiding something, we recast it by specifying just what we want to be able to do in terms of experience and behavior. For instance, the outcome of being able to respond like a certain politician who "reacts to provocative or difficult questions without trying to justify himself," could be translated into the more useful "responding to difficult questions by comfortably expressing genuine personal opinions." Similarly, the outcome of "not ruminating and being overwhelmed by one's failures" could be translated as "responding to failures as learning experiences and feeling confident."

The virtue of such a transformation into positive terms is that it specifies what you are seeking, and so provides you with a point of reference that will allow you to assess in an ongoing way whether or not the internal processes you are eliciting and eventually installing in yourself or others are in accord with your desired outcome. Without this explicit point of reference for your outcome you may find yourself gathering much information that is useless, redundant, or incoherent.

Putting Your Outcome into Context Having specified what you want to be able to do, the next important consideration is that of context: when, where, and with whom. The question to be answered here is, "In what situations do I want to manifest the outcome behavior?" It is not enough to simply set as an outcome, say, being able to comfortably express personal opinions, being confident in the face of failure, standing up for myself, following my diet, or being assertive. In addition to the behavior itself, you must also specify in what contexts you want to have access to it. In what contexts do you want to stand up for yourself? When interacting with peers? Loved ones? Superiors? All the time? If the outcome is to follow your diet, is it your intention and wish to follow it all the time, in all contexts, without exception? What about when you travel, or when you eat at the boss's home, or when you take your love out to celebrate your anniversary?

You may, in fact, have a specific context in mind for using the outcome behavior. It's important to specify the context(s) in which you want to have access to the outcome behavior because *the operative formats for the same behaviors in different contexts may be substantially and significantly different.* Thus if you want to be able to stand up for yourself to your boss at work and you elicit the operative formats for this outcome from someone who is adept at standing up for himself with his *loved ones,* you may discover the hard way that your newly acquired responses are less than satisfactory when used at the office. It's important, then, that when modeling a behavior you use as sources of information people who not only respond in the desired way, but do so in those contexts in which you want to manifest those same behaviors.

Intrinsic and Intentional Behaviors The next important outcome-related consideration is to determine whether you need to model an *intrinsic* behavior or an *intentional* behavior. Intrinsic behaviors are those that an individual has acquired as the natural result of interacting in his environment over the years. When such behaviors are recognized they are usually referred to as talents, natural abilities, gifts, or aptitudes. The youngster who quickly and easily grasps the logic underlying computer programming, and her classmate who cares not at all for computer programming but who readily appreciates those who do have such talents, both exemplify what are for *them* intrinsic behaviors. The first youngster's intrinsic behavior is the ability to understand computer programming, while the second youngster's intrinsic behavior is the ability to appreciate the talents of others. For purposes of acquisition, any behavior that is incidentally acquired (as are most of our behaviors) is simply labeled "intrinsic."

Intentional behaviors, on the other hand, are those behaviors that have been *deliberately* acquired. That is, the individual has determined the need for a particular behavior and has managed to install that behavior in him or herself. Thus the difference between intrinsic and intentional behaviors is exemplified by the difference between the person who is "naturally" good at spelling words and the person who used to be a terrible speller but eventually learned to be a good speller. Although the intrinsically good speller and the intentionally good speller both end up with the same behavior (and probably the same underlying operative formats), *there is a significant difference between them in terms of what each of them had to do in order to gain those abilities.* The difference is that the intrinsically good speller needed to do little of a deliberate nature to have access to his ability, while the intentional speller had to go through a sequence of wanting to learn to spell well, being motivated to learn this skill, actually learning it, and so on. Those responses, behaviors, and experiences that lead a person to the acquisition of a behavior, but are not themselves involved in the manifestion of that behavior, are called *precursive activities.*

A common example of the distinction between a behavior and its precursive activities occurs with regard to smoking. Most smokers know they should quit, and may even know how to go about doing it, but don't seem to be able to motivate themselves to actually quit. This is a demonstration that not only the behavioral outcome of giving up cigarettes, but also the precursive activities of deciding to do it, motivation, planning how to do it, and so on, may be critical in making it possible to quit.

In addition to the operative formats for the outcome itself, you *as an individual* may also need the operative formats for the precursive activities that make up those behaviors that lead to and support the attainment of the desired outcome. In practice, unless you are aware from the start that you lack the decisiveness, commitment, or motivation needed to make your intended outcome a reality, we suggest that you start by modeling the outcome itself. Once you have installed the operative formats for the outcome you will quickly discover whether or not you needed the precursors as well. If you have successfully adopted the ability to generate your outcome behavior but find that either you don't do it, or that you fail to *continue* generating it in the appropriate contexts, you need one or more of the precursors. Precursive activities will be discussed more completely in the "Activities" section.

Whom to Model   When selecting someone to model, you need to find a person who does what you want to be able to do in the context you want to do it in. In practice, this is not always so obvious a requirement. A common misstep at this point is to use as a subject for modeling someone who does not *strictly* fulfill the requirements of the outcome. For instance, we have often seen individuals trying to learn how to quit smoking from people who would never consider smoking in the first place. Though perhaps worth modeling, the ability to *shun* cigarettes is not the same as the ability to *give up* cigarettes. The person who wants to quit smoking needs as his model someone who has smoked and quit.

If you know at the outset that you will need the behavioral and attitudinal precursors as well as the outcome behavior itself, then you will also want to select as a model someone for whom the outcome behavior is intentional. If you don't think you need the precursors, then your subject can be either someone for whom the outcome behavior is intrinsic or someone for whom it is intentional.

If at all possible, try to witness an actual demonstration of your subject's desirable response in the context in which you are interested in having it. If you have not had the opportunity to observe this person in the context in which you want to make changes, then try to create such an opportunity, perhaps by setting up such a situation for your subject. For example, if one of your co-workers has a reputation for being particularly adept at sizing up sales prospects, but you have never been around when she makes her assessments, you could ask to sit in the next time she meets with a prospective customer. You would also want to be spend some time with her right after so that you could ask her the appropriate elicitation questions. A simpler way to accomplish the same result would be to have her interact with you as you role-play a potential customer. Either way (or in any other similar way you create), you will be able to assure yourself that your subject does in fact respond the way you would like to learn to respond. An additional virtue of creating the outcome context, and therefore the opportunity for an immediate demonstration of the subject's aptitude, is that you have a fresh example from which your subject can draw her answers to your elicitation questions.

We always try to find at least three people who exemplify what we want to be able to acquire or transfer to others. This sample allows us to make comparisons between the individuals, and to discover which patterns consistently underlie the abilities we want to model. When we use the EMPRINT method to discover patterns that are characteristic of people in general or of certain activities in general, we use a large and varied sample to substantiate our findings. If, however, our intended outcome is the personal acquisition of behavior, it is our experience that more than three examples will only lead to redundant information.

Activities

At this point you have established your outcome and have located at least one person who is already competent in manifesting that outcome from whom you can elicit the operative format information you need. Now you must recognize that what seems to be a relatively simple, straightforward, and quickly evoked behavior may actually be the end product of a whole set of activities. For example, the outcome behavior of writing a technical paper is obviously the result of successfully fulfilling other activities having to do with specifying a topic, research, formulating a structure for the presentation, picking a style, and so on.

Activities are the steps that an individual takes in order to manifest a particular outcome behavior. Thus, "select a topic" and "do research" are two of the activities that underlie the ability to write a technical paper. Similarly, using the EMPRINT method for elicitation involves the initial activities of specifying the outcome, identifying whether intrinsic or intentional behavior is needed, and identifying activities.

It is not inherent in either of the two outcomes described above (writing technical papers and doing elicitation) that they be organized in terms of the activities we have listed for each of them. The activities we listed were taken from individuals who do manifest those outcome behaviors, but the description of the underlying activities was *theirs*. That is, the set of activities elicited from an individual represents that person's way of organizing his experience, and is significant in making possible the manifestation of the outcome behavior in the particular way *that person* manifests it. For one person the behavioral outcome of "getting up and dancing" involves just one activity—doing it—while for another dancing involves a whole set of activities, including "deciding how I want to feel," "finding out what my partner would enjoy," and "imagining what I could do that would be new." For each of these dancers, the set of activities they use is "right" for responding in the particular ways each of them responds when dancing. The person whose operative formats we are eliciting is the final arbiter of how to go about doing what he does in the way he does it.

Precursive Activities   Whether you will be more successful by acquiring intrinsic or intentional behavior depends upon whether you merely need to know how to do "it," or if you also need such behavioral precursors as motivation and commitment as well. As indicated above, you can always test this by getting the operative formats for the desired outcome behavior itself from someone who has it as an intrinsic or as an intentional behavior and use those formats to guide your responses in the needed context. If you *can* do the behavior but *don't*, that is a signal that you need the additional operative formats of such precursive activities as deciding, motivation, planning, and commitment.

These four activities—deciding, motivation, planning, and commitment—are by far the most commonly significant of the precursive activities. You may already know from experience that for you a precursive behavior is either missing altogether or is inappropriate. For instance, after years of considering going back to school to get a degree in a different field, you may have already discovered that . . .

you have been unable to *decide* whether or not it would be a good idea at all, or

you have decided that it would be a good idea but have been unable to *motivate* yourself to do anything about it, or

you have been investigating the possibilities but have been unable to generate a coherent *plan* for how to proceed, or

you have a plan, but stop short of making the *commitment* to put that plan into effect.

Take as another example a father who deliberately and successfully changed his behavior from shouting to reasoned negotiation when dealing with his ten-year-old son. Someone who presently shouts at his own children might need to know . . .

How did he decide to change his responses?

How did he motivate himself to make the effort to change his responses?

How did he come up with a workable plan to change his responses?

How did he make a commitment that was strong enough to compel him to carry out his plan?

Again, the point to be remembered about precursive activities is that they include the operative formats that lead to the use of those activities and operative formats that underlie the manifestation of the outcome itself. If you know at the outset that you are personally in need of one or more of the precursive activities for a particular outcome, then be sure to gather that information first, and be sure to gather it from individuals for whom that outcome is an intentional behavior.

Activities and Operative Formats As you discovered in Chapter 3, just as an outcome may be the result of a set of distinct activities, so each of those activities may itself be made up of more than one operative format. Each of these operative formats results in some kind of external, emotional, or cognitive behavior. At this stage in the elicitation sequence, your goal should be to specify the outcome in terms of the sequence of operative formats that underlie that outcome.

You can think of the outcome as being the ultimate result of a set of sub-outcomes, with each of these sub-outcomes being activities and operative formats. Using writing a technical paper as an example of a desired outcome, we discover from our exemplar, Bob, that the outcome is made up of three activities: selecting a topic, doing research, and choosing a writing style. Upon further questioning, our subject explains that the activity of doing research is itself made up of three separate operative formats in which he decides what he needs to know, figures out where he's likely to find that information, and extracts relevant information from the references. There need not be more than one operative format for each activity, however. For the writer we are using here as an example, selecting a topic and choosing a writing style are activities that involve only one operative format each.

Although it is often the case that the completion of the evaluation in one operative format is a prerequisite for engaging in the next, operative formats may also occur simultaneously, or may be recursive, or reoccurring, and so on. Often what is being fulfilled in one operative format is the generation of information or experiences used in subsequent operative formats. In other words, the behavioral, informational, and experiential conclusions of one operative format become a source of references for another operative format. For example, consider the initial operative formats for the writing outcome.

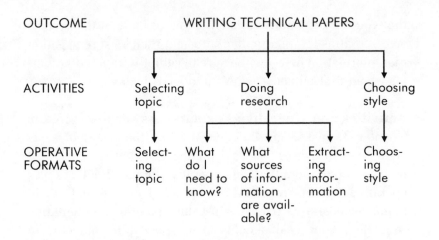

Obviously, before the sequence of operative formats that make up the activity of doing research can be appropriately engaged in, a topic must be selected. The topic that is selected will then show up as an important past reference in each of the operative formats that constitute the activity of doing research. Evaluations about what information is needed, where such information can be found, and the best way to extract the appropriate pieces of information from those sources are done by this person in relation to the past reference of the selected topic.

Although it may seem obvious that research cannot be done without first selecting a topic, for those who do not write technical papers well this may be a revelation. The fact is that many people embark upon such writing without a clear idea of their topic, or with a topic in mind that is much too broad, and so often end up wasting time and energy meandering through the literature, collecting unrelated pieces of information, and so on. The conclusions of the operative format in which this writer decides what he needs to know show up as references in the operative format he uses when identifying where to get that information and in the operative format he uses in extracting that information from his materials.

Both of the above examples are instances of the conclusions of one step *sequentially* furnishing references for another or other steps. But, as we mentioned above, conclusions from operative formats may also inform and supplement one another simultaneously, recursively, and so on. The writer's operative formats provide an example of this in the interaction that occurs between the steps of deciding what he needs to know and extracting the information. While what he needs to know is an important informational reference in the "extraction" format, the pieces of information that he extracts may also simultaneously function as important informational references for the "what he needs to know" format. That is, the information he extracts may alter his notions about what he needs to know. Often the result is a better paper.

For instance, suppose that he is researching a paper on recent advances in computer technology. While doing his research, he comes across literature references citing the long-range effects of the technology on human social interactions, an aspect he had not previously considered. Operating out of the "what he needs to know" operative format, he considers whether "social side-effects" is something he needs to find out about. Although such an evaluation may seem obvious, the fact is that many individuals, once they have chosen their area of research interest, will *automatically* pass over any information that does not match their chosen area. The capability that our writer enjoys in this context is due in part to the operative formats he uses, and in part results from his flexibility in moving new information back and forth between those two operative formats.

If you take a moment to review the material we have covered thus far you will realize that you now have guidelines to follow for determining your outcome, evaluating the appropriateness of your outcome, selecting individuals to model who manifest the outcome you want in the way you want it and in the situations you want it in, and understanding the kinds of activities and operative formats involved in fulfilling that outcome. You have just passed through the first stage. We will now move on to explore stage two, the elicitation and detection techniques that you can use to gather information about outcomes and activities, and to reveal the variables that make up the operative formats for talent and competence.

10 Identifying the Activities and Operative Formats

Whenever people talk they leave a string of clues about their internal processing. These clues are the words they use to describe their experiences. For instance, in our culture it is easy to know when a person is talking about what has happened, as opposed to what is happening or what might happen in the future; all you have to do is listen to the verb tense. But people leave linguistic markers for much more than just the distinctions of past, present, and future. They also reveal distinctions about all of the behavioral steps—the activities and operative formats—they are taking. Fortunately, all of us raised in this culture already possess linguistic decoder rings that we received as part of our biological and cultural heritage. We all use, recognize, and respond to language, and it is the key to unraveling the mystery of our internal processes.

The most important linguistic distinctions for detecting the sequence of operative formats in which a person engages are adverbs that denote sequence—such as "then," "and then," "after," "next," "following," "afterwards," "first," and so on. When used to separate verbs that specify some kind of action or activity, such adverbs are used to mark the fact that there has been a significant change in activity. For instance, in response to the purposely general question, "How do you go about writing technical papers?" Bob (our subject for the examples used in the previous chapter) replied:

I start out by *first* deciding on a specific topic, *and then* I do the research that's needed. *Then* when that's done, I decide just what writing style to use, plan it out—the paper, that is—*then* start writing.

In this statement, Bob informs us that he organizes the task of writing a technical paper into five primary activities: selecting a topic, researching, choosing a writing style, planning the paper, and writing. In all but one instance, he marked a change in activity by using either "then" or "and then." When Bob writes technical papers, those activities constitute *separate* steps—although, as we saw in the previous chapter, not necessarily *independent* steps.

Adverbs are commonly used in marking changes in activities, but they are not *always* used—Bob marked the activity of planning without using an adverb denoting sequence. In this case the change in activity is evident from the fact that the behaviors specified in each of the three phrases in his response are different behaviors. Whenever a person uses a new verb (decide, plan, write, etc.) to specify a different action, that action is the behavioral manifestation of another operative format or set of operative formats. The adverbs denoting sequencing may or may not also be there to assist in marking these shifts in activity.

To Bob, picking a writing style and planning the paper are perceived and treated as separate activities, as demonstrated by the fact that in a cursory description of the process he specifies each and does so without subsuming one within the other. Someone else for whom writing a technical paper does not include an evaluation about style, or for whom selection of writing style is simply considered part of planning the paper, would be likely to describe their process as, "I pick a topic, then do the research, then plan it out, and finally get down to writing it."

In answering our question, Bob was very helpful and apparently complete in his answer. People are not used to being asked to describe in detail their internal processes, however, and even when they are asked they can easily fail to mention a step that seems to them trivial or that they take for granted. How then can you know whether or not you have elicited the whole set of activities underlying a particular outcome? This is done by questioning your subject about the boundaries of those activities you have already elicited. That is, find out if there are any other activities that come before or after those that you already know about. The questions that will almost always elicit this information are variants of the following.

Is there anything you have to do or consider *before* you [select a topic]?

Once you have [selected a topic] are you *then* ready to start your research?

Regardless of how you put it, the function of the question is to get your subject to consider whether he has, *as far as he is concerned,* left a behavioral step out of his description.

Once you have a description of the activities that are responsible for the manifestation of the outcome behavior, you next need to determine whether or not any of those activities are themselves the manifestion of more than one operative format. You can elicit this information by applying to each of the activities the same question that was originally applied to the outcome behavior.

How do you go about [choosing a topic]?

In answering this question, your subject will either describe a set of evaluations (each of which probably denotes a separate operative format), or will start describing just one operative format for that activity. Obviously, if he offers you a set of evaluations, then each of those operative formats constitutes a behavioral step that you may need to explore and specify. If he instead answers the question by describing a single evaluation, then you can check to make sure there is only one operative format by asking questions in this general form.

Are there any other considerations that go into [choosing a topic]?

Is what you described to me the only thing you evaluate before [choosing a topic]?

This process can be depicted as follows.

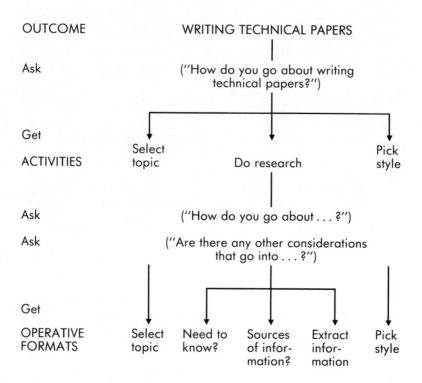

With respect to the elicitation of operative formats there is one more important linguistic distinction: the use of the conjunction "and." Like adverbs that denote sequence, the use of "and" between the description of two evaluations indicates that those two operative formats are separate steps. Furthermore, the use of "and" *by itself* also indicates that those two (or more) operative formats occur *simultaneously*. We elicited the following description from a woman who is very adept at choreography.

Well, if I have a piece of music I just have feelings about what the music sounds like *and* I feel steps that match rhythmically . . . *and after* I have a few of those pieces I make pictures in my head *and then* make pictures of connecting steps.

The sequence that she describes here involves four operative formats. She engages in the first two of these behaviors (*feel what the music sounds like* and *match steps to rhythms*) at the same time, as indicated by her use of the conjunction "and." The operative formats for each of these behaviors are different (as revealed by additional questioning, the criteria and references are different), but they engage her experience and behavior simultaneously.

The following elicitation excerpt contains examples of all of the distinctions we have made so far regarding the identification of the number and types of activities and operative formats that underlie the manifestion of an outcome. In this example the subject, Alan, has a particular genius for building things. His creations, though simple, are finely crafted. A bird feeder that Alan had recently completed was used as a content example for the elicitation. (We have added emphasis to make the distinctions more apparent.)

ML: How do you go about building a bird feeder?

Alan: Well, I spend some time *planning* it, THEN I just *build* it.

Alan's first response tells us that he makes a distinction between the activity of planning and the activity of building. These are sequential steps, as indicated by his use of "then."

ML: How do you go about planning it?

Alan: I *figure out what functions* the bird feeder will need to fulfill AND *what materials* to make it out of.

ML: What do you mean by "functions"?

Alan: It has to hold the seed and keep it dry. There needs to be a place for the birds to land. Those kind of things.

The question "How do you go about planning it?" is intended to elicit whether or not planning is, for Alan, made up of more than one operative format and, if so, what they are. Alan responds by describing two behaviors: assessing necessary functions and assessing needed materials. These two behaviors are probably simultaneous, as indicated by his use of "and" rather than "and then." As we later found out, the functions to be fulfilled affect his assessment of the materials needed. That is, the conclusions of the "function assessment" operative format show up as informational references in the "materials assessment" operative format. The question "What do you mean by functions?" was intended to begin to specify the criterial equivalence for "functions."

ML: OK. Is there anything you have to do before you start figuring out functions and so on?

Alan: No, not really, unless I'm building something for someone else. THEN I would *find out what that person wants* first.

ML: Let's assume that you're building this feeder for yourself.

Alan: OK.

The author tests for steps previous to that of "assessment of function and materials" and finds out that there is a prior behavior of "gathering information" in the special context of the project being built for someone else. (If you were interested in building things for others then you would want to find out about the operative formats that Alan uses in gathering such information.)

ML: As soon as you have figured out the functions the feeder needs to fulfill and what materials to use, are you then ready to build the feeder?

Alan: Uh, no. THEN I *decide what form* to make it AND *consider what materials I have on hand* that I could use. I like to use what materials I happen to already have, if I can.

The author then checks whether or not the function and materials assessments are all that go into Alan's project planning. They aren't. It turns out that he then "decides on form" *and* (simultaneously) "assesses on-hand materials."

ML: OK. Once you decide on a form and materials, are you then ready to make the feeder?

Alan: Well, except for getting the materials and tools together and having the time, yeah, I am.

The activity of planning the bird feeder ends when he has come to some conclusions with regard to the form and possible on-hand materials. These conclusions will show up as past informational references in the subsequent activity of getting the materials and tools, and in the activities involved in the actual building itself (informing him of how to use the materials, of the order things need to be done, and so on).

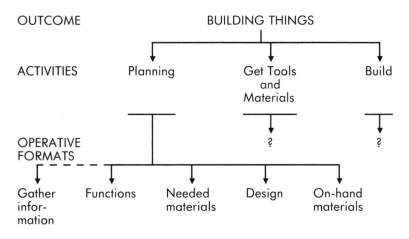

Once you have specified the set of operative formats underlying an outcome, as we have done here with Alan, the elicitation of the operative formats for each of those steps can begin. Of course, in the process of specifying the outcome, activities, and number of operative formats you will often inadvertently elicit information regarding the content of those operative formats. For instance, in describing the steps that he goes through in planning a project he is making for someone else, Alan revealed that a criterion he uses within the operative format of gathering information is *what the other person wants*.

If it seems to you that in the elicitation procedure as described thus far we are suggesting the need to be thorough, you are correct. If our only intention were to be able to appreciate Alan, we would not need to gather all this information. We could be satisfied with the appreciation we already feel as we marvel at his finely crafted work. What we discovered about Alan certainly deepens our appreciation, but we are casting our net of inquiry with the intent of capturing much more than feelings of appreciation. We want to replicate Alan's special talent in ourselves. And replication, by definition and as a practical matter, requires a precise matching of all details and variables. Replicating a skill is more difficult than just appreciating it, but the payoff in terms of expanded perceptions and competencies is immense.

11 Elicitation and Detection of the Variables

Once you have identified an outcome and determined the number of underlying activities and operative formats, you can begin to specify the seven variables for each of the operative formats. This chapter will supply you with elicitation and detection techniques for accomplishing that task.

All of the elicitation examples given in this section presuppose that the vital first steps covered in the previous chapter have already been done. The variables are discussed in the order we have found to be most useful. Elicitation of the operative format variables is illustrated with appropriate fragments taken from more extensive elicitations in order to highlight the patterns relevant to the specific distinction being described at that point.

One final point needs to be made before we proceed. As you gather information regarding the operative formats for a specific activity, you may discover that the manifestation of that activity actually depends on one or more operative formats that you were not previously aware of. When that happens, stop specifying the variables and sort out the underlying sequence of operative formats. Once you have a clear understanding of the new sequence you can pick up where you left off and continue to explore the variables.

Test Category

Time Frame and Criteria   The test category encompasses the evaluation being made within a particular operative format. The criteria are those standards that are being applied in making that evaluation, and the time frame of the test specifies whether it is important that the criteria be fulfilled in the past, present, or future.

An operative format is best elicited by first specifying the time frame of the test and criteria. There are two reasons for this. First, these two pieces of information are the most readily apparent and easily given of any of the variables. And second, specifying the time frame of the test and criteria first helps ensure that you have sufficiently specified the entire sequence of operative formats. Because each operative format will be characterized by a unique time frame and set of criteria (except in the case of simultaneous tests within an operative format), if your elicitation uncovers two or more tests for a particular operative format you can use that information to identify whether those tests really represent separate operative formats, or whether they occur simultaneously within the same operative format.

Because the time frame of the test and the criteria is almost always indicated whenever a person specifies criteria, criteria and test time frame are usually elicited together. The elicitation of criteria involves asking your subjects for the significant standards they use in making their evaluation within a particular context. Questions of the following form are effective in eliciting criteria.

What is important to you when you [behavior]?

What do you pay attention to when you [behavior]?

What is significant when they [behavior]?

When you [behavior], what are you evaluating?

The important considerations when you [behavior], then, are . . . ?

In short, any question or statement that asks your subject to reflect on and report the standards he or she uses in making an evaluation when engaged in a particular operative format will probably elicit a list of the relevant criteria. Of course, this list may include only one criterion, or it may contain many. These criteria may also be either listed according to priority or be of relatively equal importance. You can find out if the criteria that you have identified so far are all of the important ones by asking something like the following.

Is there anything else that is important (significant, you attend to, are evaluating, etc.) when you [behavior]?

Once you have elicited the criteria you can elicit the time frame of the test by asking questions that direct your subject's attention to whether he has been considering the criteria in relation to the past, present, or future. Although they are not normally at the forefront of people's consciousness, such distinctions as criteria and test time frames *are* a part of their experience and, when asked, they are almost always able to supply information regarding those distinctions. Examples of such questions include the following.

Are you evaluating the past, present, or future?

When you consider [criterion], do you think of how you have been [criterion], how you are [criterion], or how you will be [criterion]?

Are these considerations about the past, the present, or the future?

Are you attending to how [criterion] affected your past, how it affects you now, or how it will affect your future?

Any question or statement that specifies the criterion, either explicitly or by the context of the question, and asks your subject to reflect and report upon the time frame to which he is applying that criterion, will probably make it possible for him to identify the time frame he is using.

It's not always necessary to ask explicitly for either the criteria or the time frame of the test. In describing their experience and internal processes, people often include both the criteria and test time frames they are using. The previous chapter supplied the elicitation example of Alan's ability to plan projects. One of his responses was, "Then I would find out what that person *wants* first."

One of the things Alan has told us here is that a criterion he uses in gathering information is that of "want" (as opposed to, say, "need" or "appreciate").

The time frame of the test will be evident by the verb tense your subject uses when describing his criteria. For instance, in the fragment taken from Alan's elicitation, he talks about finding out what that person *wants*. The verb tense here is present, as is probably the time frame for the test of this criterion. Alan is concerned with what this person wants *now*, rather than what she wanted (past tense and time frame) or will want (future tense and time frame). Regardless of how you go about eliciting information from your subject, keep in mind that you need to specify both the criteria he is using to make his evaluations, and the time frame that is being evaluated with respect to those criteria.

The following excerpts provide many examples of the elicitation of criteria and test time frames. We have added the italics to make the distinctions more readily apparent. In the first example Bill, the man we are interviewing, has the ability to bargain effectively (outcome behavior) when negotiating the price for a piece of artwork (context). One of his operative formats is for "information gathering."

ML: What is important when you are gathering information for such negotiations?

Bill: Primarily, what is the *relative value* of the piece and what is the *lowest price possible* at which it can be had.

ML: If you were engaged in such a negotiation now, would you be concerned with the relative value and lowest possible price at present, what its value and lowest price has been in the past, or what it will be in the future?

Bill: What the lowest price is that I can get it for *now*. I do take into consideration what the prices for that artist's work have been in the past but only to give me a sense of how low it *is* possible to get it to *now*.

The criteria that Bill uses in gathering information are "relative value" and "lowest possible price," and the time frame for this test is the present.

Morgan is adept at editing (outcome behavior) educational

videotapes (context). The operative format we are asking about is that of making decisions about actual edits.

ML: As you look at the tape, on what basis do you decide to make a particular edit?

Morgan: Well, it has to be *clear*. Everything has to be clear to the viewer if they are going to learn.

ML: Are you considering whether the teaching points are clear to you right now or to someone in the future who will be watching it?

Morgan: Oh, definitely in relation to the person who I imagine *will be* watching it.

When editing an educational videotape, Morgan uses the criterion of "clarity." The time frame in which she is testing for clarity is the future. That is, she evaluates whether or not people *will be* able to understand the tape, rather than whether or not she is able or has previously been able to understand the tape.

Betty's particular genius is her ability to plan holiday meals that everybody enjoys. The following elicitation is for her operative format for deciding on a menu.

ML: What are the important considerations when deciding on a menu?

Betty: I have to settle on dishes that people find *pleasing*.

ML: Is it what you find pleasing now, or what has been pleasing, or is it what you imagine will be pleasing?

Betty: I generally go back and think about what the people who are coming *have* really *enjoyed* and try to make my menu up out of those dishes.

For Betty the criterion "pleasing" is evaluated with respect to the past. Specifically, she assesses what *have been* the most pleasing dishes for her guests and attempts to match those past menus.

Ray enjoys and is good at planning birthday parties for children. The following excerpt concerns his operative format for planning the party.

ML: When you were planning your daughter's last birthday party, what were you evaluating?

Ray: Actually, what I *would have liked to have had* for a party when I was her age.

Ray makes a past test about what he would have liked as a child, and he uses the criterion of "liked" (as opposed to understood, appreciated, benefited from, and so on). In this example, Ray's single response revealed both the criterion and the time frame for the test.

Sally responds to being complimented with embarrassment and self-deprecating remarks.

ML: What are you thinking about when someone gives you a compliment?

Sally: Whether they mean what they say or are just saying it, or even making fun of me.

ML: So whether they are being *sincere* or not?

Sally: Yes.

ML: Are you always embarrassed and self-deprecating when someone gives you a compliment?

Sally: Uh, no, not always. If I'm *comfortable* with them then I take compliments pretty well.

By asking for a counterexample, we found that there is a context in which Sally does respond differently to compliments— that of being comfortable with the person—and thereby also discovered another criterion: comfort. Sally's response to being complimented comes out of her present test regarding whether she is comfortable with this person and whether this person is sincere.

John's response to being complimented contrasts with Sally's. No matter who is complimenting him, John responds with obvious pleasure and a heartfelt "thanks."

ML: What are you evaluating when you are complimented?

John: Uh, I don't know.

ML: Well, what are you thinking about then?

John: Oh, how *good it feels.*

ML: Anything else?

John: No, not really. It just really *feels good.*

When John is being complimented he makes a present test regarding the criterion of "feeling good."

Bob and Sam were both turned down for a job. Sam's response was a sense of confidence that he would do better next time, while Bob's response was to be discouraged and quit even looking for a job.

ML: What were you evaluating when you got turned down for the job?

Bob: I wasn't evaluating anything. All I knew was that I didn't get the job. It doesn't matter what I do, I'm not *going to get a job.*

Bob makes future tests regarding whether he is going to get a job or not. Unfortunately, the references he is using in building his future test are of failing in the past and not having a job in the present. With this constellation of variables, he is doomed to feel discouraged and defeated. But consider Sam.

ML: What were you evaluating when you got turned down for that job?

Sam: Basically, what to *do different next time* — what *I could do next time* that would *work better.*

ML: Better to get you a job?

Sam: To get the job, right.

Like Bob, Sam makes future tests. Unlike Bob, however, Sam's criteria are "do different" and "work better." The difference in their responses to being turned down is largely due to the difference in the criteria they use. Bob is testing for "get a job/not get a job," which (since he has many past and present references for not having a job) makes it easy to generate a future that also does not seem promising in terms of jobs. Sam's test leads him to consider changes in his future behavior and presupposes that if he makes the appropriate ones he will get a job.

On election day, Willie stays home and Sarah goes out and votes.

ML: Did you actually decide to stay home and not vote or did you just forget?

Willie: I decided to stay home. I'm no fool.

ML: What were you thinking when you made this decision?

Willie: My vote *isn't going to make any difference*, and I *don't like* either of the candidates anyway.

ML: What about the issues on the ballot? Did you consider any of those?

Willie: No.

ML: Suppose that there was a candidate on the ballot that you liked. Would you vote?

Willie: Yeah, probably I would.

Willie's decision to stay home was the result of an operative format that contained two tests. One was a future test regarding whether or not his vote would make a difference, and the other was a present test about whether or not he liked the candidates. As long as he doesn't like any of the candidates there is no conflict between the two tests. If he does like one candidate, however, there is a conflict between the two tests. Willie resolves the conflict by subordinating criteria about making a difference in the future in favor of his criteria about liking a candidate in the present.

ML: Did you decide whether or not to vote or do you automatically vote each election day?

Sarah: The former. I was tempted not to vote this last election. I had a lot to do and it was inconvenient to get to the poll that day.

ML: What, then, was so important that you voted anyway?

Sarah: I thought about how I *would* feel about myself if I didn't vote.

ML: And how would you feel about yourself if you hadn't?

Sarah: *Irresponsible.*

Like Willie, Sarah's decision involved one operative format with two tests—one a present test with respect to the criterion of "convenience," and the other a future test regarding the criterion of "responsibility." These two tests resulted in conflicting conclusions during the last election, compelling her to subordinate the present inconvenience in favor of feeling herself to be a responsible person in the future.

Criterial Equivalence   Having a name for a criterion is not the same thing as knowing what that criterion means. As defined in Chapter 4, a criterion is a name for a certain set of perceptions or behaviors. Two people may be using the same criterion (insofar as the *name* of that criterion is concerned) but have very different ideas about what perceptions and behaviors constitute that criterion. For example, both members of a married couple may highly value "respect"; but to the husband respect means not saying or doing anything that will hurt the other, while for the wife respect means saying whatever is on her mind that concerns the other person. Both husband and wife will try to fulfill their desire to be respectful of each other, *but each will do it in his and her own way.*

Once you know the criteria your subject is using, you can elicit criterial equivalences for each of them by asking him to specify what he means by a particular criterion, or how he knows that a particular criterion is fulfilled. For example, you can use questions that follow these general forms.

What does [criterion] mean?

How do you know when you or others are being [criterion]?

What do you need to see, hear, or feel in order to know that you are being [criterion], or that others are being [criterion]?

When is someone being [criterion]?

How would you describe [criterion]?

Any question or statement, then, that directs a person to specify the particular perceptions and behaviors he uses to recognize a particular criterion will probably reveal his criterial equivalence.

Following are several examples in which we elicit criteria and criterial equivalence information. The first is with Paul, a well-known fiction writer. His special talent is creating multifaceted characters and evocative scenes.

ML: What are you going for as you write a scene? What's important to you?

Paul: Whether or not as I read it I have a *complete experience.*

ML: What do you mean by a "complete experience"?

Paul: By that I mean that *every sense is filled—what I see, hear, smell, taste, feel.* Otherwise I can be distracted. Some aspect of my experience might be filled by something that's not going on in the book. I don't want people to be able to eat while they read my book. It's a complete experience.

ML: And what if something you've written doesn't do that?

Paul: I rewrite it until it does.

The time frame of Paul's test is the present and the criterion is "complete experience." The criterial equivalence for a complete experience (that is, how he knows he or his reader is having a complete experience) is that all of the senses are occupied by the book.

Frank, an excellent teacher, was asked how he knows when he can move on to the next stage in instructing his students.

ML: When do you go on to the next piece of information or level of instruction?

Frank: When I can see that my students are *competent* with what we are presently working on.

ML: How do you know when your students are competent?

Frank: When I can see that they can to a certain extent *duplicate what I have demonstrated,* either on paper if it's calculations or in the lab, then I know that they're competent and we can move on.

Frank's criterion of "competence" is tested for in the present, and his criterial equivalence for competence is his students' ability to duplicate what he has demonstrated.

We asked Alexis, a personnel manager, what she looks for in an employee.

Alexis: I'm always looking for the right person for the right job. Not just the *best* person, but the *right* person.

ML: What does "right" mean for you in this context?

Alexis: It seems to me that the person and the job are each an *opportunity* for the other. It's kind of like the job is alive, like the person.

ML: What do you mean by "opportunity"?

Alexis: *They give each other what the other needs.* Both benefit.

ML: Well then, what do you mean by the "best" person?

Alexis: Best is *settling for what you can get.*

ML: Are you deciding whether the job and person are opportunities for each other now, or whether they will be in the future, or whether they have been opportunities for each other in the past?

Alexis: Uhh, opportunities now. People and jobs don't seem to change that much, so if they fit now it will probably last long enough to be worthwhile.

Alexis makes a present test as to whether or not the applicant is right for the job. She defines "right" in terms of opportunity. The notion of opportunity is still not at the level of perception and behavior, however, so we asked for further specification and got the criterial equivalence of *giving each other what the other needs*.

Representational Systems   It's not unusual to find a criterion that can only be fulfilled by experiences from one or another of the representational systems. In a previous example, for instance, Frank says that he knows his students are competent when he can *see* that they are able to duplicate his demonstrations. Hearing or getting a feeling about their abilities is not particularly meaningful to Frank. He needs to *see* the evidence.

The representational system is part of the criterial equivalence and, like the criterial equivalence itself, may be different for different people using the same-named criteria. For instance, while one person knows that someone is being sincere by the *tone of her voice*, another knows sincerity by *how I feel*, and yet another may recognize sincerity by how the person *looks* when she speaks.

Just as the linguistic clues of verb tense help us detect the time frame in which an individual is operating, there are linguistic clues that assist us in detecting the representational system a person is using. Words that denote certain representational systems (such as "tone," "voice," "feel," "see," and "looks" in the above examples) are called *predicates*. Following are examples of common predicates within each of the representational systems. (Gustatory and olfactory are combined because most people do not make experiential distinctions between the two.)

VISUAL   clear, focus, picture, envision, hazy, glare, show, watch, view, look, glimpse

KINESTHETIC   feel, warm, grasp, stumble, smooth, rough, firm, grope, relaxed, pressure

AUDITORY   hear, harmony, loud, chatter, whine, tune, listen, talk, shout, amplify

OLFACTORY/GUSTATORY   taste, flavor, bitter, stink, smell, reek, tang, essence, savor

Consider the role representational systems play in the following example of an interior designer, Dean, gathering information from Brian and Sue about the redecoration of their living room.

Dean: What did you have in mind?

Sue: I want the room to be very comfortable.

Dean: Well, how would you know it was comfortable?

Sue: You know, *soft and warm*; you can *flop down* anywhere.

Dean: That sound all right to you, Brian?

Brian: Well, I don't know. I wouldn't be comfortable if it *looked* cluttered.

Dean: Cluttered?

Brian: You know, pillows everywhere.

Dean: Oh, so what would be comfortable for you?

Brian: The spaces need to be *clearly* defined. I don't mind warm *colors* at all, but they need to be clean-edged, *bright, distinct*.

Certainly Brian's and Sue's criterial equivalences for a comfortable living room are different, but also striking is their specification of particular representational systems for the fulfillment of their criteria. For Sue, comfort is fulfilled *kinesthetically* (soft, warm, flop down). Brian's experience of comfort, however, is fulfilled *visually* (looked, clearly, colors, bright, distinct).

Identifying pertinent representational system information, then, is a matter of simply detecting the predicates your subjects use when they describe their tests, criteria, and criterial equivalences.[1]

Reference Category

The reference category specifies the *data base* you are using to evaluate your criteria within a particular operative format. References may be from the past, present, or future; actual or constructed; and personal or informational. When eliciting references we ask our subject to consider the basis—the experiences and information sources—he is using in evaluating a criterion. Questions that elicit this information include the following.

On what do you base your conclusion (or decision, or feeling, etc.) that there is [criterion]?

What information are you using (or did you use) to know that you are [criterion]?

We ask questions like these for each of the criteria within the operative format because the data base for different criteria may be different even within the same test. As the subject describes his references, we attend to the verb tenses used in the description. Those verb tenses tell us whether the references are from the past, present, or future.

ML: On what do you base your conclusion that you aren't a good student?

Art: On all the times I *have tried* and *failed*.

Art is using past references, as indicated by the past tense "have tried" and "failed."

ML: What information are you using to know that you have learned something new?

Sue: Easy. How I *will be* more effective in my life.

Sue is using future references, as indicated by the future tense "will be."

In making this distinction it is necessary to separate out information about the references themselves from any introduction to or explanations about the references.

ML: On what did you base your decision?

Jim: Well, on how things could turn out for the best. That's what I did last time, anyway.

Both the future and past time frames are represented in this example, but each is descriptive of a different aspect of Jim's experience. When Jim is actually saying what his reference is ("how things could turn out for the best") he reveals through the future tense "could" that he is using a future reference.

The past tense "did" belongs to an explanatory phrase that came *after* he had specified the reference itself. This is not to say that your subjects will always respond by embedding their specification of references in introductions and explanations. But this does sometimes occur, and so before noting the time frame of a reference you need to carefully pick the description of the reference itself out of the rest of your subject's responses.

Actual and Constructed References   It is usually obvious from the description of a reference itself whether it was taken from actual or constructed experience. As we described in Chapter 5, if the reference is a future one, then you know it is constructed. Likewise, if the reference is one of imagining having someone else's feelings, perceptions, or experience, then it is also constructed. If there is any doubt about whether the reference is actual or constructed, you can elicit this information by asking,

Did you actually experience that (or, Did this really happen), or did you imagine it, or read or hear about it and imagine it?

Remember, what you are ascertaining here is not whether the reference *seems* real, but whether or not it has its source in actual experience.

Personal and Informational References   Separating personal from informational references involves having your subject distinguish between having the sensations and emotions that are *of* a reference experience, and simply knowing about those sensations and emotions *without having or re-experiencing* them. The elicitation of this distinction involves questions such as,

As you recall that do you have the feelings you had then, or do you just remember that it happened?

As you imagine that, do you feel what it would feel like to be doing it, or do you see yourself doing it, or maybe just describe to yourself what you would be doing?

Is this just information to you, or is it blood and bone experience?

Do you have sensations of being there, or do you simply remember *that* you were there?

Are you feeling what it would feel like to *be* that person, or are you describing to yourself what their experience must be?

Questions patterned after these examples provide your subject with both possibilities (personal and informational) as well as the contrast between the two, thus helping them to distinguish between the two. This help is often not necessary, however. People need not be conscious of their internal processes in order to report those processes accurately. We have found that the following question is often all that is needed to elicit the information regarding whether a reference is personal or informational.

What are you paying attention to when you are [making the evaluation]?

We then attend to the person's response to discover whether or not it reveals sensory and emotional responses that are congruent with the situation he or she is evaluating. For instance, suppose we are chatting with a friend who is excited about an upcoming date. In response to our asking, "What are you paying attention to when you think about the time you will have?" she responds, "I'm excited—I can already feel his lips on mine." She is obviously using a personal reference, attending to sensations and feelings that go with being with her beau. Suppose another friend, in the same situation, responded, "I notice that people there seem to be enjoying themselves, that I'm mixing very well with the newcomers— those kinds of things. I guess I'll find out what kind of time I have when I get there." This second person is using an informational reference—she is attending to perceptions, cognitive processes, and external behaviors, but not to the sensations or emotions that go along with her upcoming date.

The following excerpts contain examples of elicitation and detection for all of the various references. As before, we have added italics to help mark key words and phrases. In addition, some of the reference information will be displayed in the operative formats in which it actually occurs. This use of the notation will help familiarize you with the effect of the interaction of references with the other variables.

In a previous section we elicited from Ray some information about his ability to plan enjoyable birthday parties for children. Ray makes past tests with respect to the criteria of "what I would have liked" and "what would have made me happy."

ML: Ray, what are you using as evidence for what would have made you happy?

Ray: I just remember *what it was like to be six and what I wanted my mom to do for me.* I also remember *other kids' parties I went to,* which ones I liked, which ones I didn't.

These are past actual references, experiences from his personal history.

ML: As you recall that, do you have the feelings of being six and wanting your mom to do certain things, or do you just recall that you wanted your mom to do those things?

Ray: Oh it's *back to being six. I feel the excitement, the expectation.* You know.

Since Ray has the feelings he had when he was actually six, this is a past actual personal reference.

ML: As you recall the other kids' parties—the ones you liked or didn't like—do you have the feelings of being at those parties, or do you just remember *that* you did or didn't like them?

Ray: I remember feeling bored at some of them, happy at others.

ML: Yes, but when you remember the boring ones do you feel something of that boredom now?

Ray: Oh, I see. *Yes, I do.*

Again, Ray's past actual reference is personal.

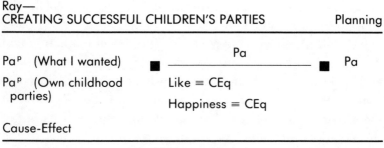

Ray—
CREATING SUCCESSFUL CHILDREN'S PARTIES   Planning

Pa^P (What I wanted)   ■ ——————— Pa   ■ Pa
Pa^P (Own childhood   Like ≡ CEq
        parties)
                              Happiness ≡ CEq

Cause-Effect

What kids would enjoy

Ann's approach to planning children's parties is quite different. Her planning involves future tests in relation to "the child's happiness" and "everything working." Her criterial equivalence for "happiness" is that the children are laughing, smiling, and engaged in friendly activities with each other. Her criterial equivalence for "everything working" is that the party can be done within the time and budget available, and that it will not require too much effort.

ML: How do you know that what you are planning will make your child happy?

Ann: *I've seen her at quite a few parties* so I have a pretty good idea of what she has liked and what she hasn't.

ML: Anything else?

Ann: Well, *I ask her about the plans* as I come up with them to sort of check them out with her.

Ann describes two references. One is a past actual reference ("I've seen her . . ."), and the other is a present actual reference ("I ask her . . .").

ML: What are you attending to as you get her feedback about the party plans?

Ann: Attending to? *What she has to say.*

ML: And as you watched her at other parties?

Ann: *Whether she looked* happy, having a good time or not . . . and *what she had to say* afterwards about it.

ML: Do you have any of the feelings she probably would have been having at the parties?

Ann: No, *just my own curiosity.*

Ann's response includes nothing about vicariously experiencing her daughter's sensations or emotions. What she was attending to was her daughter's behavior, indicating that her past and present actual references are informational.

ML: How do you know that what you are planning will work, that there will be enough time and money and effort?

Ann: I just imagine *what it will take.*

ML: And if it will take more time or money or effort than you have?

Ann: Well, then I have to change the plans.

Ann uses future constructed references as the basis for her tests regarding "everything working."

ML: What are you attending to when you imagine the time involved, the money, and how much you will have to do to get things done?

Ann: How crazy things might get . . . whether it's going to knock me out or whether I am going to get through it fairly relaxed.

ML: OK, so how crazy, and will you be relaxed. As you imagine carrying out the plan for the party do you actually feel the craziness if it does seem crazy, or feel relaxed if it seems more relaxed? Or is that just something you see happening in the pictures you're making in your head?

Ann: Uhh, *I feel it.*

Ann experiences some of the feelings that she would have if she were actually engaged in the activities she is imagining. Her future constructed references, then, are personal.

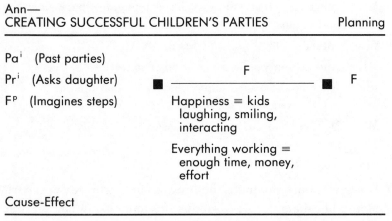

Ann—
CREATING SUCCESSFUL CHILDREN'S PARTIES   Planning

Pa^i (Past parties)
Pr^i (Asks daughter)
F^p (Imagines steps)

F

F

Happiness ≡ kids laughing, smiling, interacting

Everything working ≡ enough time, money, effort

Cause-Effect

What kids would enjoy

In a previous section we introduced Morgan, who is skilled at editing educational videotapes. We already know that when editing she makes future tests with respect to the criterion of clarity. Her criterial equivalence for clarity is that the teaching points are separate and each point follows naturally from the previous ones.

> ML: How do you know when you've edited a segment so that it is clear?
>
> Morgan: *I watch* the segment through the eyes of a beginner *and see if it is clear to I-the-beginner.*

Morgan bases her evaluation of whether or not a particular segment will be clear on her imagined perception of how the segment appears through the eyes of a beginner. This is a present constructed reference.

> ML: What are you attending to as you-the-beginner watch the segment?
>
> Morgan: As I said, is it clear? Does each point naturally follow and build on the previous points?
>
> ML: So when something isn't clear you just note that fact, or do you also feel the confusion of the beginner?
>
> Morgan: Oh yeah, that's what comes first. I'm just sitting there watching the segment as a novice and it's when *I get confused or irritated or bored* that *I look at it again and start thinking, "Now why wasn't that clear there?"*

For Morgan, then, the present reference experience of watching the videotape as a beginner is personal, and when something seems unclear to her she shifts to viewing the videotape from her own perspective as an editor, making that new reference present, actual, and informational.

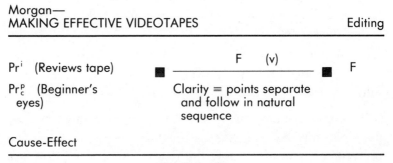

Morgan—
MAKING EFFECTIVE VIDEOTAPES   Editing

Pr^i (Reviews tape)

Pr^p_c (Beginner's eyes)

Clarity ≡ points separate and follow in natural sequence

Cause-Effect

Existing edits

We met Bill earlier as someone who is adept at bargaining for works of art. We already know that two criteria that Bill tests for when bargaining are "relative value" and "lowest possible price." To Bill, the relative value is the worth of this piece of art in relation to the price of other works by the artist. The lowest possible price means the best price he can get *while still maintaining a good relationship with the dealer.* Both of these criteria are evaluated in the present. The significance to Bill of adding the criterion of maintaining a good relationship is that it means "the dealer will want to do business with me *again* and give me preferential treatment." For the criterion of maintaining a good relationship, then, he makes a future test.

ML: What do you use as evidence for what is the lowest price that you can get it for?

Bill: Essentially, that's determined by what I know about *what this particular artist's work has been selling for* and by *the kind of responses I'm getting from the dealer as we dicker.*

Bill's reference for lowest possible price is past actual informational as to the artist's price range, and present actual as to the dealer's responses to Bill's offer.

ML: What responses are you speaking of?

Bill: Oh, are we in rapport, does he seem to be offended by an offer, is he eager, is he too eager—those kinds of things.

ML: OK, well how do you know that he's eager as compared to too eager, say?

Bill: I can see it in his eyes—if they're hard and abnormally large, then he's too eager. Also if the tempo of speech picks up or if his movements are a little jerky and exaggerated.

ML: Are you yourself feeling what it would feel like to be too eager when you see and hear those responses?

Bill: *No way. I just notice them and take it from there.*

Bill simply notices the dealer's responses without feeling the same way he imagines the dealer must be feeling. The present reference regarding the dealer's responses, then, is informational.

ML: And what do you attend to that lets you know you are going to have a good relationship with this dealer in the future?

Bill: Same thing. How he looks, sounds, and how he acts.

So Bill's present informational reference of the dealer's responses also acts as the reference for his test about a future relationship with that dealer.

Bill—
BUYING WORKS OF ART WELL   Negotiating

Pa^i (Artist's price
   history)

Pr^i (Dealer's
   responses)

$$Pr \quad (v, a)$$

Relative value ≡ par
  with other work

Lowest possible
  price ≡ still
■ maintains good ■ Compelling
  relationship   Category

$$F \quad (v, a)$$

Good relationship ≡
  want my business,
  get preferential
  treatment

Tough but fair → preferential treatment; Pr → F

What to pay

Hazel always gets her tax returns done on time. This involves the activity of planning, which itself is made up of two operative formats. The first is a present assessment of what needs to be done. The criterial equivalence for "needs to be done" is anything that will have unpleasant consequences if it is not done. The second step is the sequencing of things to do, which is a future test with respect to the criterion of "easiest." The criterial equivalence for easiest is the sequence that will take the least time and effort.

ML: How do you know what needs to be done?

Hazel: By *checking the list* my accountant gives me, and also I remember a lot of *what needed to be done last year.*

ML: What are you remembering when you recall what needed to be done last year?

Hazel: Oh, checking off the business calls from the phone bills, getting lunch receipts from business trips, post office receipts—that kind of stuff.

For her "needs to be done" operative format Hazel uses a present actual informational reference (checking the list), and a past actual informational reference (what needed to be done last year).

ML: How do you know what will be the easiest sequence?

Hazel: *I imagine what has to be done and the different ways of doing it.* If I don't know, then *I ask my accountant or someone who seems to know* about these things.

ML: As you imagine what has to be done are you simply listing what has to be done, or are you seeing yourself doing those things, or are you feeling what it would feel like to be doing those things?

Hazel: *I see myself do it.*

ML: Is there anything else you use—any information or experiences as a basis upon which to decide what needs to be done and what the easiest sequence is to do it in?

Hazel: Let me think. No, I think that's it.

In evaluating for the easiest sequence, Hazel uses a future informational reference (imagine what has to be done; I see myself do it), and sometimes a present informational reference (I ask).

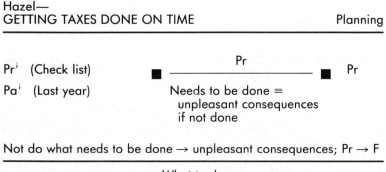

Hazel—
GETTING TAXES DONE ON TIME   Planning

Pr^i (Check list)   Pr
Pa^i (Last year)   Needs to be done ≡
                            unpleasant consequences
                            if not done

Not do what needs to be done → unpleasant consequences; Pr → F

What to do

Hazel—
GETTING TAXES DONE ON TIME   Planning

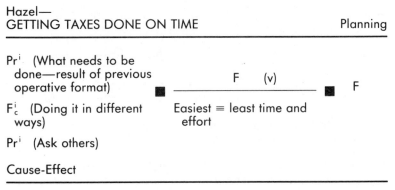

Pr^i (What needs to be done—result of previous operative format)

F$_c^i$ (Doing it in different ways)

Pr^i (Ask others)

F (v)   F

Easiest ≡ least time and effort

Cause-Effect
─────────────────────────────
What sequence to use

   Sarah votes in every election; she would feel irresponsible if she did not vote. Sarah is making a future test with respect to the criterion of "responsibility," the criterial equivalence of which is, in this context, the act of voting.

ML: What do you use as a basis for knowing that you'd feel irresponsible if you didn't vote?

Sarah: *I always go back to my mom feeling guilty about not voting for a school bond once when I was a kid.* It had just been one of those days and she was too busy. She really felt terrible and it made quite an impression on me.

ML: So you think that you would feel the same way?

Sarah: Oh yeah. I always do vote, but *I know if I didn't I would feel terrible.* Our parents taught us that voting was both a great privilege and an essential responsibility.

Sarah mentions two references. The first is a past actual reference of her mother's response after having failed to vote, and the other is a future constructed reference of how she would feel if she did not vote.

ML: You said that your mom not voting made an impression on you. When you remember her not voting what are you paying attention to?

Sarah: Her pain and shame at not having done what she knew she should have done.

241

> ML: As you remember do you feel her pain and shame, or do you just know that she felt that way?
>
> Sarah: *I feel it—the shame.* That's what makes it so powerful for me.

Her past reference of her mother is, therefore, personal.

> ML: OK. Since you have always voted, how do you know you'd feel terrible if you didn't vote?
>
> Sarah: Uh, good question. Well, I know that *I always have felt good when I have voted,* and *when I imagine not voting I imagine feeling terrible . . . irresponsible.*

Sarah describes another reference—the past actual reference of how she has felt as the result of voting—and has specified that the future reference of not voting is personal (I imagine *feeling* terrible).

> ML: When you recall how good you have felt when you have voted in the past do you feel those same feelings now, or do you just know that you felt that way?
>
> Sarah: I feel it now.

The past reference of how she has felt after voting is, therefore, also a personal reference.

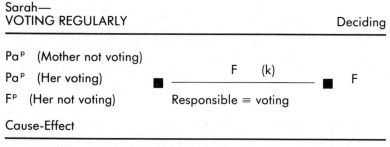

Sarah—
VOTING REGULARLY   Deciding

Pa^P (Mother not voting)
Pa^P (Her voting)   F   (k)   F
F^P (Her not voting)   Responsible ≡ voting

Cause-Effect

Whether or not to vote

Unlike Sarah, Willie rarely votes. From our elicitation we know that the operative format underlying his decision not to vote includes two tests. One is a future test regarding whether or not his vote would make a difference, and the other is a present test regarding whether or not he likes any of the candidates.

ML: What do you mean by "make a difference"?

Willie: That I can *see some change* in things, that four years from now things aren't the same as they are now or as they were four years ago.

ML: And how do you know when you like a candidate?

Willie: Know? I just know. If I like him, *I like him.*

His criterial equivalence for difference is "seeing some change," and for the criterion of "like," the equivalence is an emotional state of liking.

ML: How do you know that your vote won't make a difference?

Willie: I just know it.

ML: How? What do you see, hear, or feel on the outside or inside that is evidence of that?

Willie: Look, *there are so many people.* I'm just one person. Do the arithmetic yourself and you'll see my vote doesn't matter. Besides, no matter which party gets elected, *the same things are going on now as have always gone on.*

The references indicated here are a present actual reference (there are so many people), and a past reference regarding the results of past administrations.

ML: How do you know that?

Willie: I have a lifetime of experience. Eisenhower, Johnson, Nixon, Ford, Carter, Reagan . . . so what?

ML: Do you remember them when you consider voting?

Willie: Yeah. Vividly.

ML: What are you attending to when you remember those presidents?

Willie: *How they all did pretty much the same things* and how it didn't really matter what they did.

So, the past reference is informational.

ML: You were talking about the arithmetic involved. What are you attending to when you think about that?

Willie: *Just the numbers*—the big numbers.

The present reference, then, is also informational.

ML: I noticed that you left out Kennedy when you were listing the presidents.

Willie: I liked him.

ML: On what did you base your liking him?

Willie: I don't know, he seemed hopeful . . . sincere.

ML: And how did you know that?

Willie: Just watched and listened, watched and listened.

ML: And as you watched and listened, what were you watching for and listening to?

Willie: What he said, how he said it. *I felt so much trust* in him.

ML: Did you vote for him.

Willie: Yeah.

In evaluating whether or not he likes a candidate, Willie uses a present actual personal reference.

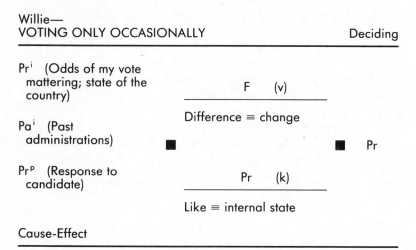

Willie—
VOTING ONLY OCCASIONALLY   Deciding

Pr^i (Odds of my vote mattering; state of the country)

$$F \quad (v)$$

Pa^i (Past administrations)

Difference ≡ change

Pr

Pr^p (Response to candidate)

$$Pr \quad (k)$$

Like ≡ internal state

Cause-Effect

Whether to vote

Cause-Effect

The cause-effect variable expresses the contingent relationships on which an individual is relying within a particular operative format. These contingent relationships can be between any combination of external behaviors, perceptions, emotions, cognitive processes, circumstances, and so on.

What characterizes a cause-effect is that "something" is believed to necessarily lead to "something else." Taking vitamin C cures colds, seeing other people happy makes me feel happy, concentrating on having a parking space causes one to be there when I need it, and being confronted with big tasks makes me perform better—these are all examples of cause-effects. They are all beliefs that the occurrence of one phenomenon is the natural or necessary *consequence* of the occurrence of some other phenomenon.

Cause-effect beliefs are an embodiment of past experience expressed as consequences. As generalizations about consequences, cause-effects provide the basis for either going toward or away from the causes of those consequences. Thus the person who has a cold and believes that vitamin C cures colds is, on account of that belief, disposed toward taking vitamin C. The person who does not want to feel bad and believes that seeing others in pain makes her feel bad is, on account of that belief, inclined to avoid people who are in pain. And the person who wants to perform better and believes that large tasks make him perform better is, on that account, disposed toward seeking out or creating large tasks.

Cause-effect beliefs are detected by attending to a person's use of any of a number of linguistic forms that presuppose cause-effect relationships. One of the two most common of these forms is "if . . . then . . . ."

If you join me, *then* I'll be happy.

If I know what I'm doing, *then* the job goes well.

He will be an asset, but only *if* he works hard.

He sees another way? *Then* he'll have to take it.

The if-then form presupposes that some "if" (the cause) leads to some consequence or "then" (the effect). As illustrated in the third and fourth examples above, the words "if" and "then" need not be used explicitly for the statement to have the form and significance of an if-then assertion.

In addition to this form, there are other linguistic forms that often mark a contingent relationship. The most common of these include "so," "therefore," "consequently," "because," and "when."

I've done things on time, *so* he will be relieved.

She has been making a lot of new contacts, *therefore* her business should pick up soon.

The *consequence* of his attention is that the job got done.

I'm happy *because* you're here.

Because I knew what I was doing, the job went well.

He will be an asset. This is *because* of his effort.

I'm happy *when* you're here.

When I knew what I was doing, the job went well.

He will be an asset, but only *when* he works hard.

The fact that a person uses "if-then," "so," "therefore," "consequently," "because," or "when" in describing the relationship between two occurrences does not necessarily mean that she has just described a cause-effect, however. Another possibility is that she is expressing a criterial equivalence. The person who says, "I like you because I enjoy being with you" may mean either "My enjoying being with you *causes* me to like you" (enjoyment → liking; cause-effect), or "My enjoying being with you is *how I know* that I like you" (liking ≡ enjoy being with you; CEq). Similarly, the statement, "If you're smiling, then you're happy," could mean either that smiling *causes* happiness, or that smiling *means* happiness.

Whether a person is speaking of a cause-effect or a criterial equivalence is often evident from the context in which the statement is made, how it is said, and what has already been elicited. If you have any doubt about whether your subject is expressing a criterial equivalence or a cause-effect, you can elicit the distinction between the two by asking,

Are you saying that [smiling] *causes* you to be [happy], or that how you know that you are [happy] is that you are [smiling]?

There is one linguistic form that is not equivocal, however. This form is marked by the use of verbs that *presuppose* causal relationships. These include the following.

Seeing you *causes* me to be happy.

Seeing you *makes* me happy.

Seeing you *results* in my being happy.

Seeing you *produces* my happiness.

Seeing you *creates* my happiness.

Statements that are of the form "Something [causal verb] something" are invariably statements of a belief in a particular cause-effect.

In addition to the content of a cause-effect (that is, what causes what), each cause-effect presupposes a causal relationship between time frames as well—for instance, that something in the present will cause something in the future, or that something in the past is the cause of the something in the present. Like all of the other variables, perceived causal relationships between time frames organize perceptions and thinking along certain lines and thereby contribute significantly to the behavior that is manifested as the result of the operative format in which that cause-effect plays a part. For example, "If I *had worked* hard I *would be* a success" is not at all the same statement, nor will it lead to the same responses, as "If I *work* hard I *will be* a success." Detection of presupposed causal relationships regarding the time frames is based upon picking out the tenses of the verbs the subject uses in identifying the cause and the effect.

"The way my parents *treated* me is the reason that I *am* the way I am."

Treatment → way I am; Pa → Pr

"If I *work* hard then I *will* eventually succeed."

Work → success; Pr → F

"I *will* always be appreciative because of what you *taught* me."

Lesson → appreciation; Pa → F

When cause-effects are not evident in what a subject has already said, you can test for and elicit them using questions of the following form.

Why is [the criterion] important?

What makes [the criterion] important?

These questions compel the subject to provide justifications for the criteria he is using; and those criteria are often in the form of a cause-effect. For example, in describing how he plans a project, Alan revealed that a criterion he uses in selecting materials is "on hand."

ML: What makes using on-hand materials important?

Alan: Using what's on hand forces me to be a little more creative about how I build things.

(Using what's on hand → more creative; Pr → Pr)

The justification for Alan's use of on-hand materials is the causal relationship he perceives between using those materials and the quality of his work.

The following examples demonstrate a variety of methods for eliciting and detecting cause-effects, as well as several different types of cause-effects and their influence within an operative format. Our first subject is Sally, who, as we have seen, responds to compliments with embarrassment and self-deprecation.

ML: Are you always embarrassed and self-deprecating when someone gives you a compliment?

Sally: Uh, no, not always. *If* I'm comfortable with them *then* I take compliments pretty well.

Sally specifies the cause-effect relationship between being comfortable and taking compliments well (comfortable → take compliments well; Pr → Pr). This cause-effect is expressed in the "if-then" form.

Mary responds to pressure situations that involve deadlines by slowing down and becoming very careful about what she does.

ML: What do you slow down for?

Mary: It's so I can be thorough about what I'm doing. I know that any mistakes I make will *make it necessary* for me to do it all over again, and I hate that.

Mary operates with a cause-effect relationship between making mistakes and having to do it again (make mistakes → do again; Pr → F). The phrase "make it necessary" indicates the cause-effect.

In describing the processes he goes through in writing fiction, Paul identified a criterion he is trying to fulfill in his writing as that of creating a "complete experience."

ML: What do you mean by a complete experience?

Paul: By that I mean that every sense is filled—what I see, hear, smell, taste, feel. *Otherwise* I can be distracted.

The cause-effect here is between all of the senses being filled and being fully attentive (filled senses → full attention; Pr → Pr). "Otherwise" is the same as saying "*if* not, *then*."

In describing how she goes about editing educational videotapes, Morgan said, "Well, it has to be clear. Everything has to be clear to the viewer *if* they are going to learn." Morgan is expressing her belief in a cause-effect relationship between clarity and learning (clarity → learning; Pr → F). As with Sally, the cause-effect is in the "if-then" form—*if* they are going to learn, *then* it has to be clear.

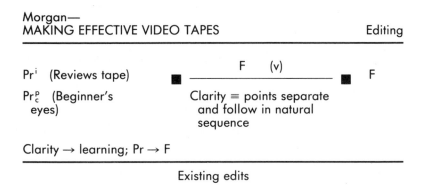

Morgan—
MAKING EFFECTIVE VIDEO TAPES   Editing

Pr^i (Reviews tape)

Pr_c^p (Beginner's eyes)

F   (v)   F

Clarity ≡ points separate and follow in natural sequence

Clarity → learning; Pr → F

Existing edits

In describing her regular voting behavior, Sarah mentions her reference experience of seeing her mother feel terrible after not voting.

ML: So you think that you would feel the same way?

Sarah: Oh yeah. I always do vote, but I know that *if* I didn't *I'd* feel terrible.

The cause-effect is between not voting and feeling terrible (not vote → feel terrible; Pr → F).

Sarah—
VOTING REGULARLY   Deciding

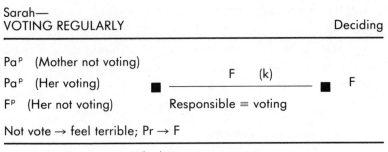

Pa^P (Mother not voting)

Pa^P (Her voting)   F   (k)   F

F^P (Her not voting)   Responsible ≡ voting

Not vote → feel terrible; Pr → F

Whether or not to vote

It is clear from the things that Willie had to say about voting that he does not perceive any causal relationship between his voting and his criterion of making a difference, or between who gets elected and making a difference. Does this mean, then, that Willie has no cause-effects in relation to making a difference?

> ML: From what you said so far, the fact that you can't see that your voting makes a difference leaves you unmotivated to vote. What makes making a difference so important?
>
> Willie: *If* I can vote and see that my vote counted, *then I know* that I count too.

Instead of a cause-effect, Willie responds by describing how seeing his vote count at least partially satisfies his criterial equivalence for "I count" (if . . . then I *know*). In other words, at least one of the ways that Willie knows that he counts is by seeing his vote count. Although this is an interesting criterial equivalence, it is not part of his operative format for deciding whether or not to vote (though perhaps it would be relevant to the operative format he uses when evaluating his own self-worth).

> ML: From what you said before, though, even if you could see that your vote counted you still wouldn't vote because it doesn't seem to you to make any difference who gets elected.
>
> Willie: I guess that's so.
>
> ML: Well then what makes making a difference important in terms of who gets elected?
>
> Willie: Because nobody, no one party or person has all the

answers. But *if* someone got in there who really did things differently *then that would make* everyone think about what they were doing and consider new ways to do things.

Willie does believe in a cause-effect relationship between doing things differently and catalyzing new approaches (different → catalyze new approaches; Pr → F).

ML: You said you also consider whether or not you like the candidate. In fact, you voted for Kennedy because you liked him. What makes liking a candidate important?

Willie: Because *if* you like him *then* at least you'll be able to feel that you could relate to that person, even if you don't like what they're doing.

Willie expresses a cause-effect relationship between liking a person and feeling you could relate to that person (like → able to relate; Pr → F).

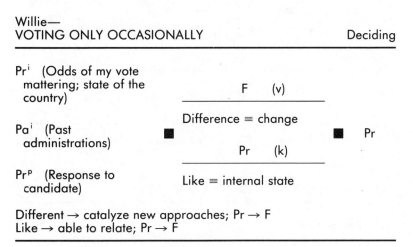

Willie—
VOTING ONLY OCCASIONALLY   Deciding

Pr^i (Odds of my vote mattering; state of the country)

F   (v)

Pa^i (Past administrations)

Difference ≡ change

Pr   (k)

Pr

Pr^p (Response to candidate)

Like ≡ internal state

Different → catalyze new approaches; Pr → F
Like → able to relate; Pr → F

Whether to vote

Compelling Category and Subordination

The compelling category specifies which of the tests that are made in an operative format results in behavior. The significance of the compelling category is that, although it is possible to make many different representations and evaluations, some of those representations and evaluations will, more than others, lead to behavior.

To identify the time frame of the compelling category we need only know what the tests, criteria, and actual behavioral responses are for a particular operative format. The compelling category time frame will be the same as the time frame of the test that results in manifesting behavior. For example, the actual planning that Ray did for children's parties was a function of past tests he made regarding what made him happy as a child. What is compelling for him in this context, then, is the past.

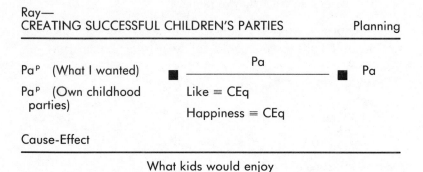

Ray—
CREATING SUCCESSFUL CHILDREN'S PARTIES   Planning

Pa^p (What I wanted)   ■ ——————— Pa ——————— ■ Pa
Pa^p (Own childhood   Like ≡ CEq
        parties)
                                    Happiness ≡ CEq

Cause-Effect

What kids would enjoy

Ann's planning, however, was the behavioral manifestation of *future tests* regarding happiness and everything working out.

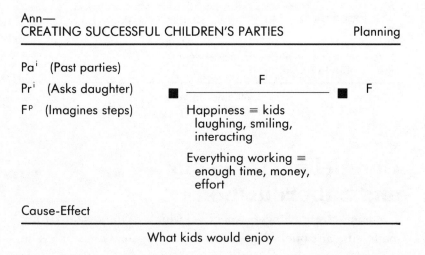

Ann—
CREATING SUCCESSFUL CHILDREN'S PARTIES   Planning

Pa^i (Past parties)
Pr^i (Asks daughter)   ■ ——————— F ——————— ■ F
F^p (Imagines steps)   Happiness ≡ kids
                                    laughing, smiling,
                                    interacting

                                    Everything working ≡
                                    enough time, money,
                                    effort

Cause-Effect

What kids would enjoy

If, as in these two previous examples, only one test is being made, then the time frame of the compelling category is, by default, the same as that test. It is often the case, however, that more than one test is being made within a particular operative format. Suppose that it is ten o'clock at night and that you have not yet begun a report that is due tomorrow morning. In deciding whether or not to stay up and do the report you consider both that you *are tired and want to go to bed* (present test) and that you *will be called on the carpet tomorrow if you do not have the report done* (future test). In order to come to a decision you need to subordinate one of those tests. You will either go to bed and face the carpet tomorrow (subordination of the future criteria), or drink coffee tonight and have your report in hand tomorrow (subordination of the present criteria).

In describing his voting behavior, Willie provided another example of subordination. The result of his future test regarding whether his voting will make a difference and his present test regarding whether he likes a candidate is that he rarely votes. Usually the results of those two tests are compatible with one another (that is, he does not see that his voting will make a diffrence *and* he does not like any of the candidates). Willie offered an exception, however, when he revealed that he had voted for John Kennedy because "I liked him."

ML: When you voted for Kennedy did you believe that your vote would make a difference?

Willie: No, not really.

ML: Well, did you think that Kennedy would make a difference?

Willie: To be honest, I'd say no. The odds were against him, but I liked him, so, what the hell, I voted.

Willie had to subordinate one of his competing tests. For Willie in this context, liking a candidate is a more compelling experience than his calculations about what impact his vote will have, and so he subordinates the future for the present. That he votes only occasionally is in large part due to the fact that he rarely finds a candidate he likes.

Willie—
VOTING ONLY OCCASIONALLY   Deciding

Pr^i (Odds of my vote
   mattering; state of the
   country)

$$\frac{F \quad (v)}{}$$

Difference ≡ change

Pa^i (Past   ■   ■   Pr
   administrations)

$$Pr \quad (k)$$

Pr^p (Response to   Like ≡ internal state
   candidate)

Different → catalyze new approaches; Pr → F
Like → able to relate; Pr → F

Whether to vote

During the elicitation of an operative format involving more than one test, your subject may not volunteer an example of subordination. In that case, you won't be able to identify which of the tests is more compelling. An example of this was Bill's operative format when negotiating for works of art. When negotiating he makes two tests. One is a present test regarding relative value and getting the lowest price, and the other is a future test regarding having a good business relationship with the dealer. Since Bill did not give us any examples in which these tests cannot both be satisfied, we don't know which of those tests he finds more compelling and which he would subordinate.

We could find out which of the tests is more compelling, however, by asking, "Recall some time when you thought you could get a piece of artwork at a good price but only at the expense of not maintaining a good relationship with the dealer. What did you do?" Or we could get him to respond to an imagined situation by asking, "Suppose you could get a piece of artwork that you wanted for a really good price, but that doing so would jeopardize your relationship with the dealer. What would you do?" Either of these approaches will create a situation of competing tests, and the answer will tell us which of the tests is more compelling.

ML: What if you were in a position to persuade a dealer to sell you a piece at an extremely good price, but that if you did it would damage your long-term relationship?

Bill: I wouldn't do it, no matter how good the price.

ML: Have you ever been in a situation like that?

Bill: Sure, but it just wasn't worth ruining a working relationship that might someday be even more valuable in terms of getting good treatment, first look at new pieces, and so on.

And so, if necessary, Bill subordinates the present for the future. The future possibilities of the good relationship are more compelling for him than is the good deal in the present.

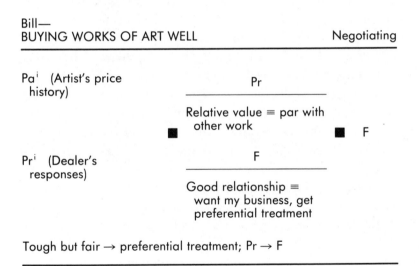

Bill—
BUYING WORKS OF ART WELL   Negotiating

Pa^i (Artist's price history)   Pr
_____

Relative value ≡ par with
other work   ■ F
■

Pr^i (Dealer's responses)   F
_____

Good relationship ≡
want my business, get
preferential treatment

Tough but fair → preferential treatment; Pr → F

What to pay

A final note about the compelling category and subordination: The act of having to subordinate a test and its attendant criteria generally creates internal conflict. *If we detect indications of internal conflict as a subject describes his tests, criteria, and behavioral responses, we check to see if he is evaluating anything else within the operative format that he has not yet described to us.*

Summary of Elicitation and Detection Procedures

The elicitation procedure for the EMPRINT method begins with specifying the desired outcome, followed by determining whether you need as a model someone for whom the outcome is intrinsic or for whom it is intentional, then selecting a subject, then gathering information from the subject as to the number and kinds of activities and operative formats that underlie that person's ability to manifest the outcome.

The *outcome* is the specification of what you would like to be able to do that at least one other person in the world is already able to do. Outcomes include not only external behavior, but emotional responses and cognitive processes as well. The outcome needs to be stated in the positive ("sleep soundly" versus "not be restless"), and needs to be specified as to the context in which you want to manifest it.

Intrinsic behaviors are those that an individual has coincidentally acquired as the natural result of his or her life experiences, while *intentional behaviors* are those that an individual has sought out and installed in him or herself. The primary difference between intentional and intrinsic behaviors is that the acquisition of an intentional behavior is almost always preceded by a set of *precursive activities* that include such considerations as motivation, commitment, planning, and so on. The operative formats underlying either intrinsic or intentional behaviors will probably be useless to you *if* you do not already have precursive responses that are congruent with engaging and utilizing those operative formats.

The selection of a subject to model involves finding someone who does what you want to be able to do in the contexts in which you want to be able to do it. Furthermore, if you need the precursive responses your subject will also need to have the outcome behavior as the result of intentional (rather than intrinsic) acquisition. If at all possible, witness or create a demonstration of your subject's ability to actually engage in the behavior you want to model. Also, if possible, model at least three people who manifest the outcome behavior in order to sort out the significant patterns of operative formats.

Activities are the behaviors that combine to make possible the manifestation of the outcome behavior. Each activity is the result of one or more operative formats. *Elicitation* of the sequence of activities and operative formats begins with asking the subject to describe how he goes about accomplishing the outcome. *Detection* of the activities and operative formats depends upon recognizing linguistic clues in the subject's description that specify different behaviors. Each distinct activity or operative format is usually marked as a phrase and/or by the use of such conjunctions as "then" and "and then." Additional or overlooked steps are elicited by asking, "Is there anything you have to do *before* you _____?" and "Once you have done _____, are you then ready to go on to the next step?"

The *operative format* is a set of seven variables that can be specified by means of a combination of detection and elicitation skills. The most efficient and useful sequence for the elicitation of these variables begins with tests and criteria, followed by criterial equivalences, references, cause-effects, and subordination. Remember, however, that much of the information specifying these variables is simultaneously present in the descriptions a subject offers about his experience, and so the information is available to those who are adept at detecting the variables without necessarily resorting to the recommended sequence.

The time frame of the test and criteria is generally detected and elicited together since the test *is* the application of criteria to a specific time frame. *Criteria* are any standards that are applied to, or used within, a particular context, and the *test time frame* is detected by attending to the verb tenses used in specifying those criteria ("Will I be happy?": criterion of "happy"; future test). Elicitation of criteria is accomplished with questions that ask the subject to consider the standards he uses in a particular context ("What is important to you when you [behavior]?"; "When you [behavior], what are you evaluating?"). The time frame of the test is elicited by asking questions that direct your subject to specifically attend to his evaluations in relation to the past, present, and future ("Are you evaluating the past, present, or future?" "Are you attending

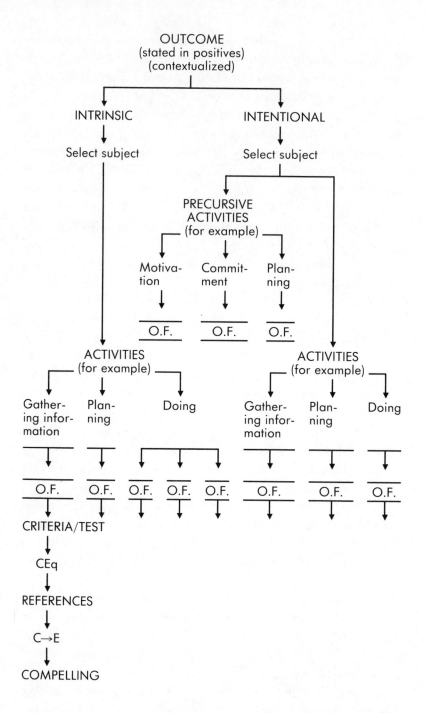

General Elicitation Sequence

to [criterion] in the past, [criterion] in the present, or [criterion] in the future?").

Criterial equivalence is detected when a subject either explicitly or implicitly explains what he has to see, hear, and/or feel in order to know that a criterion is fulfilled. Explicit descriptions of criterial equivalences can usually be detected by the subject's use of linguistic forms such as "[criterion] *means* [criterial equivalence]", or "When [criterial equivalence] I *know* that [criterion]." Elicitation of criterial equivalence involves asking your subject to specify how he knows when a specific criterion is being fulfilled ("What does [criterion] mean to you?" "How do you know when you are [criterion]?").

References normally require elicitation. References are elicited by asking variations of the question, "On what do you base your [test]?" Each reference will be characterized by being from one of the time frames; by its authenticity (either something that actually happened or that was constructed); and by emotional involvement (either personal or informational). The time frame of the reference is detected by the verb tense the subject applies to a particular reference. Whether the reference is actual or constructed is detected by the context and your subject's descriptions of his experience. If the distinction is not clear, it can be elicited by asking, "Did you actually experience that, or did you imagine it, or did you perhaps read or hear about it and imagine it?" All future references are constructed. Personal and informational references can often be detected by attending to the presence (personal) or absence (informational) of sensory and emotion-specific words in your subject's description of that reference. The distinction can be made explicit by asking such questions as, "As you recall that, do you have the feelings that you had then, at the time, or do you just remember *that* it happened?"

Cause-effects are detected by listening for linguistic forms that indicate a presupposition of a contingent relationship between any two occurrences ("occurrences" being any experiences, behaviors, perceptions, situations, etc.). These linguistic forms include "if-then" constructions, "so," "therefore," "because," "when," and the class of verbs denoting causal relationships (such as "causes," "makes," "leads to," and so on).

Specification of the cause-effect includes not only the content of the relationship but the time frames as well (for example, $Pr \rightarrow F$). Time frame relationships of cause-effects are detected on the basis of the verb tenses that are used in conjunction with each "side" of the cause-effect ("If I run now, then I will be tired"; $Pr \rightarrow F$). The cause-effects that are relevant to a particular operative format are those that provide the experiential justification for the criteria. Cause-effects are elicited by asking a person to justify his criterion in terms of its consequences, using such questions as, "What makes [criterion] important?"

The *compelling category* time frame in an operative format is the same as the test that is manifested in behavior. When there are two or more irreconcilable tests, the test that is not subordinated (and therefore manifested in behavior) is the compelling test. The compelling test can be elicited by having the subject recall a situation in which his tests were irreconcilable, or by having him imagine such a situation.

This EMPRINT method elicitation procedure enables you to convert complex human behavior into a code that you can use as the basis for understanding, predicting, and transferring aptitudes to others, or replicating them in yourself. This coding process is rigorous. To gain facility in elicitation and detection you need to practice. And each time you practice you will be moving another step closer to gaining access to the storehouse of human competence.

12 Reproducing Competence

Once you have identified an outcome behavior worth modeling and made it appropriate for elicitation, found at least one other person who does it well, identified the underlying activities and operative formats, and elicited the variables for each of the operative formats, you are ready to transfer those operative formats to another person, or to adopt them yourself. This final stage bridges the gap between appreciating a skill or trait through comprehending its underlying structure, and the ability to reproduce that skill or trait in yourself or in others. The information and examples in this chapter are intended to act as such a bridge.

As we begin exploring how to transfer a skill it's important to remember that all skills, including character traits, are the manifestation of underlying operative formats. And operative formats are themselves made up of certain constellations of seven different internal processing variables. When you transfer a skill, then, what you are really transferring is one or more operative formats—the operative formats that result in that particular skill. And when you transfer an operative format, what you are really transferring is a set of variables— the variables that make up that particular operative format. Transferring any skill, therefore, is a matter of transferring individual variables, no matter how many operative formats are involved. The only difference between transferring a skill composed of one operative format and a more complex skill made up of many operative formats is how much time it takes. The more complex skill will take longer to transfer not because it is more difficult to accomplish, but because you are changing or placing into effect more variables.

What does it mean to "transfer a variable"? When you transfer a variable you install the use of that variable in a person's internal processing in a particular context. For example, if one of your business associates tests for the criterion "What could go wrong" every time you discuss a new opportunity, and you succeed at getting him to test instead for "Does this have merit," you have transferred a variable. You have installed a new criterion in the context of evaluating new opportunities. Before rushing into specific installation techniques and examples, we want to give an overview of the installation process.

Overview

In installing operative formats, you will do best if you concern yourself with one variable at a time. This process has the advantage of being relatively uncomplicated. For instance, suppose you have elicited from a successful colleague her operative formats for negotiation skills, and you now want to transfer those operative formats to a friend. If you try to teach your friend how to generate and use several of the variables of one of the operative formats at once (or worse, several operative formats at once), both of you will probably end up overwhelmed, and your friend will undoubtedly be confused. If on the other hand you introduce one variable at a time, *making sure that variable is in place before proceeding to the next*, it will be easy for your friend to follow your lead. Forcing too many variables on your friend at the same time and expecting him to be able to use them is like cranking up the volume on six different radios at once, all tuned to different music stations, and asking him to pay attention to the lyrics. Or it's like asking him to pay close attention to one of the sensations in his body while you have five other friends touch, tug, pull, and push him with varying intensity and in different directions at the same time. Remember, *when you transfer a skill, install one variable at a time.*

When you start to transfer a skill you may discover that many of the requisite variables are already in place. That a person does not manifest a particular behavior does not mean that he is not using at least some of the same variables that underlie the outcome behavior. For example, we were working with a husband and wife business team who often have very different responses to upcoming business meetings: he is optimistic and confident, she feels worried and inadequate. We discovered that both were making future tests of how the meeting would go, both were testing for the criterion of being successful, both had a future-to-future cause-effect that how they did in the meeting would determine whether or not they would be successful, the future was compelling for both, and they were using the same references. What was different? For her, success meant negotiating and securing agreement to a deal *by the end of the meeting.* As a result of this criterial equivalence, she would worry about failing and feel inadequate to the task if she could imagine *any* possibility of something getting in the way of concluding a deal before the meeting adjourned. Her partner knew he was going to be successful if he could imagine *taking a step* toward securing an agreement, and a step might include anything from responding to problems to making additional presentations to establishing a personal relationship that might pay off in the future. He could walk away from a meeting without shaking hands on a deal and not feel that he had failed. Each took their own criterial equivalence for granted, as most people do. It never occurred to either of them that the other had a different idea of what constituted success:

She: What if things don't work out?

He: What are you talking about? Of course they will. This is a great opportunity.

She: I just hope I don't blow it. It would be so easy to lose this one.

He: We haven't even met with them yet! Why do you always have to be so negative?

There was only one difference in their operative formats in this context, and when we showed her how to change her criterial equivalence for success to match his, she immediately became more resourceful. Not every change is this easy, of course. We also work with people whose operative formats in a particular situation are completely mismatched to the ones needed for the skill they desire. That does not disqualify them from being able to acquire the skill; it only means that more adjustments need to be made and therefore more time needs to be devoted to the process. Once you know what the variables are, the time involved in the acquisition of a complex skill comprising a dozen operative formats can be measured in hours spread out over several days. The acquisition of a skill comprising only a few operative formats can be accomplished in two or three hours. (The change we made with the woman in the above example took five minutes.)

Later in this chapter we present examples of how to change criterial equivalences, as well as methods for either changing or placing in effect all of the other variables. It is rarely the case that all of the variables in every operative format must be adjusted when transferring a skill. If you gain facility with all of the variables, however, and if you are willing to invest the time, you will have the tools you need to transfer any skill, to any person, in any context.

Once you are ready to install in yourself or someone else a particular skill, it is not necessary to first model the operative formats that you or that person are already using. For each skill you model using the EMPRINT method you will possess, if you have been thorough and followed all of the guidelines, a list of activities and operative formats that is plenary—a complete package. That is, you will have a recipe that lists all of the ingredients and includes all of the cooking instructions for that particular skill. You know how to make the dish, and you have all the ingredients. Nothing prevents you from clearing the workspace, hauling out the ingredients, and assembling the meal.

The recipes are like software programs for human beings. We all share the same biological and neurological "hardwiring," which allows us to perceive and evaluate information in the five sensory systems. We can see the things around us as well as make internal images, we can hear others talk as well as chat internally with ourselves. We can differentiate between cold and hot, heavy and light, smooth and rough, salty and bitter. We can recall music, emotions, sights, sounds, conversations, and so on. The information we are *actually processing* through our sensory systems in a particular context—the evaluations we are making, the memories we are recalling, the feelings we are attending to, and so on—is the software program we are using in that context. Change the software and you change the outcome. If you boot a word processing program into your computer you will get word processing. Boot up the program for PacMan and your computer will not change, but the task it performs *will* change. You can't use your computer to write a letter while the Pac-Man program is running. Operate the program for optimistic and confident and you will get optimistic and confident. Operate the program for worried and feeling inadequate and that is what you will get.

Once you have the recipe or program for a skill, you can proceed directly to putting it into effect. This is the approach we have taken in another of our books, *Know How: Guided Programs for Inventing Your Own Best Future*. That book contains instructional sequences that install in the reader the operative formats for several important life skills. These installation formats are worth studying. They contain hundreds of examples of our actually transferring each of the variables in the EMPRINT method. Most of the examples used throughout the rest of this chapter are from *Know How*. [1]

Another approach you can take when you want to install a new skill is to first identify the variables that you or someone else is using, then add or change only those variables that need changing, as we did with the businesswoman in the example given above. You are familiar with the method for determining the variables that a person is already using in a particular context; the method is the elicitation and detection process presented in the previous chapter. The only difference is that now you are using the same techniques for identifying existing activities, operative formats, and variables not to model a skill, but in order to determine what is already in place that can be used, and what needs to be added or changed. Because of the added elicitation step, this approach will take more time than the other, more direct, approach. Despite this apparent drawback, however, the second approach has one advantage, and is often our preference.

This advantage is exemplified in our previous example of the husband and wife business team. We could have simply elicited his operative format and then transferred it to her without first eliciting her operative format. After all, her operative format resulted in her feeling worried and inadequate, not an outcome that most people would consider a skill worth modeling. But there is a gem tucked away in a corner of her operative format. Before she goes into a meeting, she thoroughly considers potential objections and problems. As a result of this future test, she is well informed of any stumbling blocks that are in the way or are likely to occur. Her criterial equivalence was worth changing. However, the future test she makes is valuable and worth keeping. It provides her with a set of references she can use to plan for and head off possible difficulties. It's a test that her husband needed to temper his unbridled optimism. It's a test that many people could use, and we might have missed discovering it if we had not elicited her operative formats. Modeling operative formats from anyone, for any context, is likely to yield at least a few interesting pieces that are valuable either in some other context, or when used in the same context with a slightly different constellation of variables.

Once you know the operative formats you want to transfer, installing a skill using the EMPRINT method involves two main steps. The first is teaching your "student" (or yourself) how to access or generate each of the required variables. The second step consists of installing the variables through repetitive use—practice—and a special form of rehearsal called *future-pacing*.

Learning how to generate variables and then practicing using them is analogous to the process you would go through to learn a sport. For example, suppose you are on vacation at a resort that has several tennis courts. If you are attracted by the aggressive but fluid movement of the best players and the squeal of tennis shoes on the playing surface, but have never played tennis, you might introduce yourself to the resident pro and arrange for a beginning lesson. During that lesson the pro would explain the basics of the game. He would show you how to grasp your racket and how to move your feet, knees, shoulders, arms, and head when you want to hit a forehand or backhand. He would hit balls to you so you could practice your strokes. All the while he would be watching carefully, telling you when to bend your knees, where to look, when to move your right foot instead of your left, how and when to take your racket back, and so on. He knows the movements are new to you, and that you need practice to master them. He also knows that the form you use when you practice will be the form that gets installed, so he makes sure you are developing the right habits.

Like any beginner, you would be trying to concentrate on everything at once. You would probably be awkward and certainly not yet accomplished, but after your first lesson you would have an experience of what it is like to play tennis, at least at a novice level. As you continue to practice, the movements become more and more automatic, until you are playing tennis and are able to pay attention to other things, like strategy, without having to think about the basics at all. It is your practice—the repetition of the individual required movements—that is responsible for improvement and eventual mastery.

Similarly, when you teach someone how to generate variables and operative formats you need to appreciate that she is learning something new, and you need to help her practice until she gets the hang of it. Being with her as she practices a few times allows you to check to make sure she is generating and using the variables correctly. In other words, the installation procedure in the EMPRINT method does for mental aptitudes and abilities what other teaching methods have accomplished for physical skills such as skiing, golf, and tennis.

After your student has practiced her new operative format a few times, she will be familiar with the outcomes to expect from using it. You then need to make sure she will use the new operative format in the contexts in which she needs it. Connecting the operative format to future contexts is accomplished through future-pacing. Future-pacing is a form of mental rehearsal. By imagining actually being in the situations she expects to occur in the future, and imagining using her new operative format and fully manifesting the outcome behavior, she attaches the operative format to those future contexts. This additional practice helps ensure that she will automatically use the new operative format in the future.

The order in which variables are best installed is different from the order in which we suggested they should be elicited. When you model a skill to reveal its underlying variables, the process you are engaged in is analogous to taking apart a pocket watch to inspect and clean its works. You begin by removing the outer case, which gives you access to the first layer of wheels and springs. You then proceed one layer at a time, with each piece you remove revealing access to the next piece, until the task is completed. To rebuild the watch, you reassemble the parts in a different order than the one you used to take them out. The same is true for transferring a skill.

Each operative format resembles a separate structure, with the references and cause-effects forming a foundation for the tests, which together give the compelling time frame its continued support. If you were building a house you would pour the foundation first, and you would install the roof only after the walls were in place. Likewise, when you transfer a skill it is necessary to install the references and cause-effects first. These are the materials from which the tests are constructed. And because the compelling time frame is the manifestation of one or more tests that are being made, it would be inappropriate (if not useless) to concern yourself with the compelling category before installing the requisite tests.

One last point needs to be made to complete this overview of the installation process. The following is not an exhaustive presentation. Volumes could be written about the various methods for installing operative formats. There are many different themes that can be followed for installing variables, and there are variations on each of those themes. In our trainings we spend more time on installation than on any other aspect of the method; sometimes more time is devoted to installation theory and technique than is allotted to all of the other aspects combined. The topic of installation cannot be fully explored in one book, and certainly not in one chapter. Therefore only the basics are presented here.[2]

We now turn to the basic installation techniques for each variable. The variables are discussed in the order in which we suggest they be installed.

References

Whether you realize it or not, you are already proficient at getting others to use specific references for their evaluations, and you practice incessantly on your family, friends, and co-workers. You access the use of past references when you say to a child, "Before you do, you better remember what happened last time you hit your sister," or when you ask, "I know asparagus looks funny, but you thought broccoli looked funny the first time you saw it—but when you tasted it you liked it. Remember that?" You are requesting that your mate start using a present reference when you say, "I know you want to go out tonight, but just look at everything that needs to be done around the house," or "Is the laundry dry?" You are creating and bringing a future reference to the fore when you say to a colleague, "Just imagine how happy and relieved you're going to feel when you finish that report."

Past, present, and future references are accessed by asking questions or making statements that (1) in order to answer or respond, require that your subject consider or recall the information or experience you want referenced, and (2) contain the verb tense that is consistent with the time frame of the reference you want to access. For example, if you were installing a health-related operative format and wanted to access a past reference for having a particular level of stamina you might say, "Search through your *past* until you find an example of *having had* the kind of stamina you want to have again." If you were installing an operative format that required an evaluation of how a person is better off financially today than in the past, and therefore required a past reference, you might say, "*Recall* what your financial situation *was like five years ago.*" If you were installing an operative format that would result in a discouraged worker once again feeling encouraged and motivated you might access a past reference for hard work having paid off in the past, by asking, "When *have you worked* hard and *attained* a goal and, as a result, *enjoyed* a great amount of pleasure or satisfaction?" If you are installing an operative format for planning the best way to ask for a raise, one of the needed references would be past information about how the person's boss has responded in the past to similar requests, and you could access the information by asking, "How have you or any of your fellow employees successfully negotiated a raise from your boss in the past?"

The only difference when instructing a person to use a present reference is that of the verb tense you use in your questions and statements. Using the same examples as in the previous paragraph, if the operative format for implementing the plan for asking for a raise called for a present reference of the boss's responses in order to make tests for whether to continue or change the plan, you might say, "Now imagine that you are meeting with your boss and asking for the raise. As you begin to follow your plan, notice carefully how he *is* responding. *Does* he look receptive or amenable to what you *are* saying? *Does* he sound sympathetic or agreeable?" For the financial evaluation you might also need a present reference, which you might access by asking, "What *is* your financial situation like today?" or "Now consider the *current* state of your finances."

Similarly, if you needed to install a future reference of the benefits of having stamina in your health-related operative format you might say, "Now as you begin to evaluate whether or not you want to exercise, remember what it *will be* like having that kind of stamina in the future, being able to effortlessly accomplish your tasks, feeling healthy and strong." If the person does not already have such a future reference you could first generate one by saying, "Imagine what it *will be* like having that kind of stamina in the future, being able to effortlessly accomplish your tasks, feeling healthy and strong." If you wanted to generate in your discouraged worker a future reference of the worth of hard work you could say, "Imagine having attained your goal, and at the same time imagine how much pleasure and satisfaction you *will* feel."

You could help install its use by saying, "As you consider the work that still needs to be done, be sure to keep in mind the pleasure and satisfaction you *are going to feel* when you finish it."

The following examples of accessing and generating different references are taken from *Know How*, as are the rest of examples in this chapter unless otherwise noted. The first is from the installation format for healthy eating habits and is an example of generating a future reference for the negative effects of overeating. This reference is made personal by including directions that lead the reader to experience the feelings associated with this future possibility.

Imagine yourself six months in the future suffering from the results of overeating, and most especially from overeating fat-producing foods. You can imagine seeing yourself in the mirror, nude, looking at yourself from the front, side, back, seeing the tone of your flesh as well as the overall configuration of your body. Using this future body, imagine touching your toes, doing some sit-ups and leg lifts, feeling the effort and exertion these small tasks require of your abused body. Hear your future self say, "If only I had what I want now instead of this. Instead, now I am even deeper into the hole of my own indulgence." (p. 100)

After creating another future reference for the benefits of eating well, we give directions that ensure that this reference also is personal.

Regardless of how you went about creating this compelling, desirable future, feel the pleasure of being this future self by first stepping into the picture you have made, seeing everything as you would from your future self's eyes. Then feel yourself move, beginning with how it feels to walk, bend, and dance from within this desirable body. Feel the sensual experiences of vitality and grace this future self offers. Be sure to hear yourself say, "I'm so glad I changed my ways, and I'm so proud." (p. 102)

References can also be generated by having a person engage in a task, as illustrated in this example (from the same installation sequence) of generating a present actual personal reference.

You can provide yourself with these experiences by deliberately choosing and behaving (for one meal) in accordance with some explicit choice of your own, in the following way. Choose to

271

*accompany friends out to eat but choose not to eat anything yourself
while still having a good time (if necessary for your comfort, eat
before going out with them). Or, choose to eat and enjoy exclu-
sively vegetables for a dinner (if necessary, creating the enjoyment
from, perhaps, the surroundings in which they are eaten, an in-
depth exploration of their textures and flavors, experimentation
with ways of preparation, or any other arrangement that makes it
possible for you to have at least one experience of enjoying a chosen meal of vegetables). Each experience of the kind we have just
exemplified will provide you with meaningful reference experiences
capable of positively influencing you in the future as you progress
toward your desired goal. (p. 108)*

The next three examples are from the installation format for
avoiding or stopping the use of harmful drugs. The first accesses a past actual informational reference.

*Even if you yourself are not bothered by substance abuse prob-
lems, take the time to call up visions from your past—memories
of yourself or others—and identify people who have drug related
problems. (pp. 126-127)*

The reader is then instructed to use this past reference to
identify the manifestations of a drug problem by asking himself questions that will generate the tests we want him to
make.

*Then answer these questions. How do you know that they do have
a drug problem? What are the ways in which they respond that
are indicators of a drug problem? (p. 127)*

After having the reader use that reference to identify the
manifestations of a drug problem, we give directions that use
that criterial equivalence to generate a future constructed
personal reference for the harmful effects of abusing drugs.

*Once you have identified the manifestations of a drug problem
you are ready to take the next step. When you reach the end of
this paragraph, imagine actually having that drug problem and
its attendant manifestations and symptoms. Make this scenario as
real as possible by paying close attention to who you are with and
what you are doing, how your vision is affected, how your sense
of hearing and taste are altered, and how you feel. Include in
this future the possibility that other people, people you care for
and respect, recognize that you have this out-of-control drug prob-*

lem. Your evidence that you have done a sufficient job of stepping into this problem is the degree to which you experience this possibility as devastatingly unpleasant. While still within this awful, projected future, picture the drug that is its cause. In this way the unpleasant future is associated with the drug that is its cause. Do this now, and then be sure to free yourself from that terrible future and come back to the present. (p. 127)

We follow the same procedure of accessing the appropriate past reference and then using it to generate a future reference in the installation format for quitting smoking. Here is the first step of accessing an appropriate past reference.

To this end you need to imagine your own experience in the future to be devastatingly bad as a direct result of having smoked cigarettes on a habitual basis. You can start with any memory of having been confined to a hospital (or a bed). *If you don't have a memory like this,* remember visiting someone confined to a hospital (or a bed) and how good it was when you left. Locate this memory now *so you will have it to use in the next step.* (p. 139)

The installation formats for temperate drinking habits include two steps that access and then generate present informational references.

To begin, identify someone who manifests the behavior (or significant aspects of the behavior) that you intend to acquire, and does so in the appropriate situations.

Now run a short movie inside your head in which you watch and listen to your role model. Pay attention to how they use their body (the way they move, how they position themselves in relation to others, the gestures they use, their facial expressions, and so on) as well as what they say and how they say it (the tempo of their speech, the tonality and timbre qualities of their voice, and so on). Evaluate carefully whether or not you are satisfied with what they do and how they do it. If not, pick someone else and repeat these initial steps. (If no acquaintance comes to mind you can use movie or literary personalities in your movie.) (p. 154)

The installation format for the ability to enjoy sex contains many examples of accessing and generating present references. In these three examples, we include directions that ensure that the references will be actual and personal.

At the end of this paragraph, close your eyes and feel various objects which are similar but still different. For example, you could use an avocado, an orange and a lemon. First, using your hands, feel the differences between them in texture, in moisture, in firmness, weight, warmth, and so on. Second, smell each one, comparing their odors and pungencies. Then feel and taste each one with your lips and tongue, using your lips and tongue to feel the same textures, temperatures, firmness that you felt with your fingers. Do this now, before you go on to the next step.

Now let's consider internal experience. This involves bringing the associations between specific experiences and their meanings into alignment with the fact that sexuality is sensory experience. *Drop your awareness internally down through your body. As you go through your body, feel the mass, the substance of your physical being. From inside this living cylinder, feel your left arm, your right, your left and right thighs, your heart beating and your lungs expanding and contracting within your torso. Once you are aware of these sensations, identify just where you interface with the nonliving world—that is, your clothes, shoes, the chair, the floor, and so on. In doing this you are identifying the evidence of being* alive. *Continue to concentrate on those sensations which allow you to* know *you are alive. Be sure to take all the time you need for this step.*

Next, without looking at or touching yourself, become aware of the internal sensations that let you know that you are a man or a woman. If you are a man there is the feeling of hair on your face, of your testicles, penis, the awareness of changing pressures in your penis and in the pelvic muscles that attach to it. If you are a woman, there is the presence and weight of your breasts, your vaginal lips and orifice and the muscles surrounding this sensually rich opening, your uterus, and ovaries. Feel your body completely. Next, direct your consciousness into feeling your lips, teeth, and tongue. Touch your tongue to your lips, feeling their warmth, moisture, softness, and surface texture. Then take your awareness through the rest of your body—the evidence of your sexuality is on the same level as those feelings that lie within your body that are evidence of your being alive. At this most basic level of sensory experience, your sexuality can no more be separated from you than can your breathing or your heart beat. You may not always be aware of those sensations that are evidence of your sexuality, but they are nevertheless always there, part of your being, part of your well-being. (pp. 162–163)

The installation format for establishing and maintaining satisfying relationships includes three steps that demonstrate one way to access, generate, and use past, present, and future references. These steps are part of a sequence we call the "threshold neutralizer." When someone is over the "threshold" he is associated into the past painful memories concerning his partner, and dissociated from the past pleasures. He can remember both, but the pleasurable ones have become *informational* and the painful ones have become very *personal*, and are therefore much more real and compelling. In addition, his pain and dissatisfaction are attached to, and associated with, his partner. The purpose of these steps is to begin to separate the pain and dissatisfaction from the partner, and to regain access to the positive feelings that result from accessing pleasant memories. Thus the following examples also demonstrate one way of changing a past personal to a past informational reference and vice versa.

The first step generates a present constructed reference and uses it to help gain access to the emotional state we want the person to have.

Think about the qualities and characteristics, large and small, that make you uniquely yourself. Look at yourself through the eyes of someone you know loves you (whether or not you love them is not important right now), and enjoy the positive attributes that can be appreciated in a fresh and new way through the eyes and perception of someone who loves you. Use this fresh perspective on your wonderful qualities to help you get in touch with strong feelings of self-appreciation. Hold on to those feelings throughout the entire process that follows. *(Being able to feel good about yourself while seeing the other person separates the bad feelings from being attached to all aspects of the other person, as well as giving yourself more of the experience of choice concerning your responses when around that person.) (p. 207)*

In the second step we give instructions that change the past and present personal references into informational ones. This is accomplished by changing the way the person is viewing the other person ("as if in a photograph") and directing the person's attention to feelings of self-appreciation rather than letting him attend to the angry/hurt feelings that previously were attached to memories of the other person. Once that is accomplished we direct the reader to make a future test that generates a future reference. Finally, with the memories "de-fused," we access past references that need to be used in the next step and whenever the reader thinks about this person in the future.

Picture the other person in a still shot (that is, as if in a photo-graph) as he or she looked when you first met. While you are looking at that picture, be sure to maintain your feelings of self-appreciation. When you can look at the remembered image of that person and maintain your feelings of self-worth, view that person as being separate from you, an individual in his or her own right, who lived a life that did not include you up until that point in time. Recognize that he or she is a complete person, separate and distinct from you, with his or her own unique set of qualities and characteristics. Picture him or her in the future, living in a differ-ent place, with friends and loved ones that are strangers to you. Then, recall the qualities or attributes that drew you to him or her in the first place. (p. 207)

In the third step, we access a past reference and give instructions that ensure it will be accessed as a personal one.

Having done that, recall a past pleasant memory you share with that person. Recover this memory in as full a representation as you can, seeing what you saw, hearing what you heard, smelling what you smelled, and feeling what you felt at that time, recog-nizing as you do, that this is your memory, and that nothing should be allowed to take it away. *(p. 207)*

In a different sequence from another section in the relation-ship chapter, we access a past actual reference to be used as the basis for several past tests. The result of this step is to generate several new past constructed references for enabling the reader to act differently, and more appropriately, than he or she actually did in the past.

As you consider your own qualities that you most value, and the ways in which you manifest those qualities through your behavior, go back to some awful past interaction involving your mate. Pay attention to yourself and to what your mate's feelings were behind his or her behavior. Identify how you also were not being all of who you want to or could be. See yourself there in that situation.

Choose one of your highly valued attributes that would be useful in that situation and see yourself generate different forms of behavior that are reflective of those attributes. Notice how the entire interaction is transformed by your living out your own attributes. Repeat this process with at least two other awful past interactions. (p. 211)

In this example from the parenting section we generate a present constructed informational reference.

In order to orient yourself to a present assessment of your child which is congruent with your child, the first thing to do is to identify at least two other children who are two or three years younger than your child. In your mind's eye, imagine those two younger children standing beside your child. As you look at them, compare their bodies; compare height; torso, limb and head proportions; weight; musculature; development of facial features. Make this simple comparison before going on. (p. 238)

Later in the same section we give a task that will generate a present actual personal reference.

In this regard, we know of no better way of keeping in touch with your child's world (and, thus, the various distinctions we have been describing) than occasionally to interact with him or her in his or her environments and on his or her terms. Match your tempo to that of your child by talking, moving, and reacting at the same rate as he or she does. Attend to the words and concepts he or she uses. Talk about and do the things that he or she wants to do, and in the way that he or she wants to talk about and do those things. (p. 242)

In the next three steps, also from the parenting section, we access a series of references in order to build a particular cause-effect between a child growing older and the child's ability to master skills and develop attributes. In the first step we access a past actual reference and, because it is going to be used as a basis for a new cause-effect, we give directions that make it personal and therefore more compelling.

First, identify some important skill (e.g. count to one hundred, go without diapers, make friends) or attribute (e.g. concern for others, shares, tries new things) that your child has recently mastered. Go back to that incident or moment when you realized that this skill or attribute was now in your child's repertoire, recapturing the feelings of pride and relief (and perhaps surprise and satisfaction) you had when you realized this. Relive that incident or moment; it is important that you get in touch with and re-experience these feelings before proceeding. (p. 245)

In the second step we access the other past reference that will be used to build and support the cause-effect.

Next, travel back through time until you reach that era in which your child had not yet mastered that skill or attribute, but a time that you nevertheless expected or wanted that skill or attribute from your child. (For instance, you notice that your son, Bobby, is now able to share his things with others. Moving back through time you come to an incident six months ago in which, despite your suggestions, encouragement and admonishments, Bobby's friends had to be sent home because he would not let them touch any of his toys.) Locate that time now. (pp. 245–246)

Finally, we have the reader access the references and cause-effect in order to change the outcome of a test.

Reliving that moment, step into the frustration, disappointment or anxiety of that past, but this time do it knowing (now) what you did not know then: that your child will eventually acquire that skill or attribute, but that it is not YET a feature of his or her development. *Notice how your response changes (probably becoming more patient, perhaps even curious about the future) in relation to and within that situation. Go back through this same sequence with several other skills or attributes that you once expected and fretted over, and that your child has now mastered. (p. 246)*

Cause-Effects

As the previous example illustrates, cause-effect relationships are born out of and sustained by the references a person accesses. To generate a particular cause-effect, then, you first need to access references that are compelling and that can serve as evidence for the "cause" and the "effect," and thereby support the linkage of the two. Once accessed, you need to direct your subject's attention to them in such a way that she connects the references as being contingently related. There are many ways of accomplishing this. The following examples are representative of the methods for installing cause-effects that we have found to be easiest and most effective. The first example is from the format for evaluating a troubled relationship. It contains instructions that lead the reader to make past tests that generate past references that support a past-to-present and past-to-future cause-effect.

Do a thorough evaluation of how being with your mate has made you more than you would have been without him or her. Regardless of whether all of your experiences felt good or comfortable, how have you been compelled to be more of who you want to be (or appreciate being) because of the experiences you have had together? How will you be more of who you want to be in your future as a result of your past together, regardless of whether you stay together now? (pp. 209-210)

The operative formats for regular and healthy exercise habits include a present-to-future cause-effect. Here is one of the ways we generate it.

The reality that exercise will lead to the fulfillment of the criteria you have identified for yourself must be based upon personal experiences. This step is intended to give you those kinds of personal experiences. Acquaint yourself with the instructions, then follow the instructions when we ask you to.

Supposing again that one of your criteria is stamina, go back through your personal history until you find an example of your having the kind of stamina you would like to have again (or preserve). From there, work backward through time from that point, farther into the past, noticing how your behavior and activities made that stamina possible. If you do not have such experiences in your personal history, you can get vicarious examples of them from other individuals who do have stamina. Then step into what you believe their ongoing experience is. That is, imagine what it must be like to be them. This gives you the basis of a cause-effect relationship between actions and results regarding stamina. Now carry this into the present and future by creating a you in the future that has your desired level of stamina. (You can choose several ages of self, from the near future on into old age.) Work backward from each future to the present, identifying what you will have done to achieve that desired future. In this way you will build a set of cause-effect relationships between what you do now and the future physical shape you want for yourself. Go ahead and build those cause-effect relationships now. (pp. 115-116)

It takes strong present-to-future cause-effects to lead to and support the compelling future tests required in the operative formats for a person to quit smoking, or for an ex-smoker to remain a non-smoker.

The next step in this sequence is to identify five existing behaviors that you carry out on a daily basis, behaviors that you know will lead to a desirable future. These behaviors can be as seemingly insignificant as brushing your teeth. It might seem like a small thing, but brushing your teeth does contribute to a desirable future, one in which you have your own teeth as well as healthy gums. Another behavior might be expressing some kind of affection to your loved ones on a daily basis. This contributes toward a future of meaningful and significant relationships. You will probably be able to identify many of these beneficial behaviors, but five will do for now. Identify them now and jot them down below.

What is common to all five of these behaviors is that they all carry you toward desirable futures. Take a moment to imagine the positive futures that you are creating by manifesting each of these behaviors. Make sure these futures are ones that your future self also wants and appreciates. Now determine how not *doing these behaviors could lead to* undesirable *futures. Imagine the futures that will greet you if you fail to carry out the five behaviors. Be sure to finish this step before going on to the next.*

Now identify four behaviors that you do not *engage in and, if you did, would result in you experiencing terrible consequences. These could be behaviors like stealing, lying, abusing others, not paying taxes, or ignoring the needs of your loved ones. Perhaps you do not drink alcohol, eat red meat, or cheat on your spouse. These are all examples of behaviors that could result in you feeling bad about yourself, or other dire consequences. So for this step, you need to specify four behaviors that you do* not *do— behaviors that you are* glad *you refrain from doing.*

Now add a fifth behavior to this list: either smoking, or smoking as much as you presently do.

Imagine the positive future that you are headed for by not *participating in these five undesirable behaviors. Imagine moving into that positive future a day at a time, a week at a time, and a month at a time. Take the time to make each of the stages real. In this way you can know and appreciate that for* each day you do not engage in those behaviors you move one step closer to realizing your desirable future, *and one step further away from an unwanted and unpleasant future. (pp. 144-146)*

There are two cause-effects being installed in the following two steps, which are taken from the relationship sequence. The first is a present-to-present between internal experience and external behavior, which tends to lead the reader toward understanding and away from developing or clinging to blanket judgments in the form of negative criterial equivalences. The second is a past-to-past that will be used later in the sequence to establish a future-to-future belief that the reader will be able to elicit different responses in the future if he changes what he is responding to.

Describe some of the behaviors that your mate does to which you strongly object. Going through them one at a time, determine what would have to be going on inside of you so that you would generate the same behavior. (So, if you really hate his walking out of the room while you are arguing, imagine yourself doing just that, walking out in the middle of an argument. What's going on with you that you would be compelled to do that? Is it the intensity of how angry, frustrated, or threatened you feel? What are the possibilities of what lies behind that objectionable behavior which make it understandable—not necessarily likeable or even acceptable—but at least understandable?)

While reviewing each of several situations where your mate has expressed such behavior, attend to the possibilities which compel him or her to be expressive in that way, and imagine how it would have been different if you had responded or behaved differently. Try a few different forms of behavior for yourself in each of those past situations and recognize how it could have been different if you had responded to how your mate was feeling on the inside, instead of what he or she was doing. (p. 210)

Here is another excerpt from the relationship section that establishes a cause-effect, and also demonstrates to the reader the value of paying attention to cause-effects.

Probably the best way to avoid expectation and habituation in your relationship is to be aware of the cause-effect connections which make possible your and your lover's moods, behaviors and the satisfaction of your and your lover's criteria. For example, suppose you appreciate and value the fact that your husband helps out with the housework. You might determine that the cause of his helping is his experience of doing something together *with you. As soon as you recognize this cause-effect relationship, two things happen. The first is that his helping becomes much less possible to expect and, so, ultimately less possible to take for granted. His helping with housework, as you now recognize it, is not an inherent response of his, but one that is caused by certain conditions, namely, the perception that it is a joint endeavor.*

The second thing that happens as a result of recognizing the cause-effect relationship is a shift from stacking to what might be termed interaction. Instead of the passive noticing when things are there or (more commonly) are not there that characterizes stacking, you become an active *member of an interaction, determining how to bring into experience those moods or behaviors that you and your partner want and value. For instance, if you are not considering cause-effect, and you ask your husband to take down the drapes to be washed* and he balks, *the common response is to notice that he doesn't seem to want to help with the housework the way he used to; and the incident gets stacked upon previous, similar examples that you are storing up. Perceived as cause-effect, however, your response becomes one of wondering what about your request and this particular situation led to his demurring, rather than eagerly jumping in. If you know that the sense of teamwork makes the difference in his response, you can then approach the situation accordingly. You could suggest taking the drapes down together, ask him to take down the drapes as part of a general house cleaning that you are also involved in, or indicate it would help you get to other things that* both *of you recognize need to be done.*

Now it is time to apply what you have learned about cause-effect to your situation. Identify several areas within your present relationship that are sources of disappointment to you in that they are examples of behaviors and responses that were once characteristic of your partner and that you appreciated, but which your partner no longer seems to be willing or able to do. For example, when you were courting, your lover may have been prompt, or generous, or helpful, or concerned, but now, months or years later, he or she no longer evidences those qualities and responses, and you miss them. You will use this information in the next step, so identify these sources of disappointment before proceeding.

Next, for the response you want to have, determine what caused it when it was there, and what caused it not to be there when it wasn't. If you have difficulty in finding the cause-effect relation-

ship, try the following: Take the first one of those situations, re-call an example of when your partner did *have the response you cherish, and an example of when your partner* did not *have that response. Comparing the two incidents, ask yourself the question, "What is the same and what is* different *about these two exam-ples?" In order to check out and refine the cause-effect relation-ship you have discovered, check the differences you find against a couple of other examples of the response being there and not being there. You can then use this information to create an atmosphere which is appropriate for the natural elicitation of the kinds of in-teractions that you and your mate want and appreciate (as in the drapery example). Taking one of your examples, discover the causes involved and then create ideas for how to interact in the future to elicit the responses you appreciate. (pp. 203-204)*

Establishing a future-to-future cause-effect is different from the other time frame possibilities only in that the tests and references you direct your subject to make are all con-structed, and all in the future.

Now, having accumulated several examples of new, more useful behavior to influence your interactions, take them into one of those possible futures you created in the previous step and play them out. How differently do events transpire? How much more of what you want do you get? (p. 211)

And here is an example taken from the installation se-quence for controlling drug abuse.

Now generate a future reality of yourself being in control of your own well-being, confident and secure in your independence. Look-ing back from this future, find examples of saying no to the op-portunities for using the drug, examples which have contributed so greatly to this desirable future. (p. 127)

Criteria

Each operative format you install will require the use of a particular criterion or set of criteria. Generating the use of particular criteria for any test is accomplished by asking questions or giving directions that lead to an evaluation, and that include the criteria in the question or task. For example, when you ask your friend, "Are you thirsty?" you are asking a question that requires your friend to consider the criterion

EMPRINT

of "thirst." When you ask, "Was the movie funny?" you are requesting that a test be made using the criterion of "funny." When you say, "Look at the intensity of colors in that rainbow" you are directing your friend to evaluate the rainbow in terms of "intensity of color" as opposed to any other possible criteria that could be tested for in that same context, such as "How do you *feel* as you look at that rainbow?" or "Do you think you will *want* to come back to this spot tomorrow?" and so on. Any time you ask a question or make a statement you are, by the criteria included in that question or statement, influencing what is being considered.

In all of the following examples we establish the use of particular criteria by directing the reader to answer questions or engage in tasks that presuppose the standards we want him or her to use. The examples are different only in the criteria being established and the additional instructions included. In the operative formats for nurturing your child, for example, it is necessary to consider what you want your child to *learn* at different stages. The criterion is "learn," and it is established in the evaluation by making a simple statement and posing a question.

Take a moment to consider what you want your child to learn in the long run. What do you want your child to learn as a young-ster, a teenager, a young adult, and an adult? (pp. 247-248)

In this next example from the section on how to set and attain goals we instruct the reader to apply four different criteria to something he or she is considering pursuing as a goal. In some cases the additional instructions direct the reader to use certain criterial equivalences for the criteria we are establishing.

The second thing that needs to happen in turning a wish into a want that is worth pursuing is for you to ask and answer the well-formedness questions. These questions should also be an-swered for each of your wants to make sure they are worth pur-suing to fulfillment. Before you do this for each of your wants, however, take one of your wishes to which you are strongly attrac-ted (after having completed the previous step), and evaluate it with respect to each of the following questions.

Is It Within the Realm of What Is Possible?

That is, is there at least one other person who has achieved a similar goal, or are the necessary basic resources, body of knowledge, etc., available to utilize? In terms of possibility, there is a big difference between wanting to live on Mars this year and wanting to be an astronaut, or wishing your feet were two sizes smaller and wanting to be financially independent. While a goal may be possible in the world, existing factors may make it not possible for you. For instance, the possibility of your becoming an astronaut is greatly reduced if you are a paraplegic or seventy years old. Evaluate your wish using the question above before you proceed.

Is It Worth Having?

That is, is this goal that you want in harmony with those attributes, ideals, and predilections which are important to you and by which you define your self? For example, our would-be astronaut might conclude that participating in the space program is tantamount to giving approval to increasing militarization of space, something which he is very much against. Or perhaps the goal of being an astronaut is not worth having when the long hours away from home and family are taken into consideration. Now use the question, "Is it worth having?" to evaluate your wish.

Will It Get Me What I Really Want?

You have probably had the experience of really wanting something that looked, sounded and seemed worth wanting, only to discover once you finally did get it that it was not at all worth having (and perhaps even worth avoiding). For example, you might have wanted, worked for and acquired a large, lovely, prestigious home, only to discover that maintaining it and the grounds around it is a consuming and undesirable burden. Similarly, owning and running a business (long hours, unpredictable pay), or owning an expensive but delicate car (lots of shop time, expensive repairs), or having your own horse (daily care, vet bills), may seem like things worth wanting until you are actually faced with the (perhaps unpleasant) reality of having them. At this point, you need to step into the vivid representation you previously generated of having your wish—step in so that it is as if you are there, seeing what you would see, hearing what you would hear and, most especially, feeling what you would feel. Is

your experience what you would want it to be? If not, can your
wish be adjusted or amended in order to make it satisfying? Step
into that representation and make the evaluation now.

Is It Worth Doing What It Would Take
To Attain the Outcome?

Before devoting yourself to a goal it is important to evaluate
whether or not it is worth the effort you will probably have to in-
vest in pursuing it. For this evaluation, first imagine some of
what is involved in making that which you are wishing for a re-
ality (in our astronaut example, giving up a present job, moving
to NASA in Houston, low pay, stretches of time away from home,
etc.), then step into the undertaking itself and assess your feelings
about it. Do you feel that it is worth doing what it will require?
Make this assessment for your wish before you go on. (pp. 78-79)

In the sequence for installing moderation in connection
with drinking alcohol we want the reader to evaluate, and
adjust or update if appropriate, the criteria currently being
used in drinking situations. We also want to give the reader
an experience of how the use of different criteria lead to
different outcomes; and we want the reader to evaluate a wide
range of criteria and choose the particular criteria that work
best for him or her to ensure future well-being. We accomplish these outcomes in the following steps.

In social drinking situations, do you return to the teenage days of
chug-a-lug contests? Is a man someone who can hold his liquor,
no matter how much? Is getting drunk still an assertion of your
daring, maturity or independence? If so, evaluate your present
criteria with respect to their appropriateness for who you are now
and the world you are now living in. This reordering of criteria
should include not only eliminating those which are no longer
relevant, but adding those which you think more appropriate. For
instance, do you want a person to whom you are attracted to
know you, or to know you drunk? Perhaps in social drinking sit-
uations you will want to continue to treat yourself and others with
respect and integrity. As you did before, prepare for yourself a
menu of possible criteria, then imagine what, how and when you
would drink in a social situation using each one of those criteria
in turn. For example:

drunkenness

good time

escape

taste

health

my well-being tomorrow

being in control of my behavior

respect of others

pride

In applying these different criteria pick a situation, such as a mid-week evening after a particularly grueling day. It is evening and you are on your way home after this exhausting day. Now consider how you will spend your evening with respect to drinking. Try applying the criterion of escape, *letting it become the experience you want. How do you plan and anticipate getting it? After doing this in relation to escape, return to the beginning and reorient yourself to your journey homeward after that grueling day, considering how you will spend the evening, this time applying the criterion of* well-being tomorrow. *The contrast of experience and effect between escape and well-being tomorrow will bring into sharp focus the behavioral differences made by such criteria considerations. Try this now for the criteria of escape and well-being tomorrow, imagining as vividly as possible actually being in this situation and using these different criteria.*

Run through the above situation (or one of your own choosing) again and again, each time changing the criterion you are using (taken from the list above or from your own list). How does your experience and behavior change as you apply each of those criteria? Which criteria naturally lead to the kinds of experiences and behaviors which are supportive of your determination to be free of alcohol dependency? This is an important step, so take all the time you need to make these evaluations. (pp. 151-153)

The criterion "pleasurable" is called for when evaluating emotions and sensations in the operative formats that lead to enjoyable sex.

As you did before, direct your awareness to your sensory experience and notice what of a pleasurable *nature you are presently experiencing, including emotions and places of comfort, warmth, and stimulation in your body and at the surface of your body.*

For instance, the emotion you are experiencing right now as you read this sentence might be one of curiosity, with the lower part of your face relaxed, the muscles around your eyes and in your torso pleasingly tense, and warmth in your mouth and in your hands. Before reading any further, explore your sensory experience to discover those pleasurable emotions and sensations. (pp. 164-165)

The effects of voice tones are important to consider in certain operative formats having to do with the attraction phase of relationships. In the following example we establish "voice tone" as a criterion.

The next quality to consider is the sound of that person's voice. Voice tones—shrill, resonant, nasal, soft, loud, flat, breathy— very much influence people's emotional states but, unfortunately, discriminations of voice tonality are usually out of consciousness for most people in our culture. Taking voice tonality for granted, you can spend a lifetime around someone who generates an unpleasant emotional state in you without your connecting that emotional state to the tonality of that person's voice. So, the next question to ask is, "How does that person's voice sound to you?" This will, of course, require much closer proximity (perhaps even engaging that person in conversation). Going back to the two people you had selected above (the nonattractive person and the attractive person you did not meet), recall now the sound of each of their voices and attend to how your emotional state changes as you listen to their tonalities. (p. 193)

Criterial Equivalence

Once a criterial equivalence is established it usually exerts its effect on a person's experience without being considered, unless circumstances happen to force a reevaluation. People rarely evaluate the evidence they use for knowing whether or not a criterion of theirs is fulfilled. But a new criterial equivalence can be generated by directing a person's attention to references that are compelling to that person and that support the new criterial equivalence. Once a person is given credible evidence (in the form of references), he can easily incorporate that evidence into his considerations of what constitutes fulfillment of an important standard. For example, in the following excerpt from a therapy session, one of the authors

(LCB) is working with a client who is discussing her feelings about her husband. In this excerpt a criterial equivalence is changed from "Wanting my husband to be happier with me than he could be with anyone else ≡ selfish" to "Wanting my husband to be happier with me than he could be with anyone else ≡ expression of being loving and responsible." First, past and present references are accessed and used as evidence to support the desired criterial equivalence, then future references for the negative consequences of not adopting the desired criterial equivalence are generated. The weight of this evidence results in the acceptance of the new criterial equivalence.

Hazel: I do want him to be happy.

LCB: It's just that you always want to know that he can't be as happy with anyone else as he can be with *you*.

Hazel: Is that all right?

LCB: Yes! (Both laugh) Do you want me to say it again? Yes!

Hazel: It seems a little selfish, but it would be nice.

LCB: (laughs) Go for it, Hazel.

Hazel: Oh, ok.

LCB: Yes, it's all right. You *can want* him to be happier with *you* than with anyone else. (Pause) You love him. You are happier with him than you would be, are, with anyone else. Yeah? (Hazel is crying and nodding affirmatively) Yes, yeah—it is. It's fine for you to want that. The basis of your wanting that is not about penning him in, it's not about locking him up, it's not about wanting him to be happy with you by denying him anything. The basis is his being more of who he wants to be when he's with you. You know, through the up times and the down times. It's like, the two of you have made a commitment about spending a good piece of your life together. Probably, I mean I don't know if you have a commitment that goes til death do us part no matter what, but I *know* your commitment absolutely is not to deny one another anything, but to contribute and to give . . . absolutely. And it's not just about in the moment, it's about over time. So it's like wanting him to be happier with you than with anyone else—that's not a selfish thing. I mean it's not like you're saying, "I'm going to keep you and I don't give a damn if you're miserable. You said 'I do' and that's it turkey! Forget that. What's this happiness crap." (Hazel is laughing) Besides that, your wanting him to be happier with you, more fulfilled with you, is the motivator for you to give to him. So I want you to, it's like jealously, that feeling, it's a feeling that goes "that man is very important to me." Ok, and . . . that's a wonderful thing to know. What would happen, Hazel, if you didn't have it? What if you didn't have anything that said, "This man is really important to me?"

Hazel: Oh, gosh, we wouldn't be together.

LCB: No. And you'd be apt to make terrible mistakes.

Hazel: Terrible mistakes?

LCB: Like ignoring him.

Hazel: Oh, yeah.

LCB: Like not keeping track of his well-being.

Hazel: Right.

LCB: If you had nothing that went "This man's really important to me and he's really precious to me and *it is possible* in the world to lose him . . . it is *possible* in the world to lose him. If you had nothing that let you know that, there wouldn't be anything to engage those behaviors, to check on how things have been and are with you, and how you want them to be.

Hazel: That's true. (slight pause, then Hazel giggles)

Now we're going to look again at a portion of an excerpt we used earlier as an example of accessing and creating present references. These two steps also demonstrate how to establish a desirable criterial equivalence, in this case that sexuality is rooted in sensory experience (sexuality $\equiv$ sensory experience).

Now let's consider internal experience. This involves bringing the associations between specific experiences and their meanings into alignment with the fact that sexuality is sensory experience. *Drop your awareness internally down through your body. As you go through your body, feel the mass, the substance of your physical being. From inside this living cylinder, feel your left arm,*

*your right, your left and right thighs, your heart beating and
your lungs expanding and contracting within your torso. Once
you are aware of these sensations, identify just where you interface with the nonliving world—that is, your clothes, shoes, the
chair, the floor, and so on. In doing this you are identifying the
evidence of being* alive. *Continue to concentrate on those sensations which allow you to* know *you are alive. Be sure to take all
the time you need for this step.*

*Next, without looking at or touching yourself, become aware of
the internal sensations that let you know that you are a man or a
woman. If you are a man there is the feeling of hair on your
face, of your testicles, penis, the awareness of changing pressures
in your penis and in the pelvic muscles that attach to it. If you
are a woman, there is the presence and weight of your breasts,
your vaginal lips and orifice and the muscles surrounding this
sensually rich opening, your uterus, and ovaries. Feel your body
completely. Next, direct your consciousness into feeling your lips,
teeth, and tongue. Touch your tongue to your lips, feeling their
warmth, moisture, softness, and surface texture.* Then take your
awareness through the rest of your body—the evidence of your
sexuality is on the same level as those feelings that lie within
your body that are evidence of your being alive. At this most
basic level of sensory experience, your sexuality can no more be
separated from you than can your breathing or your heart beat.
You may not always be aware of those sensations that are evidence of your sexuality, but they are nevertheless always there,
part of your being, part of your well-being. *(pp. 163-164)*

One of the things you can do with criterial equivalences is
change them by expanding them. This immediately gives a
person who is using that criterial equivalence more opportunities to experience satisfaction of that criteria, which in
turn creates more choice and flexibility of behavior.

*As we have noted several times (and illustrated with respect to
eating) it is often the case that people eat, drink, smoke and take
drugs in order to satisfy important criteria, such as pleasure,
fulfillment, control, and confidence. But how many ways are there
to satisfy any one of these criteria? Pleasure may indeed be the
result of chocolate fudge melting in your mouth, but it can also
come from:*

■ *your body gliding through warm, silky waters*

■ *bounding lithely up the stairs*

- *clean, crisp sheets on a muggy evening*

- *hot cider on a cool evening*

- *powerfully racing down a ski slope*

- *great music on a fine stereo (or in person)*

- *a good cup of coffee and the Sunday paper in bed*

- *the multi-hued greens and browns of a forest on a warm afternoon*

- *listening to your own footfalls as you stroll under the evening stars*

And, of course, the menu goes on. What could your list of pleasurable experiences include? Taking each of your criteria for losing weight, make up a menu of possible ways of satisfying those criteria, other than eating. (pp. 108-109)

One of the evaluations in the relationship sequence involves identifying behaviors that are appropriate manifestations of certain emotional states. Those behaviors then constitute a criterial equivalence. But before that evaluation is made, it is necessary to make sure that a person is able to distinguish which emotion he is experiencing. It's surprising how often related but different emotions—such as fear, anger, and revulsion—are not adequately separated. The result is that a person may not really be aware of which specific emotion he is experiencing, responding instead to a general feeling of anxiousness, unhappiness, etc., and therefore he may not respond in ways that are in his best interests. For instance, the responses that are appropriate if you are afraid are often very different from the responses that are appropriate to being angry. Specifying the criterial equivalence for different emotions and then identifying the behaviors that would be appropriate for each (another criterial equivalence) are included in these two steps from the sex sequence.

Now, how do you know, in terms of sensory experience, one emotional state from another? When you reach the end of this paragraph, select one of the emotional states on your list and identify for yourself the sensations that combine to make up your experience of that emotional state. For example, affectionate could be smiling with your mouth and eyes, relaxed face and torso, warmth throughout your body, feeling in your arms and hands the desire to reach out and touch your lover, and so on. Identify those sensations now.

Once you have done that, identify at least three behaviors that are appropriate, useful and fulfilling in the expression of that emotion. Using affectionate *as our example, such behaviors might include gently stroking or patting your lover, surprising your lover with a strong hug and a smack of a kiss, complimenting your lover on a special quality, and telling your lover that you love him or her. Before you go on, identify and list at least three of the behaviors that express the emotion you have chosen. (pp. 165-166)*

Here is an example of how to access and examine an existing criterial equivalence that also points out the importance of doing so in this context.

So now you have a list of short-term and long-term criteria that are important to you with respect to love relationships. In addition to knowing what those criteria are, however, you must have ways of knowing if and when the qualities that those criteria represent are present or absent in your prospective lovers and mates. Suppose that one of your criteria is considerate responsiveness to others. *What behavior would be evidence that this quality was there? Perhaps as you and your date are passing an elderly lady who struggles upstairs with a bag of groceries, your date greets her and offers to help her with the bag in a way that says, "I know you can do it, but let me help your day go a little easier." Evidence of the* lack *of the quality of considerate responsiveness to others might be cutting in front of people in traffic or in waiting lines, or pushing past others to beat them into elevators. (Of course, these same behaviors could be taken as evidence of ability to survive if you are in New York City.) If you do volunteer work at the local SPCA and Audubon Society, a woman who wants a sealskin coat, thinks big game hunting is sexy and buys black market ivory is not evidencing behavior which is likely to represent the kind of criteria that you value.*

Go through your list of criteria and consider what kinds of behaviors and responses would constitute evidence of those criteria being shared by another person, and what kinds of behaviors and responses would constitute evidence that your criteria are not shared by another person. This will give you the basis for informed responses to others, thus making your selection of mates and the fulfillment of your wants and needs much less haphazard.

*Give yourself this gift right now by identifying those behaviors
and responses. (pp. 190-191)*

Breaking undesirable criterial equivalences and expanding
desirable ones are covered in the following sequence of steps
from the relationship section.

*In changing such criterial equivalences, the first thing to do is to
identify* counterexamples. *That is, search through your personal
history (or even the world itself) for examples which are inconsis-
tent with your unwanted criterial equivalence. The importance of
finding and recognizing the counterexamples is that it turns the
default response of a criterial equivalence ("that's the way it is")
into something about which there is at least the possibility of a
choice response. For example, if you believe that commitments
mean the subordination of oneself, search through your memories
and find at least one example of a time when your character and
needs were allowed complete expression and satisfaction within a
committed relationship. If you are unable to find even one counterexample in your own experiences, you can search through the
experiences of friends and acquaintances for such examples so
that you can know that at least it is* possible *to be in a committed relationship without sacrificing one's self. If you have a
fear of committing to a relationship, spend a minute or two right
now to identify your undesirable criterial equivalences. Once
identified, find counterexamples to each one.*

*It is also important to consider the flexibility of your criterial
equivalences when making a commitment. It is especially significant to consider after a commitment has been made and you are
living together in the security phase. For Jill, the way that she
knew that Sam cared was that he called her during the day to see
how she was doing. Accordingly, when he didn't call, she felt un-
cared for. Having only one way of satisfying a criterion means
that you will be able to experience fulfillment with respect to that
criterion* only *if the necessary circumstantial requirements are
met. The world is complex and capricious enough to guarantee,
however, that there will be times when those circumstantial requirements will* not *be met. What then?*

*It is far more useful (as well as gratifying) to have many ways
of satisfying your criteria. Obviously, the more ways there are for
you to feel loved, the more often you will get to have that experi-*

ence. For example, if you are a woman you could feel loved when he calls if he's going to be late; when he locks the house up and turns the lights off at night; when he asks what movie you would like to see; when he makes fine love to you; when he says no if he really doesn't want to make love; when he turns down business opportunities that would take him away from you for long stretches; when he doesn't flirt with other women; when he challenges you if you need it; when he tells you the truth even if it is not what you want to hear. All of these (and much more) could serve as indicators that you are loved. (It is particularly helpful if they are all behaviors your mate can't not do—that is, if they are behaviors which naturally occur as byproducts of his or her own personality.)

In this regard it is important to note and realize that it is very likely that your lover is letting you know that he or she loves (respects, cares for, enjoys, appreciates) you in many ways that you do not recognize as examples of that love. Asking you what you want to see at the movies may be just common courtesy to you, but to your lover it may be an expression of love for you.

At the end of this paragraph, identify some experience (like having fun, or feeling believed in or trusted) you very much like to have within your current intimate relationship, but that you don't have as often as you would like. Then sort through your interactions with the other person and try to identify ways in which that person is actually trying to give you that experience, ways that you have, until now, not recognized. Once you have identified those ways you can, if you wish, ask that person directly what their intention is in doing whatever it is that they do in that situation. (Several good examples of this were given at the end of the "Threshold" section.) Complete this step before moving to the next.

Having done that, consider the criteria (standards, matters of importance) that you want to be sure are satisfied within your relationship. Pick three or four of these criteria and, for each of them, think of at least four ways (other than those you are accustomed to) that would serve as examples to you of this person fulfilling your criteria. Do your very best to make your choices with regard for your partner's existing behaviors. Remember, the more ways that your criteria can be fulfilled, the better your ongoing experience, and the richer and more secure your relationship will be. Before you go on, make this important evaluation. (pp. 198 and 200–202)

Test Time Frame

Directing a person to make an evaluation in a particular time frame is easy and natural—you do it all the time without thinking about it (although that will probably change now that you have read this book). For example, you request a present test be made when you ask, "Are you thirsty?" or when you say, "Look at the intensity of colors in that rainbow," or "How do you feel as you look at that rainbow?" You are directing your friend to make a past test when you ask, "Was the movie funny?" And you are requesting your friend to make a future test when you ask, "Do you think you will want to come back to this spot tomorrow?" Because time frame is inherent in the verb tense you use, when you want an evaluation to be made in one of the time frames you need to use the verb tense that designates that time frame. For example, these questions instruct the listener to make present tests.

What do want from a relationship right now in your life?

What does your mate do now that satisfies your wants and needs?

These questions instruct the listener to make past tests.

Go back to several years ago and, looking through younger eyes, see what it was you wanted then. What attracted you, what filled the needs that you had back then?

Which of your wants and needs has your mate satisfied in the past?

What has your mate given you in the past that you didn't even know to ask for? (p. 209)

This next instruction generates a future test. It is followed by a question that asks that a specific present reference be used (what your mate does now) to inform another future test.

Moving from the past to the present and now into your future, go forward in time to discover what you will be wanting and needing in the future that differs even from now.

What does your mate do now that would satisfy you in the future? (p. 209)

This example from the parenting sequence generates a present test that uses a past and present reference.

*Now see in your mind's eye your child as he or she was a year
ago, and your child as he or she appears now. Compare those two
images in the same way that you did with the younger children.
(If in looking at the two images, your child appears the same in
both, get a photograph of your child taken about a year ago and
use it to refresh your memory of how your child looked then.) As
before, notice how your child's body, face, voice, movements,
physical and academic interests, school subjects, reasoning, and
responses to various situations have changed. (p. 238)*

This is followed by instructions that generate other present
tests, but this time with different present references.

*The next step in appropriately orienting yourself to who your child
is is to make the same kinds of comparisons described above between your child and children who are older. To begin with, select two or three adults you know. Picture those adults and your
own child side-by-side, and compare them in terms of physical
development. Then compare them in terms of behaviors, intellectual abilities and interests, kinds of emotional responses, and
so on.*

*Having done that and noticed some of the gulfs that still sepa-
rate your child from the adult world, select a couple of children
that you know who are about two years older than your own
child. Again, make comparisons between those two children and
your own child with respect to physical, physiological, behavioral,
intellectual, and emotional differences. As before, the only goal
here is to make you aware of some of the ways in which your
child is different from individuals who are older. If you do not
find the comparisons compelling, then we suggest that you actually get your child together with two or three adults, and then a
few somewhat older children, and make your comparisons by actually watching and listening to their interactions. (pp. 238-239)*

The example from the sex sequence used previously (under
present references and criterial equivalences) is also a good
demonstration of generating present tests. Throughout its
lengthy instruction the reader is kept in the present by use of
present tense verbs. The following excerpt, taken from a
different step in that sequence, also generates present tests.

*Next put your consciousness out to your extremities. Hold out your
arm and move it back and forth until you can feel the air passing*

around it. Tap the table with a pencil, then tap it with your finger. What is the difference in how each feels? How much sensory information do you get from using the pencil compared to using your own finger? After answering that question, repeat the exercise (tapping first with the pencil, then with your own finger) attending this time more to the range of information that is available from each. (p. 162)

This instruction generates a present test in the relationship sequence.

Begin making present tests by taking an inventory of your mate's behaviors that are worth appreciating. Identify at least five things that he or she does on a regular basis that you really appreciate. They could be that your mate tells you the truth, keeps commitments, keeps the car's gas tank more than half full, lets you crawl into bed at night while he or she locks up and turns out the lights, throws his or her dirty clothes in the hamper, remembers to buy you a present on your birthday, picks up the dry cleaning, or treats your parents well. They can vary in importance, but they all should be behaviors that warrant appreciation. (p. 195)

An excerpt used earlier to demonstrate how to generate future references is also a good example of generating future tests. (Remember that all future references are constructed, and thus require a future test to be generated.)

There are several ways to begin building your compelling future for healthy eating habits. After you have read the instructions in this paragraph, imagine yourself six months in the future suffering from the results of overeating, and most especially from overeating fat-producing foods. You can imagine seeing yourself in the mirror, nude, looking at yourself from the front, side, back, seeing the tone of your flesh as well as the overall configuration of your body. Using this future body, imagine touching your toes, doing some sit-ups and leg lifts, feeling the effort and exertion these small tasks require of your abused body. Hear your future self say, "If only I had what I want now instead of this. Instead, now I am even deeper into the hole of my own indulgence."

Regardless of how you went about creating this compelling, desirable future, feel the pleasure of being this future self by first stepping into the picture you have made, seeing everything as you would from your future self's eyes. Then feel yourself move, beginning with how it feels to walk, bend, and dance from within this desirable body. Feel the sensual experiences of vitality and grace this future self offers. Be sure to hear yourself say, "I'm so glad I changed my ways, and I'm so proud." (pp. 100 and 102)

The example used earlier in the section on Criteria is also an example of directing the reader to evaluate criteria by making a future test.

Take a moment to consider what you want your child to learn in the long run. What do you want your child to learn as a youngster, a teenager, a young adult, and an adult? (pp. 247–248)

Representational Systems

Just as you use a specific verb tense to direct a person to make a test in a particular time frame, you use sensory-specific predicates to direct a person to represent that test in a particular sensory system. You can instruct a person to *see* what they *look* like, or to *listen* to the *sound* of their *voice*, or to remember how they *felt* —and they will. When it is important that a test or a reference be generated in a particular representational system, you can generate the test you want by including representational system instructions as you direct your subject to make the test or access the reference. For example, in an excerpt with which we are already familiar, we instruct the reader to build a test that includes the visual, kinesthetic, and auditory systems. We include all three systems because we want this test to be compelling, and the richer and fuller an evaluation is in terms of sensory-specific details, the more real and compelling it will seem.

There are several ways to begin building your compelling future for healthy eating habits. After you have read the instructions in this paragraph, imagine yourself six months in the future suffering from the results of overeating, and most especially from overeating fat-producing foods. You can imagine seeing yourself in the mirror, nude, looking at yourself from the front, side, back, seeing the tone of your flesh as well as the overall configuration of your body. Using this future body, imagine touching your toes, doing some sit-ups and leg lifts, feeling the effort and exertion these small tasks require of your abused body. Hear your future self say, "If only I had what I want now instead of this. Instead, now I am even deeper into the hole of my own indulgence." (p. 100)

In the sequence for installing temperate drinking habits there is a test that is best made only visually.

If generating a future self as an alcoholic is too unreal for you (that is, you steadfastly believe that such a reality is in no way a real possibility for you), do the following. Imagine problem situations where a single occurrence of overindulgence causes very unpleasant consequences (like being arrested for drunken driving, or worse, causing an accident and injuries to others as a result of drunken driving; or behaving in ways that bring you much personal shame while drinking). These should be specific, likely situations that you can imagine occurring to you. While we realize we are directing you to imagine very unpleasant experiences, we also know that they are better imagined and used to avoid the behaviors which cause them, rather than experienced directly, along with their attendant feelings of grief, remorse, guilt and shame.

To create these avoidable future experiences follow the same sequence as you have in previous sections WITH ONE EXCEPTION: BE SURE TO SEE A PICTURE OF YOURSELF IN THESE EXPERIENCES. The reason for this is that if you fully step into these imagined experiences you will be stepping into the numbing, blurred perceptions of the drunk. In dealing with excessive drinking, it is better to see yourself from an outside point of view *that definitely motivates you to avoid such experiences.* (p. 151)

The drinking sequence includes the steps for a technique called the *new behavior generator,* which is useful for evaluating and adopting external behaviors. One of its steps requires a visual and auditory test.

Now run a short movie inside your head in which you watch *and* listen *to your role model. Pay attention to how they use their body (the way they move, how they position themselves in relation to others, the gestures they use, their facial expressions, and so on) as well as what they say and how they say it (the* tempo of their speech, *the* tonality and timbre qualities of their voice, *and so on). Evaluate carefully whether or not you are satisfied with what they do and how they do it.* (p. 154)

The operative formats for enjoyable sex include many kinesthetic tests and references. Many people don't make the appropriate kinesthetic tests during sex, however, which is often the cause of sexual dysfunction (see *Solutions* by Cameron-Bandler). The following four steps are part of a sequence designed to teach the reader how to generate kinesthetic tests. The first step instructs the reader in making a test that also includes the olfactory-gustatory system. (Some of these steps have been used as examples in previous sections. We are repeating them here because they exemplify the role predicates can play in generating references, criteria, criterial equivalences, and tests.)

Begin with external stimuli. At the end of this paragraph, close your eyes and feel *various objects which are similar but still different. For example, you could use an avocado, an orange and a lemon. First, using your hands,* feel *the differences between them in* texture, *in* moisture, *in* firmness, weight, warmth, *and so on. Second,* smell *each one, comparing their* odors *and* pungencies. *Then* feel *and* taste *each one with your lips and tongue, using your lips and tongue to* feel *the same* textures, temperatures, firmness *that you* felt *with your fingers. Do this now, before you go on to the next step.*

Pet *a cat or a dog with a wooden spatula, then with your hand, and remember the differences in the* sensations *that you experienced with each, as well as noting differences in the animal's responses to your* stroking. *With your hands, explore your hands, feeling* for areas of *roughness, smoothness, hardness, softness, warmth, cold, and so on. Then use your hands to explore the rest of your body, discovering differences in* sensitivity, texture *and* temperature *on different portions of your skin.*

Next, with a partner or friend, pick some communication to give that person but do not tell them what it is. Any communication such as affection, passion, concern, caring, or trust is appropriate. Take hold *of that person's hand and using* only *your hand, communicate to them the message you have selected. Ask your partner what he or she understood the communication to be. Continue using just your hand to convey your message until the meaning that your partner is receiving matches the message you are intending. Having done that, expand the range of touch to include* hugging, caresses *and so on, using each to experiment with conveying other messages to your partner.*

Next, without looking at or touching yourself, become aware of the internal sensations *that let you know that you are a man or a woman. If you are a man there is the* feeling *of hair on your face, of your testicles, penis, the awareness of changing* pressures

EMPRINT

*in your penis and in the pelvic muscles that attach to it. If you
are a woman, there is the presence and weight of your breasts,
your vaginal lips and orifice and the muscles surrounding this
sensually rich opening, your uterus, and ovaries. Feel your body
completely. Next, direct your consciousness into feeling your lips,
teeth, and tongue. Touch your tongue to your lips, feeling their
warmth, moisture, softness, and surface texture. Then take your
awareness through the rest of your body—the evidence of your
sexuality is on the same level as those feelings that lie within
your body that are evidence of your being alive. At this most basic
level of sensory experience, your sexuality can no more be separated from you than can your breathing or your heart beat. You
may not always be aware of those sensations that are evidence of
your sexuality, but they are nevertheless always there, part of your
being, part of your well-being. (pp. 162–164)*

The following four steps from the relationship sequence are
designed to generate visual, then kinesthetic, then auditory,
and finally kinesthetic tests, in that order. (Note that some
visual *references* are used for the kinesthetic tests.)

*Take a moment when you reach the end of this paragraph to list
seven or eight qualities or characteristics that you value in any-
body. After making your list, identify someone of the desirable sex
whom you were around recently (possibly at a social gathering) to
whom you were not attracted, someone you could have met but
declined to. Then identify someone recently to whom you were
attracted but did not meet. Making as clear an internal image
as you can of the first person, look at him or her and ask yourself
the kinds of questions we described above, using your list of
valued character traits as the content for those questions (e.g.
"Does he look caring about others?").*

*Next, consider how you feel as you look at that person. Do you
feel good, bad, sad, curious, bored, careful, hopeful? Having
done that, switch to the image of the person to whom you were
attracted but did not meet, and take him or her through the same
sequence of evaluation with respect to your list of valued character
traits, the traits that are there that you have not considered, and
how you feel looking at that person. Make these evaluations before proceeding to the next step.*

*The next quality to consider is the sound of that person's voice.
Voice tones—shrill, resonant, nasal, soft, loud, flat, breathy—
very much influence people's emotional states but, unfortunately,*

discriminations of voice tonality are usually out of consciousness for most people in our culture. Taking voice tonality for granted, you can spend a lifetime around someone who generates an unpleasant emotional state in you without your connecting that emotional state to the tonality of that person's voice. So, the next question to ask is, "How does that person's voice sound to you?" This will, of course, require much closer proximity (perhaps even engaging that person in conversation). Going back to the two people you had selected above (the nonattractive person and the attractive person you did not meet), recall now the sound of each of their voices and attend to how your emotional state changes as you listen to their tonalities.

Now reconsider how you feel when you are with this person. Is your experience enriched? Are you happy to see this person? Do you feel valued and appreciated when with this person? Do you feel comfortable with this person? Sensually stimulated? Intellectually stimulated? If you now take a moment to search through your acquaintances for a person to whom you are not visually attracted but with whom you feel valued, and a person to whom you are visually attracted but with whom you do not feel valued, you will recognize immediately that an attraction strategy that is based upon matching external, visual criteria in no way guarantees that the person will be a satisfying and gratifying partner. Try this now. (pp. 192–194)

The next excerpt was used previously as an example of changing a personal reference to an informational reference. Notice the key role that representational systems play in this conversion process. We do this by having the personal reference represented only visually, while the kinesthetic system is occupied with a set of feelings that belong to an experience other than the reference. Thus a kind of dissociation is created, changing the reference to an informational one. In the second step, we take advantage of this change to have the reader access a *pleasant* memory of this person. We make *this* a personal reference by enriching the memory with all of the representational systems. The reader now has access once again to a past personal reference that, because it *is* personal again, will be compelling.

Picture *the other person in a* still shot *(that is, as if in a* photograph*) as he or she* looked *when you first met. While you are* looking at that picture, *be sure to maintain your* feelings of self-appreciation. *When you can* look *at the remembered* image *of that person* and *maintain your* feelings *of self-worth,* view *that person as being separate from you, an individual in his or her own right, who lived a life that did not include you up until that point in time. Recognize that he or she is a complete person, separate and distinct from you, with his or her own unique set of qualities and characteristics.* Picture *him or her in the future, living in a different place, with friends and loved ones that are strangers to you. Then, recall the qualities or attributes that drew you to him or her in the first place.*

Having done that, recall a past pleasant memory you share with that person. Recover this memory in as full a representation as you can, seeing what you saw, hearing what you heard, smelling what you smelled, *and* feeling what you felt *at that time, recognizing as you do, that this is your memory, and that nothing should be allowed to take it away. (p. 207)*

An excerpt from the parenting sequence that was used earlier as an example of generating a present test is also an example of creating a *visual* test.

In order to orient yourself to a present assessment of your child which is congruent with your child, the first thing to do is to identify at least two other children who are two or three years younger than your child. In your mind's eye, *imagine those two younger children standing beside your child. As you* look at them, *compare their bodies; compare height; torso, limb and head proportions; weight; musculature; development of facial features. Make this simple comparison before going on. (p. 238)*

Compelling Time Frame

If only one test is being made in an operative format, that test will be compelling—by default. However, if the person you are working with is making tests that are competing for compelling status with the one you want to be compelling, you need to make your desired test most compelling. How do you build up the "compellingness" of a test? As we discussed in a previous chapter, one of the elements of a compelling test is that it involves criteria that very important to the person. The more significant the criteria, the more compelling the test will be.

Another element is the sensory richness of the evaluation. The more representational systems used in the evaluation, the more "real" and compelling the test will seem. Tests are also usually more compelling if they include representations of positive gain as well as negative consequences, as demonstrated in a few of the excerpts used earlier. Obviously, if the references being used are personal and actual, as opposed to informational and constructed, the cause-effects underlying the tests and the tests themselves will be more compelling. The following six steps from the healthy eating habits sequence illustrate one of the ways to generate a compelling future test. You are already familiar with two of the steps. They are presented here in context to give you a better idea of how they interact with and support other steps.

There are several ways to begin building your compelling future for healthy eating habits. After you have read the instructions in this paragraph, imagine yourself six months in the future suffering from the results of overeating, and most especially from overeating fat-producing foods. You can imagine seeing yourself in the mirror, nude, looking at yourself from the front, side, back, seeing the tone of your flesh as well as the overall configuration of your body. Using this future body, imagine touching your toes, doing some sit-ups and leg lifts, feeling the effort and exertion these small tasks require of your abused body. Hear your future self say, "If only I had what I want now instead of this. Instead, now I am even deeper into the hole of my own indulgence." Do this now.

If that is not real enough for you, spend some time doing the following, then repeat the steps above. Look for fat people of your own gender wherever you go. Watch them climb stairs, squeeze into chairs, maneuver down airplane aisles, and struggle in and out of cars. Imagine being them as you watch, feeling the additional flesh straining your heart, draining your vitality and spirit. Watch how others respond, how they look at these people and what they say as that very overweight person walks by. It's a cruel reality, but the unpleasantness serves to make that reality compelling.

Enough of that. Now at the end of this paragraph imagine yourself six months into the future after having carried out impeccable eating habits. Look at your future self in the mirror again from the front, back and side. Be sure to compare this future self with your previous dire projection and present appearance *and only with that previous dire projection and your present appearance. In this way you will be comparing the best you can be with what is, for you, less than acceptable. Note that your skin and hair has also benefited from your changed ways. Feel the ease and joy of movement this thinner, healthier, cared for body can experience with movements like toe-touching, sit-ups, and walking up stairs. Review these instructions, if necessary, and complete this step before proceeding.*

If you have trouble making this projection of your future self real to you then take the time to do the following. Recall a time in your past—even back as far as your teen years—when your body was at a weight and tone you appreciated. Recall how this felt and looked. Step back into some pleasant memories of the ease with which your body moved at that weight, possibly including the freedom from concern about your weight at that time. Having recalled that past self, transfer those weight and vitality characteristics out into your imagined and desired future self. In making this transfer, be sure to keep characteristics of your actual age, but change the weight and vitality you experience having. And especially keep your wisdom, that which you have gained in life experiences and worthwhile criteria since those earlier years.

If you have never been at what you consider a desirable weight and level of vitality it is essential for you to begin by imagining a childhood and adolescence at a more ideal weight and level of vitality, and then carry that imagined history into your future. If this seems difficult, go out into the world to gather your examples. Watch people of all ages who are at an appropriate weight. Identify with them. Imagine moving within and along with your chosen example's body. (Remember: Only learning, behavior and a little time stand between you and what you want.) Translate these examples from others into your own representation of your future self. If this step is appropriate for you, now is the time to engage in this interesting experiment.

Regardless of how you went about creating this compelling, desirable future, feel the pleasure of being this future self by first stepping into the picture you have made, seeing everything as you would from your future self's eyes. Then feel yourself move, beginning with how it feels to walk, bend, and dance from within this desirable body. Feel the sensual experiences of vitality and grace this future self offers. Be sure to hear yourself say, "I'm so glad I changed my ways, and I'm so proud." Once you have accomplished this, slowly step back into the present. (pp. 100–102)

Here are two steps from the smoking sequence that are designed to help make the future test regarding consequences more compelling than a present test regarding the desire for a smoke.

To this end you need to imagine your own experience in the future to be devastatingly bad as a direct result of having smoked cigarettes on a habitual basis. You can start with any memory of having been confined to a hospital (or a bed). If you don't have a memory like this, remember visiting someone confined to a hospital (or a bed) and how good it was when you left. Locate this memory now so you will have it to use in the next step.

Now imagine that you are the patient instead of the visitor. You need to include in your projections the desirable experiences that your smoking will have robbed from you, such as not seeing your grandchildren, not making love, not being able to smell a spring morning, not being able to take that special trip, and so on. Get in touch with the feelings of sadness, regret, pain, longing or disappointment that belong in this reality. It will be challenging for you to make this real, because as soon as it is you are going to be very uncomfortable when trying to smoke a cigarette. Thus we suggest you begin to make this compelling future real enough to motivate you now, and return to it again after doing the upcoming steps. In this way you will be fully compelled into action when you have more of the other necessary steps in preparing yourself to comfortably become a nonsmoker. Take the time now to complete this step. (pp. 139–140)

Know How includes an entire installation sequence (pages 22–32) that teaches the reader how to generate compelling futures. The ability to generate a compelling future is important in almost every endeavor. You need to be able to generate a compelling future whether you want to lose weight, or invest wisely, or change your opinion of yourself, or set and attain goals. The compelling future installation sequence contains examples of accessing, generating, and installing most of the variables used in the EMPRINT method. We suggest you read through the sequence and then review this chapter.

You may have noticed that in some of the examples in this chapter, despite our admonishment in the overview, more than one variable is being generated as a result of a single instruction. For example, when we ask that a criterion be evaluated, we usually suggest the test time frame to be used by the verb tenses in our instruction. In the same instruction we might include predicates that direct the test to be made in the appropriate representational systems, and all this might add up to make this test time frame compelling. One instruction, and four variables accessed or generated. You can work this way when you are installing a skill, but you don't need to. Until you are comfortable with dealing with each variable, take them one at a time. The end result will be the same. As your experience and confidence build so will your ability to structure your questions and statements to accomplish multiple outcomes.

Future-Pacing

After accessing and generating the necessary variables for an operative format, you need to install them through practice. After you (or the person you are installing them in) have practiced generating the entire operative format several times, you are ready to use a form of rehearsal that helps ensure that the operative format will indeed be used in the future. This "future-pacing" allows you to try out your new operative format in an imagined future situation. Such additional practice helps install the operative format, and also helps identify any adjustments that might need to be made. These adjustments, if any, may be obvious, or they may require additional modeling on your part. Any adjustments can then be made and installed, and the operative format future-paced again for practice and to check on its efficacy. Each new operative format should be future-tested in this way.

The most important function of future-pacing is to create a conscious and unconscious connection between an operative format and the situations in which you want it to be used. Your new operative formats are replacing other operative formats that you have probably been using for a long time. The new operative formats need to be accessed as automatically in the future as the old ones have been in the past. By mentally rehearsing the use of the operative format in the desired contexts, you are more likely to remember to use it, or to use it automatically, when the appropriate time arises. The more future-pacing you do, and the more times you use your new programs in actual situations, the more automatic they will become. Like almost everything else you have learned in your life that seemed complicated or overwhelming as you were learning it—such as learning to ride a bike or to drive a stick shift—after a while it becomes automatic and you are able to master it without giving it conscious thought.

When you future-pace a skill you are generating a future test of manifesting the skill. The future-pacing will be most effective if you make that future test as rich a representation as possible, filling in as much detail as you can in all of the sensory systems.[3] The following four examples are from the installation sequences in *Know How*. The first is from the eating habits sequence.

Because you are acquiring new strategies for yourself, it is neces-sary to rehearse them internally, practicing by placing them in the situations in which you want those programs to function in the future. For example, when we ask you to, rehearse (internally) arriving at a party and asking for mineral water instead of beer or champagne—hear yourself ask for the mineral water. If, for instance, you overeat when you are tired, rehearse (internally) coming home tired and climbing into a warm bath or a comfy chair with a favorite magazine (or whatever behaviors you have determined will satisfy the need created by being tired), instead of making a snack-laden beeline from the fridge to the TV.

In rehearsal it is important that you represent to yourself only what you will do, rather than what you no longer want to do. The reason for this is that we respond to imagined experience, and even negations must still be represented in order to be ne-gated. (It is like European road signs, which picture some possi-bility, such as walking, passing, or bringing your dog in, then put a big slash mark across the picture to inform you further that it is not to be done.) For instance, say to yourself, "I won't eat the piece of chocolate cake." In order to comprehend the meaning of that injunction you probably made a picture of that piece of chocolate cake. Perhaps you imagined the taste, smell and texture of the cake as well. The richer the representation, the more irre-sistable it becomes. The words—or a slash mark across a picture of the cake—simply can not compete with the responses elicited by that sensory rich representation of the cake. In terms of the

*goal of losing weight, then, it is more useful to say, "I will eat
the fresh, juicy nectarine" than to say, "I won't eat the New York
cheesecake."*

*In short, as vividly and thoroughly as possible, imagine your-
self behaving and responding in the ways that you want to in the
situations in which you need those behaviors and responses. Try it
right now. Spend a few moments rehearsing your new strategies.
(pp. 109–110)*

This is the future-pacing step from the exercise sequence.

*You are acquiring new strategies for yourself, and further practice
is necessary to insure that these new ways of thinking and behaving work effectively in the future. Fortunately, this kind of practice is as easy and enjoyable as it is profitable. When you come to
the end of this paragraph, mentally rehearse how you will be exercising during the next two weeks. Imagine the events of each of
those upcoming days—where you are, what you are doing, who
you are with—from the time you wake up in the morning to the
time you retire in the evening. Feel the flow of time and activities,
making sure to participate in your chosen exercise program in a
way that makes your exercising a natural part of that flow. Be
sure to include any necessary preparation or travel time. Feel the
movement of your body and the attendant sensations as you carry
out the steps or stages of your exercise program. If at any time
you imagine yourself thinking or behaving in an undesirable way,
back up and adjust your mental rehearsal until it is in keeping
with your exercise goals. For instance, if you imagine coming
home from a tiring day at work and plopping down in front of
the TV and staying there until it is time to get up and go to bed,
you might want to start over and imagine how glad you are that
you took a brisk and refreshing walk around the block (or to that
evening exercise class). Take a minute or two right now to mentally rehearse your new exercise habits. (p. 118)*

This is the rehearsal step from the drinking sequence.

*Having updated your criteria and made alcohol a choice variable
through your behavioral flexibility, you may want to be able to
resume drinking in certain situations, such as a party. Doing this
in such a way as to perserve your desired future requires some
future-pacing. In order to get to work or to an engagement on
time you plan ahead, alotting the necessary time for travel, show-
ering, breakfast, and so on. Do the same kind of planning for
drinking. Before going to the party, assess for yourself the amount*

of time between the first drink and its effects, the amount of time between the second drink and its effects, the third drink, and so on, keeping in mind the time when you plan to leave and the amount of time it will take to sober up prior to leaving. In this way you can preset yourself for how many drinks to have, how far apart, and when to quit in time to leave sober. The effectiveness of such future-pacing was demonstrated by an acquaintance of ours who had set six o'clock as the time at which she would stop drinking champagne at an afternoon party. She forgot her resolution. At one point, while standing in the kitchen, she inexplicably let her full glass of champagne drop from her hand. When she bent to clean up the broken glass, she suddenly remembered her resolution and, looking up at the clock, noticed that it was precisely six o'clock.

So, take a social evening and plot it out for yourself as to time and experience in relation to alcohol intake. And be sure to take into account how far beyond that social evening the effects of drinking (including a hangover) extend. Any plans to get drunk should include considerations that go through the entire day/ evening (i.e., driving home), as well as through the following day (i.e., having a hangover at work). (p. 155)

And finally, here is the future-pacing step for one of the installation sequences from the parenting section.

Having done that, it is important to take the time to insure that your new responses will occur in the future. Identify two or three upcoming situations in which you want to respond to your child with these new, more patient and assured responses. Taking them one at a time, fully imagine being in these futures; seeing everything around you, hearing other's voices, feeling the sensations that are present in that future. Mentally rehearse responding to your child as you intend to, making any adjustments necessary for your response to be aligned with your new perceptions and emotional state. Be sure to notice and appreciate how you have learned to convert problem situations into opportunities for loving and supportive expressions. (pp. 246–247)

Taking the Next Step

You now possess a method capable of revealing previously inaccessible human resources. The organizing principle, distinctions, elicitation and detection techniques, and installation procedures that make up the EMPRINT method are now yours to use to explore skills, aptitudes, attributes, and competence. With the EMPRINT method, you are free to set out on a path that leads to a future rich in human excellence. The questions that confront you now are, Where will you turn first? What is the best next step?

You may already have a notion of the skills and attributes you want to acquire. Perhaps you want to be a more patient teacher, or more effective at recruiting employees, or more creative, or a more tender and romantic lover. Or perhaps you want to understand how successful investors analyze world economic events, or how to appreciate modern art or classical music, or how to persevere when you are mired in frustrations and setbacks, or how to enjoy your good fortune when everything is going right. If you know what you want, find someone who already has it and, modeling camera in hand, discover the internal processes that underlie their success. You will in no way diminish them—in fact you will probably flatter them—and you will be adding to your own, and therefore the world's, resources.

If you don't already know what you want to model, you could begin by taking an inventory of your existing skills and attributes. Then make a list of the talents manifested by the people you most admire. Compare this list to the list of your existing qualities and identify those skills or attributes that you admire but don't already possess. This list of talents you admire most but don't presently possess becomes your "shopping list." Pick one of the items on your list and begin your search for an exemplar.

Individuals are not the only ones who can benefit by applying the EMPRINT method. If you are a member of an organization—such as a business, school, public agency, or service club—you could use the method to build a file of the collective talents of all of the members of the organization, which you could make available to all other members of the organization. This happens to be one of our goals. For instance, we intend to inspire business leaders to create corporate "skill centers" that would contain, in coded form, the best individual talents of all of their employees. The staff in these centers would be well trained in the EMPRINT method elicitation and installation techniques. In each of these centers, each skill, each coded operative format, would be filed together with an installation sequence developed for that particular skill. In this way, the information about the skills would be preserved, and they could be passed on to as many other employees as desired, as far into the future as desired, regardless of whether or not the exemplar employee was still associated with the business.

We have heard hundreds of business owners and managers utter a variation of the phrase, "I wish I had a few more like Jim." In the past this wish usually remained just that—a wish. They knew that Jim was special, and that they would be lucky to be able to find or afford one more Jim, let alone several more Jims. In wishing for a few more like Jim, however, they were actually expressing their appreciation of, and desire for, what Jim possessed in terms of skills or attributes. Jim is a unique human being—*he* can't be reproduced. But his skills and attributes *can* be reproduced. Jim's special talents could be coded into the corporate skill center and then installed in any number of employees, at any time. The result would be an improvement in the business's productivity and bottom line. But those outcomes are not the motivating force behind our commitment to this goal. The fuel that fires our commitment is the unprecedented avenues of education and opportunities for advancement that would result for every person in the workplace.

Regardless of the goal you set for yourself, the next step is to begin noticing and modeling the people around you. The application of the EMPRINT method is a rigorous process. Like any skill you have learned in your life, you need to practice to achieve a level of proficiency. And only practice stands between your existing abilities and your ability to reproduce competence.

13 Conclusion

The EMPRINT method is not the product of spontaneous generation, but is part of the lineage of extensional models through which human beings have been evolving their perceptions of the world and, thereby, of themselves as well. As our scientific, philosophical, sociological, cultural, and psychological viewpoints change and evolve, so do our sciences, philosophies, society, culture, and psychology. None of us is immune to this unfolding of new perceptual and cognitive filters. These ways of thinking permeate our society, language, and thoughts, and soon are taken for granted. These days, even the layman knows that "Everything is relative," and that "If I go out into space on a long journey, when I get back you'll be old and I'll still be young!" That is the way the world is, and we can't imagine it being otherwise—for now.

But the fact that we as individuals and societies continue to evolve does not necessarily mean that we are evolving toward being *better* individuals and societies, only that we are continuing to change and trying to adapt. We may be approaching a crisis with respect to our limits of adapation, however. For better or worse, the tempo patterns of our culture continue to accelerate, demanding a frequency of adaptation that already shows signs of being beyond the present adaptive abilities of many of us. The flood of information, technological advancement, and social fluctuations is overwhelming.

Pitted against the kaleidoscopic nature of our modern lives is our current understanding of the world, which is, in part, based upon the presupposition that each of us has certain *inherent* abilities, and therefore certain inherent limitations. The effect of this presupposition is usually one of resignation to being the way one is, and of having to forgo certain experiences that others are blessed with. At best, this leads to efforts at coping with a "deficiency" that must be endured, a cross that must be borne. At worst, the discrepency between what we would like for ourselves and what we have been alotted leads to feelings of helplessness and even despair. At the same time, the possibilities and dangers presented by our society keep multiplying, as do the demands on our abilities.

Obviously, we have to keep growing. But how? First we need to learn how to become more competent, not only for the joy it brings, but also to understand how we are capable of committing acts of folly and unspeakable self-destruction. The question of how we can grow is urgent. And we must not limit our quest by falling back on the convenience of heredity, or on the justifications provided by our personal histories, or on the distinctions or assumptions with which we are already familiar. If we fail to seek out and absorb new and evolutionary notions we may indeed be, as many suggest, on the brink of jeopardizing our own survival. Medical researcher and essayist Lewis Thomas sounds a similar warning and plea.

Our behavior toward each other is the strangest, most unpredictable, and almost entirely unaccountable of all the phenomena with which we are obliged to live. In all of nature there is nothing so threatening to humanity as humanity itself.

I wish the psychiatrists and social scientists were further along in their fields than they seem to be. We need, in a hurry, some professionals who can tell us what has gone wrong in the minds of statesmen in this generation. How is it possible for so many people with the outward appearance of steadiness and authority, intelligent and convincing enough to have reached the highest positions in the governments of the world, to have lost so completely their sense of responsibility for the human beings to whom they are accountable? Their obsession with stockpiling nuclear armaments and their urgency in laying out detailed plans for

using them have, at the core, aspects of what we would be calling
craziness in other people, under other circumstances. Just before
they let fly everything at their disposal, and this uniquely intel-
ligent species begins to go down, it would be a small comfort to
understand how it happened to happen. Our descendants, if there
are any, will surely want to know.[1]

The last-ditch efforts on the part of our current methods for understanding ourselves can be found in scientific research into the neurochemical basis for emotions, learning, memory, intelligence, creativity, and so on. The technological goal of this research is the development of what will be, essentially, the equivalent of a pill that will make it possible for those who take it to be creative, or have better recall, or feel happy, or act respectfully, or learn a new skill. We are not saying that these pills should not be developed. To the contrary, we are very much for anything that helps make it possible for more people to lead more gratifying and fulfilling lives.

But even such truly wonderful scientific advances are still in the service of the supposition that you are inherently limited as a result of the circumstances of your birth and upbringing—thus the necessity for chemical intervention. This supposition avoids (in fact precludes) taking what we think is the next step in an *ascending* evolution of our culture's understanding of the world. That next step is an approach that allows for—in fact, presupposes—*the evolution of models of the world.*

Such an evolutionary approach assumes that our experiences of the world, and our responses to the world, are a function of the models through which we are perceiving that world. Korzybski suggested this supposition when he stated that "the map is not the territory." By changing our models we can change our world and ourselves. The change that we are proposing here is the difference between understanding the workings of a television well enough to be able to enhance its picture and to pull in more stations, and *generating new ways of transmitting information.* Once the paradigm of evolving models is taken for granted (like the notion of relativity), the world immediately shifts from an ongoing obstacle course of limitations to a world of opportunities and possibilities.

Throughout this book we have tried to illuminate those possibilities. It is possible to gain a more insightful understanding of the genesis of the cacophony of behaviors that exist in our often discordant world. It is also possible to seek out the behavioral compositions that would result in a harmony of voices. The resulting score would provide not only a way of analyzing the structure of those compositions, it would also provide a means of transferring to anyone capable of reading that score the ability to reproduce the music itself. Our world is already peopled with individuals who possess the aptitudes we need to grow and prosper. Aptitudes are the great experiential and behavioral compositions of human beings, and our goal is to provide musical scores capable of making those compositions available for the enjoyment of everyone.

We developed the EMPRINT method because we wanted to see every individual participating in the full range of opportunity that could and should be the birthright of every human being. How you use the method will help determine how quickly that dream is fulfilled. We hope that as you begin to search out and acquire new aptitudes this book will lead you to experience and appreciate the value of diversity in our amazing species. And finally, we want to remind you that the journey you are embarking on holds the possibility of great rewards, but has no end. Rather, this journey is part of the evolution of our extensions, and through them, of man.

Chapter Notes

Chapter 1: Taking Camera In Hand

1 As representations of reality, models are always going to be less than inclusive, yet utterly compelling. When El Nino (a stupendous upwelling and shift of warm water currents in the Pacific beginning in 1983) began producing unusual meteorlogical readings, meteorologists were at first kept uninformed of the phenomenon because they had programmed the computers that analyzed their data to throw out such readings. Such a phenomenon was considered impossible, so they told their computers that any such readings should be considered spurious and tossed out. The dramatic shifts in global weather patterns could not be tossed out, however, nor could they be adequately explained under the current model. Even after the readings of tremendous temperature shifts were eventually confirmed as real, many meteorologists refused to believe that El Nino was real, because such an occurrence was clearly not possible under their existing models.

2 It should not be assumed that "evolution" presupposes "better" or "advancement." All that "evolution" presupposes is "change." To be sure, many changes are for the better and do advance an organism (or us) in terms of adaptibility, security, longevity, and so on. But such changes may also evolve an organism toward nonuseful ends—or even toward oblivion. For example, a certain kind of English stag evolved larger and larger antlers until they became so huge that they are easily entangled in the underbrush, making the stag easy prey.

There are important cautions with respect to extensions. The subtlest, most prevalent, and most important of these is the ease with which we forget that our extensions *are* extensions, and are not reality. Thus the fact that the clock says noon/lunchtime comes to take precedence over whether or not we are actually hungry at that moment. You should bear in mind that, regardless of how homomorphic and effective it may be, the model we are presenting here is not reality but a way of *representing* reality (as are *all* models). For those interested in a discussion of the cautionary aspects of extensions, we recommend *Beyond Culture*, by Edward Hall.

3 We do not mean to imply that the implicit transference of models is inferior to an explicit approach, but that explicit transference offers choices (in terms of efficiency and consistent effectiveness) that implicit mentoring does not. Implicit mentoring eliminates, through attrition, those individuals who are not highly motivated to learn. However, the transference of models may be more thorough for those who do endure the long apprenticeships.

4 Examples of such explicit models for these kinds of skills include the spelling and math strategies described by Dilts et al in *Neuro-Linguistic Programming, Volume I*, the interactional models for successful intimate relationships detailed by Leslie Cameron-Bandler in *Solutions*, and the EMPRINT formats presented by the authors in *Know How*.

5 Our self-concepts are formed in childhood in much the same way, with our parents (rather than ourselves) as the primary labeling agents.

6 In making a distinction between external and internal behaviors we are not implying that these constitute mutually exclusive classes. In fact all internal processing is manifested in external behavior, although such behavior is often very subtle. For example, if you ask a person to make an arithmetic calculation "in his head" you will notice that each time he does so he assumes a characteristic posture or sequence of postures, moves his hands, eyes, and mouth in a

certain way, and so on. Asking this same person to make a decision about tomorrow will elicit a different—but characteristic—set of simultaneous external behaviors.

7 Of course, you could also take your eager anticipation of something pleasant (having a good time on a date) and turn it into a hope by simultaneously imagining *not* getting what you want (having a rotten time on a date). In general, the effect of this is to blunt the keenness of the excitement you had been feeling about the future.

8 The supposition of replicability is itself based on two other presuppositions: that *The map is not the territory* (see Korzybski, 1951 and 1958), and that *The mind and body are part of the same cybernetic system* (see Feldenkrais, 1949 and Lynch, 1985); and the observation that each of us has essentially the same sensory and central nervous system "equipment."

9 For the reasons already given, the method we are presenting is representative only of individuals brought up in the culture of modern America. Although the method will usefully overlap to a certain extent the internal processes of European countries, just how applicable it is and what changes would have to be made to bring it into accord with those and other cultures is not yet known. Indeed, as Cassirer stated,

> There is no rigid and pre-established scheme according to which our divisions and subdivisions might once for all be made. Even in languages closely akin and agreeing in their general structure we do not find identical names. As Humbolt pointed out, the Greek and Latin terms for the moon, although they refer to the same object, do not express the same intention or concept. The Greek term (men) denotes the function of the moon to "measure" time; the Latin term, (luna, luc-na) denotes the moon's lucidity or brightness....The function of a name is always limited to emphasizing a particular aspect of a thing, and it is precisely this restriction and limitation upon which the value of the name depends. (E. Cassirer, 1944)

Chapter 2: The Organizing Principle

1 We present some of the practical results of the EMPRINT method in *Know How* (1985), in which we describe patterns of successful and unsuccessful internal processing and behavior within a number of contexts (including goal setting, substance abuse, sex, eating, parenting, and loving), as well as provide instructional sequences intended to assist the reader in incorporating those patterns that underlie contextually successful internal processes and behaviors.

2 As noted previously, the method we are describing here by no means exhausts the possibilities for partitioning human cognitive processes, experience, and behavior. Some of the more recent models that have been developed include the TOTE (Miller, Gallanter, and Pribram, 1960), computer (Newell and Simon, 1971), cybernetic (Ashby, 1960), and holographic models (Pribram, 1971; Wilber, ed., 1982). The method we are presenting here is to be measured by its ability to provide a set of conceptual and behavioral presuppositions (in the form of distinctions and syntax) that make it possible both to better understand and to have some useful impact upon our experiences and behaviors.

3 The biological roots of our experience of time go deeper than most of us are aware. For instance, J.J. von Uexkull demonstrated in a series of ingenious experiments that different organisms, including man, have different perceptions of the rate of flow of time. These rate perceptions were determined by finding the shortest duration of time perceivable by an organism. He called this duration "moment signs," and defined them as "the smallest receptacles that,

by being filled with various qualities, become converted into moments as they are lived." According to von Uexkull, a subjectively discontinuous moment for a human being is one twenty-fourth of a second (the speed at which the individual frames of a motion picture are run). For a snail a discontinuous moment may be as long as a quarter of a second, and for the cattle tick waiting on a stalk of grass for a cow to happen by it may be eighteen *years*. (Reported in, among other places, John Bleibtreu's *Parable of the Beast*, 1968.)

4 All of these examples of intercultural time differences were taken from *The Silent Language* (1959) and *The Dance of Life* (1983), both by Edward T. Hall. Many additional examples can be found in these books, both of which are well worth reading.

5 Movies with unresolved plots are not often made in this country; and those that are usually flop at the box office. If you would like to compare the film syntax of American culture with that of an Asian culture, we recommend *Chan Is Missing* (1982), in which there is no resolution, only movement in a direction.

6 As you did with the "anticipation" ↔ "hope" example in Chapter 1, you can change your subjective experience of disappointment by identifying something about which you are disappointed, then believing for a moment that the possibility of getting what you want still exists. Similarly, you can identify something with which you are frustrated, then believe for a moment that the possibility of having what you want has passed. For a complete presentation of the structure and means to alter emotions, see *The Emotional Hostage* by two of the authors (LCB and ML).

7 We want to point out that the causality we typically "find" in the past is not inherent in the past, but is an interpretation we apply to events in the past. There are other schools of thought, such as Zen, which devote much of their instruction to an acausal, nonlinear comprehension of events.

Chapter 3: The Distinctions

1 In fact, if you extend our discussion of responses to the relatively molecular level of neurophysiology, it can be said that *all* responses are the behavioral manifestation of hierarchies of tests. See *Plans and the Structure of Behavior*, by Miller, Galanter, and Pribram.

Chapter 4: Test Category

1 *Know How*, by the authors, provides many detailed examples of appropriate and inappropriate test time frames for a wide range of contexts, such as goal setting, eating, drinking alcohol, exercise, sex, relationships, and parenting, as well as for general change formats.

2 Of course, criteria may be imposed by a context (as when you attend a lecture and "decorum" and "politeness" become relevant criteria), or imposed by an individual (as when your supervisor tells you to make your written reports "crisp" and "brief").

3 The notion of criterial equivalences extends far beyond the specification of criteria. Every discrimination we make, whether it be "blue," "chair," "happiness," or "future," is a label for a set of perceptions, behaviors, and/or functional relationships. The color "blue" is light of a frequency falling within a certain spectral range. "Chair" is an object made for one person to sit on. "Happiness" is a certain set of kinesthetic sensations in oneself, or (in someone else) smiling and expansive body movements. And "future" is anything that happens after right now. You may or may not agree with these criterial equivalences, but that agreement or disagreement is itself a demonstration that you

have for each of these classes of experience criterial equivalences which you use to evaluate what is and what is not blue, a chair, happiness, and the future. Because you have criterial equivalences for every discrimination you make, criteria constitute a special class of criterial equivalences: "Criteria" are those criterial equivalences which *an individual considers significant* within a particular context.

4 For a complete presentation of all of the variables involved in adopting and maintaining healthy eating and exercise habits, see *Know How* (Cameron-Bandler, Gordon, and Lebeau).

5 The implications and technology of representational systems (much of which is not relevant to the method presented here) extend far beyond what we have described here. For those interested in therapeutic and additional modeling applications of representational systems, see *Solutions* (Cameron-Bandler), *Frogs Into Princes* (Bandler and Grinder), *Neuro-Linguistic Programming, Vol. 1* (Dilts et al), *Patterns of the Hypnotic Techniques of Milton H. Erickson, M.D., Vol. 2* (Grinder, DeLozier, and Bandler), and *Therapeutic Metaphors* (Gordon), all of which are listed in the References.

6 The EMPRINT format in Chapter 8 of *Know How* (Cameron-Bandler, Gordon, and Lebeau) teaches the reader how to make present kinesthetic tests that lead to sexual arousal.

Chapter 5: Reference Category

1 As A.J. Leggett pointed out in his paper, "The 'Arrow of Time' and Quantum Mechanics," this apparent barrier to actual experience of the future may someday be surmounted.

> *And what I want to suggest is, that at least in the absence of a much more detailed understanding of the workings of the human brain than we at present possess, it is not entirely obvious that the laws of physics, even when combined with the given overall direction of biological process, exclude any possibility of genuine precognition over fairly small distances in time—or, by the same token, of a very limited ability to "affect the past." Needless to say, such a possibility, were it to exist, would have profound implications not only for philosophy but also for our view of physics itself. . . . I do strongly suspect that if in the year 2075 physicists look back on us poor quantum-mechanics-besotted idiots of the twentieth century with pity and head-shaking, an essential ingredient in their new picture of the Universe will be a quite new and to us unforeseeable approach to the concept of time: and that to them our current ideas about the asymmetry of nature with respect to time will appear as naive as do to us the notions of nineteenth-century physics about simultaneity. (Leggett, 1977)*

Nevertheless, the arrow of time is currently a pervasive and prominent feature of our subjective experiences, and any model of experience and behavior must take it into account if it is to be in accord with those experiences.

Chapter 6: Cause-Effect

1 In addition to individual differences in contents and patterns of cause-effect relationships, there are also differences between individuals in terms of the *frequency* and *proximity* necessary to create cause-effects. "Frequency" refers to the number of times two sequential events must occur before a person concludes that A causes B. How many times do you have to have engine trouble after filling up at Bill's Gasamat before you decide that Bill's gas affects your car adversely? How many times do you have to fly in an airplane comfortably to conclude that you are no longer afraid of flying? How many times do you have

to embrace your lover before you conclude that your embrace causes that person to feel good? How many times do you have to get a ride by flailing your arms before you conclude that this technique is more likely to make people stop?

Just how many repetitions of an experience are needed in order for you to generate a cause-effect relationship depends partly upon contextually determined expectations. When a scientist injects a group of cancerous mice with a serum and those mice experience remissions of their cancers, those results must wait for at least two or three retrials of the experiment before most scientists would be willing to say that a cause-effect relationship exists between the serum and the remission of cancer in mice. Similarly, most people recognize that more than one day of exercise is required before you can legitimately decide whether or not that particular form of exercise makes you feel better. Beyond these contextually determined expectations, however, there are still the idiosyncratic test requirements that each of us uses. For some individuals, one example is all it takes to generate a cause-effect, while others, even after the twentieth example, will concede only that "Well, maybe" there is indeed a cause-effect relationship at work.

"Proximity" has to do with the closeness in time with which events occur. For example, if you take an aspirin for a headache and that headache does not go away until the next day, you are not likely to attribute the disappearance of the headache to the aspirin. If, however, your headache vanishes within twenty minutes of taking the aspirin, you are likely to give credit to the medicine— even though, of course, the aspirin may not have actually been the cause of relief (everyone has had headaches that either persisted even after several doses of aspirin, or have gone away without aspirin). As with frequency, there will be contextual as well as individual differences as to what constitutes a decisive time interval. For instance, in the context of taking a pain reliever, it is expected that the drug will take effect within an hour.

Similarly, each of us is characteristically satisfied by certain time intervals in making our cause-effect determinations. For some, two events must almost immediately follow one another in order to be recognized as being cause and effect, while for others days and even years are not too long to establish such relationships. We know of one person who thinks about getting a parking space, three days later finds a parking space when she needs it, and is sure that her thinking about getting a space was the cause of her finding one three days later. While for most people such an extended time interval falls into the realm of "coincidence," for this particular woman a time interval between two events of "only three days" is *proof* of a cause-effect relationship. (More thorough descriptions of the inferential processes underlying cause-effect computations can be found in *Patterns of Plausible Inference* by Polya, and in *Clinical Inference and Cognitive Theory*, by Sarbin, Taft, and Bailey.)

Of course, what we have just described is the structure of how superstitions are generated. Superstitions need not be as blatant as that of the woman who turns internal images into parking places. We have all fallen under the spell at one time or another. You wear your yellow shirt to take a test that you expect to do poorly on, you make an "A," and thereafter the yellow shirt becomes your "test-taking shirt." Or you knock over the salt shaker, that night you have an automobile accident, and from then on you always throw salt over your shoulder. Or perhaps your car is a bringer of rain—all you have to do is wash it.

We want to point out, however, that the cause-effect relationships that we label as superstitions are no different *structurally* than those we use to justify taking vitamin C in order stave off colds or putting gasoline in our cars to make them run. What difference there is between "superstitious" and "rational" thinking lies in the frequency and/or proximity of contiguous events that satisfies us that those two events are necessarily linked.

Chapter 8: The Method At Work

1 If you would like a free copy of "The EMPRINT Format for Converting Mistakes into Learnings," or if you want to know the next time the authors will be presenting the format in a public workshop, contact us at FuturePace, Inc., P.O. Box 1173, San Rafael, California 94915.

Chapter 11: Elicitation and Detection of the Variables

1 For a thorough presentation of the use of behavioral cues (known as *accessing cues*) as a means of detecting representational systems, as well as more information about the significance of representational systems, see Cameron-Bandler, *Solutions*; Dilts et al., *Neuro-Linguistic Programming, Volume I*; and Bandler and Grinder, *Frogs into Princes*.

Chapter 12: Reproducing Competence

1 The instructional sequences, or *EMPRINT formats*, are designed to transfer the patterns of variables we distilled after interviewing hundreds of people with exceptional talents. Included are the EMPRINT formats for the five essential steps for setting and accomplishing goals (wishing, wanting, planning, doing, having); for healthy and sustainable eating and exercise habits; for abstaining from drugs, cigarettes, and alcohol; for enjoying sex; for creating and sustaining a satisfying relationship; and for parenting. Half of the book is filled with short vignettes describing people who are successful and people who consistently stumble in particular contexts, and how their behavior indicates the kind of internal processing they are using in those contexts. The other half of the book contains installation sequences that install in the reader the operative formats gleaned from the successful people for each context. For the reader of this book, *Know How* is an advanced course in detection and installation techniques.

2 Fortunately, other sources are available if you want to extend your study of the installation process. We have already mentioned *Know How*. Two other excellent sources are the videotape training packages titled "Lasting Feelings" and "Making Futures Real," produced by two of the authors (LCB and ML). These videotape packages include a client session in which Leslie Cameron-Bandler elicits existing operative formats and installs new and more useful ones, a modeling segment in which Leslie Cameron-Bandler and Michael Lebeau explain the outcomes that were achieved in the client session, as well as the techniques Leslie used to accomplish those outcomes, and an annotated transcript of the client session. Because the installation techniques demonstrated in these videotapes are tailored to a specific individual, they are different in many respects from the ones contained in *Know How*. For more information contact FuturePace, Inc., P.O. Box 1173, San Rafael, CA 94915.

3 *Solutions*, and the videotapes "Lasting Feelings" and "Making Futures Real" contain many additional examples of future-pacing.

Chapter 13: Conclusion

1 Both of these quotes are taken from Lewis Thomas's *Late Night Thoughts on Listening to Mahler's Ninth Symphony*. The first is from the essay titled "Making Science Work," and the second is from the essay titled "On Medicine and the Bomb."

Glossary

Activity   A "sub-outcome" underlying the successful manifestation of an outcome behavior. An outcome may involve more than one activity.

Actual (references)   Experiences that you really have had or are really having.

Cause-Effect   Experiences, occurrences, situations, etc. that are, or are perceived to be, contingently related to one another, such that the expression or occurrence of one leads to the expression or occurrence of the other.

Compelling (time frame)   The time frame that an individual experiences as most subjectively "real" and that therefore leads to behavior.

Constructed (references)   Experiences that are imagined, but that never really occurred.

Criteria   The standards on which an evaluation is based.

Criterial Equivalence   The specification of what behaviors, perceptions, qualities, circumstances, etc. constitute fulfillment of a criterion.

Emotional State   Specification of an individual's overall feelings at a moment in time (such as happy, curious, confident, etc.).

Evaluation   The process of applying your criteria to a specific context in order to determine whether or not, or to what extent, your criteria were, are being, or could be fulfilled (also referred to as a "test").

Future-Pacing   A technique for helping to ensure that new responses will occur when needed by stepping into the future and imagining as fully as possible the experience of using those new responses in the appropriate context.

Informational (references)   Experiences left as data, devoid of those emotions or sensations that are of the experience.

Intentional Behaviors   Those behaviors that an individual has sought out and learned or installed in him or herself.

Internal Processes   An individual's beliefs, thoughts, evaluations, representations, feelings, and emotions that are in operation within a specific context.

Intrinsic Behaviors   Those behaviors that an individual has coincidentally acquired as the natural result of his or her life experiences.

Operative Format   The set of interacting internal processing variables underlying the manifestation of a particular activity.

Outcome   The internal or external behavior that one would like to understand or replicate.

Precursive Activities   Those activities leading to the acquisition of new behaviors, usually including such activities as "motivation," "planning," and "commitment."

References   The sources of information an individual is using when making a particular evaluation.

Representation   The internal pictures, sounds, and feelings that a person is using when making an evaluation.

Subordination   Ignoring or overriding evaluations about one time frame in favor of evaluations about another time frame (for example, ignoring the future in favor of the present).

Test   The process of applying your criteria to a specific context in order to determine whether or not, or to what extent, your criteria were, are being, or could be fulfilled. (Also referred to as an "evaluation.")

Time Frame   The past, present, or future.

Vicarious   Gaining experiential information by imagining what someone else's experience is.

References

Aaronson, Bernard S. "Behavior and the Place Names of Time." In *The Future of Time*, edited by Henri Waker. New York: Doubleday & Co., 1971.

Ashby, W. Ross. *An Introduction to Cybernetics*. London: University Paperbacks, 1956.

_____. *Design for a Brain: The Origin of Adaptive Behavior*. New York: John Wiley & Sons, 1960.

Bandler, Richard and Grinder, John. *The Structure of Magic*. Palo Alto, CA: Science & Behavior Books, 1975.

_____. *Frogs Into Princes*. Moab, Utah: Real People Press, 1979.

Bateson, Gregory. *Steps to an Ecology of Mind*. New York: Ballantine, 1972.

Bleibtreu, John N. *The Parable of the Beast*. New York: Collier Books, 1968.

Cameron-Bandler, Leslie. *Solutions: Practical and Effective Antidotes for Sexual and Relationship Problems*. San Rafael, CA: FuturePace, 1985.

Cameron-Bandler, Leslie; Gordon, David; and Lebeau, Michael. *Know How: Guided Programs for Inventing Your Own Best Future*. San Rafael, CA: FuturePace, 1985.

Cameron-Bandler, Leslie and Lebeau, Michael. *The Emotional Hostage: Rescuing Your Emotional Life*. San Rafael, CA: FuturePace, 1986.

Cassirer, E. *An Essay on Man*. New Haven, CN: Yale University Press, 1944.

Cheek, F. and Laucius, J. "Time Worlds of Drug Users." In *The Future of Time*, edited by Henri Waker. New York: Doubleday & Co., 1971.

Comfort, Alex. *Reality and Empathy*. Albany, NY: State University of New York Press, 1984.

Dilts, Robert et al. *Neuro-Linguistic Programming, Vol. I*. Cupertino, CA: Meta Publications, 1980.

Feldenkrais, Moshe. *Body and Mature Behavior*. New York: International Universities Press, 1949.

Gordon, David. *Therapeutic Metaphors: Helping Others Through the Looking Glass*. Cupertino, CA: Meta Publications, 1978.

Grinder, John; DeLozier, Judith; and Bandler, Richard. *Patterns of the Hypnotic Techniques of Milton H. Erickson, M.D., Vol. II*. Cupertino, CA: Meta Publications, 1977.

Hall, Edward T. *The Silent Language*. New York: Doubleday & Co., 1959.

_____. *The Hidden Dimension*. Garden City, NJ: Doubleday & Co., 1966.

_____. *Beyond Culture*. Garden City, NJ: Anchor Press/Doubleday, 1976.

_____. *The Dance of Life*. New York: Anchor Press, 1983.

Korzybski, Alfred. "The Role of Language in the Perceptual Processes." In *Perception: An Approach to Personality*, edited by Robert Blake and Glenn Ramsey. New York: The Ronald Press Co., 1951

_____. *Science and Sanity*. Lakeville, CT: The International Non-Aristotelian Library Publishing Company. 1958.

Kuhn, Thomas S. *The Structure of Scientific Revolutions*. Chicago: The University of Chicago Press, 1970.

Leggett, A.J. "The 'Arrow of Time' and Quantum Mechanics." In *Encyclopedia of Ignorance*. New York: Pergamon Press, 1977.

Lynch, James J. *The Language of the Heart: The Body's Response to Human Dialogue*. New York: Basic Books, 1985.

Mann, Harriet; Siegler, Miriam; and Osmond, Humphry. "The Psychotypology of Time." In *The Future of Time*, edited by Henri Waker. New York: Doubleday & Co., 1971.

Miller, G.A.; Galanter, E.; and Pribram, K. *Plans and the Structure of Behavior*. New York: Holt, Rinehart & Winston, Inc., 1960.

Miller, Jonathan. *States of Mind*. New York: Pantheon Books, 1983.

Newell, A. and Simon, H.A. *Human Problem Solving*. Englewood Cliffs, NJ: Prentice-Hall, 1971.

Pei, Mario. *The Story of Language*. Philadelphia, PA: J.B. Lippincott Co., 1965.

Polya, G. *Patterns of Plausible Inference, Volume II*. Princeton, NJ: Princeton University Press, 1954.

Pribram, Karl. *Languages of the Brain*. Englewood Cliffs, NJ: Prentice-Hall, 1971.

Sarbin, Theodore; Taft R.; and Bailey, B. *Clinical Inference and Cognitive Theory*. New York: Holt, Rinehart & Winston, Inc., 1960.

Thomas, Lewis. *Late Night Thoughts on Listening to Mahler's Ninth Symphony*. New York: The Viking Press, 1983.

Whorf, Benjamin Lee. *Language, Thought and Reality*. Edited by John Carroll. Cambridge, MA: The MIT Press, 1956.

Wiener, Norbert. *The Human Use of Human Beings: Cybernetics and Society*. New York: Avon Books, 1954.

Wilber, Ken. *The Holographic Paradigm and Other Paradoxes*. Boulder, CO: Shambala Publications, 1982.

Full Table of Contents

Dear Reader,

If you would like information on trainings in the EMPRINT method or on other workshops given by the authors, or if you want to know more about the authors' other books and video-tape training packages, contact us at FuturePace, Inc., P.O. Box 1173, San Rafael, California 94915.

Do you have these important
FuturePace Books?

If you have found THE EMPRINT METHOD valuable, you will want to take advantage of this special offer to complete your FuturePace Library.

The Emotional Hostage, *Rescuing Your Emotional Life,* $11.95

Solutions, *Practical and Effective Antidotes for Sexual and Relationship Problems,* $11.95

Know How, *Guided Programs for Inventing Your Own Best Future,* $11.95

SAVE! ORDER ANY TWO BOOKS AND SAVE $2.40.
ORDER ALL THREE BOOKS AND SAVE $5.00.

YES! Please send me the FuturePace books I have checked here:

I want a copy of:

☐ **THE EMOTIONAL HOSTAGE at $13.45** ($11.95 plus $1.50 postage and handling.)
☐ **SOLUTIONS at $13.45** ($11.95 plus $1.50 postage and handling.)
☐ **KNOW HOW at $13.45** ($11.95 plus $1.50 postage and handling.)

☐ I am ordering the two books checked above for $23.50 (includes $2.00 postage and handling).

☐ I am ordering all three books for $33.35 (includes $2.50 postage and handling).

☐ I enclose my check for _____   ☐ Charge to my credit card.

Visa # _____   Expires _____

Mastercard # _____   Expires _____

Signature _____

Name (please print) _____

Address _____

City _____ State _____ ZIP _____
California residents add 6% sales tax

Mail this card with your payment to:
FuturePace, Inc.
P.O. Box 1173
San Rafael, CA 94915